The Republic
of Childhood

The Republic of Childhood

A CRITICAL GUIDE TO
CANADIAN CHILDREN'S LITERATURE
IN ENGLISH

Second Edition

Sheila Egoff

Toronto
OXFORD UNIVERSITY PRESS
1975

ISBN 0-19-540231-6 (clothbound)
ISBN 0-19-540232-2 (paperbound)

1 2 3 4 5 — 9 8 7 6 5

Printed in Canada by
THE BRYANT PRESS LIMITED

contents

illustrations

introduction to the second edition

In an age when an international bestseller, *Future Shock*, can be fashioned out of the simple theme that the world is changing very quickly, it is perhaps not inappropriate to bring out a second edition of this book seven and a half years after the first. Canadian writing for children—like the whole Canadian society out of which it has developed, like its sister branches of Canadian literature—has altered and grown since 1967.

Characteristically enough, the changes have been cumulative rather than abrupt, with progress discernible in terms of an overall advance rather than specific achievements. In Australia an Ivan Southall, in Sweden a Maria Gripe has been able to produce children's books of such distinctiveness and distinction as to rally a whole new school of writing about them. In Canada the changes have been more modest and the successes—apart from picture-storybooks—less notable.

Although there has been a sharp increase in the production of Canadian literature for adults, there has been no corresponding increase in books for children. In fact, depending somewhat on how one classifies, the number of children's books issued per year may have actually declined in absolute terms in relation to population growth. However, there are some offsetting factors. Much more *attention* is now devoted to Canadian children's books than was evident before 1967. A distressing lacuna began to be filled, for example, by the inauguration in 1967 of the quarterly *In Review*, a journal devoted exclusively to the reviewing of Canadian children's books (English and French), published by the Provincial Library Service of Ontario. *In Review* does not, unfortunately, reach a wide audience: for the most part it is seen only by librarians and teachers, who use it as an aid in book selection. It is thus a 'professional' rather than a 'literary' review, but at least it gives every Canadian writer for children some kind of hearing and response and it performs its function very well indeed. In a country where serious reviewing is generally a neglected craft and where children's books in particular are reviewed summarily or not at all, *In Review* is probably as much of an aid to authors as to the librarians and teachers for whom it is intended.

Government interest and support have also been shown by the Ontario Royal Commission on Book Publishing whose *Background Papers*, issued in 1972, included articles on writing and publishing for children; by the first exhibit of Canadian children's books sponsored by the National Library of Canada (1972); by the first appointment of a children's librarian at the National Library; and by the support of the Canada Council in respect of grants for the writing and publishing of children's books.

Periodicals provide the indispensable continuing attention for any subject and fortunately two new magazines can be mentioned. *Canadian Children's Magazine*, launched at the end of 1974, is the first general magazine for children published in Canada since the late nineteenth century. A scholarly magazine for adults, *Canadian Children's Literature*, will presumably do for children's writing what *Canadian Literature* has done for the adult counterpart. If so, we will at last have the full-dress literary criticism that Canadian writing for children has lacked. Also on the verge of fruition, at this date of writing, are the first two general conferences on children's literature to be held in Canada—one in Toronto in 1975 and one in Vancouver in 1976.

There are other new rumbles of interest in Canadian children's books that signify a belated change in the general attitude towards them. They can be noticed in the 'little books' for children that have appeared from new small or private presses and in the concern of pressure groups such as feminists to propagate or stifle certain kinds of children's books. Above all, the new interest is discernible in the number of inquiries made of those who work in the field of children's literature about how to get published.

Several publishers have taken the step—long an ordinary practice in other countries but unprecedented in Canada—of appointing a special children's book editor.

This surge of attention may do something to change the circumstances and patterns of authorship. It has always been puzzling and disappointing to realize the number of one- or two-book authors we have. A James Reaney, Paul St Pierre, Doug Wilkinson, or George Clutesi makes an excellent start and then writes nothing more for children. Perhaps even more discouraging has been the fact that Roderick Haig-Brown and Farley Mowat, for example, who produced several good children's books in the fifties and sixties, have done nothing of the like since.

It would seem that Canada has hitherto not encouraged its authors enough, critically or monetarily, to persuade them to continue. The result has been that the progress of Canadian children's literature is to be measured not author by author but book by book. One must continue to speak of Canadian literature for children in terms of genres and trends rather than of 'name' writers.

The movement, then, has been an inching forward rather than a leap-frogging. Building on a distinctive tradition of outdoor fiction and tales of our native peoples, we have produced a strong —though narrow, conservative, and unambitious—body of writing firmly rooted in the land that equals the best fiction of this kind from other countries. Up to the present the tradition thus established has been strong enough to resist modern trends— good and bad—that are apparent in children's books from other countries, especially from the United States. We can regret that the *tour de force*—the kind of imaginative, introspective departure from the norm that has blossomed forth in other countries—is unknown to us in a Canadian context, but we can hardly deplore the fact that facile, simplistic, sterile novels with sociological 'meaning', which are dominating without enriching American children's books, have hardly been tried by Canadian writers. However, while additions to our literature for children over the past eight years and their scope have been unexceptionable on the whole, there have been some notable gains. Eskimo and Indian legends, fantasy, biography, and illustration are definitely richer. The record is not dramatic, but it is substantial, and it is the intent of this new edition to examine it in some detail.

A few words about the revision. While much of the text of the first edition has been used unchanged, there are numerous revisions and of course additions. Not only discussions of recent books but whole sections have been added. The sections on Eskimo legends, poetry, plays, picture-books and picture-storybooks are new and the general discussions of legends, historical fiction, and fiction have been revised to include observations that have grown out of nearly eight years' reading. Discussions of some ephemeral books have been omitted from the main text, though they have been retained in the annotated check lists at the end of each chapter.

introduction to the first edition

Children are intensely curious, impressionable, and avid for experience. In their quest for knowledge and comprehension of the larger world, books have a power to engage their minds that is quite unmatched in later life. When we remember the thrill of anticipation we had as children when we picked up another book by a favourite author, the deep absorption that made us oblivious to everything around us, the revelations of worlds and lives other than our own, we can believe with Graham Greene that 'it is only in childhood that books have any deep influence on our lives'.

In adult society the reading of books is a pursuit for the few—probably only ten per cent of the population. Most children, however, read quantities of books, a fact attested to by the high circulation of children's books in Canadian public libraries, where it is common for children to borrow more than adults. Supermarkets and drug stores find it profitable to stock children's books. On behalf of their children, parents will buy encyclopaedias from door-to-door salesmen to an extent that they would not buy such books for themselves; and when the school library lacks books they will dutifully attend bazaars, raid their attics, and buy raffle tickets to increase its size. In the last few years there has been a great increase in school and public libraries. There has also been an explosion in the writing and publishing of children's books. For Canadians this means a choice of incomparable richness: all the books published in England and the United States as well as Canada.

Quantity and easy access, however, may mean that quality will be lost sight of. Many adults believe that *any* reading by children is itself a Good Thing and often ignore the need for standards. If reading is so important to children, is it not essential that from the enormous stock of titles available we give them books of superior quality? Indeed, considering that children lack the experience and knowledge to choose the best books for themselves, should not children's books be subjected to even closer review and assessment than adult literature?

It is in such a spirit of critical inquiry that I have approached this study of Canadian children's books. My aim has been to indicate in general the standards by which one may select and guide children's reading and, more particularly, to show the degree to which certain Canadian publications have met them.

I have been chiefly concerned with the literary evaluation of the Canadian children's books of this generation—that is to say, the Canadian books that constitute the basic stock from which children of today may select their reading. Most of the books discussed were issued after 1950, but a few older publications that have made a place for themselves are also included. In addition, for the sake of the historical record I have given in the last chapter a brief account of some early books that have a place in the development of Canadian children's literature. It should be understood, however, that this book is basically a study of contemporary writing and not a literary history.

I undertook to write this study first of all because there exists a group of children's books that can be identified as 'Canadian', just as we speak of Australian books or French books or American books, and it seems beyond human nature not to investigate something that exists.

Moreover, a study of the children's books of any one country cannot help but reveal a good deal about that country. J.R.R. Tolkien's *The Hobbit* is a fantasy set in a world that never was and in a time that never happened, and yet it is English to its core; the children in Paul Berna's *The Horse Without a Head* are the children of the respectable poor, the kind of carefree, resourceful children that one expects to find around the world, and yet the book has a tone and a charm that are essentially French. It is surely no accident that most of the great children's fantasies have stemmed from England—a country with a long, rich, varied, and imaginative literature. So too it is logical that the best children's stories of the Second World War have come from countries where the agony of war was an everyday occurrence—Poland, Greece, Denmark, Holland, and England. A study of Canadian children's books, therefore, can throw some light on the nation itself. I have in no way made an explicit study in this area, but the books whose literary qualities are here discussed reveal more than content and style. They show what Canada and Canadians are like, what values we respect, how we look at ourselves today and at our past. Just as *Alice in Wonderland* tells us much about Victorian England, so children's books in Canada reflect many of the forces in our own society; it is a reflection in miniature, of course, but accurate and indicative.

It is surely important to know what a society offers its children in the way of literature. While there are always going to be books that are better or poorer than other books, and some that are outrageously bad, it is well worth trying to see if there is any kind of 'norm'. Do we mainly have *real* writers who can express themselves to the young and who have a deep and genuine interest in the subjects they write about? Or do we offer children books by people who can't write very well, who take on subjects they don't care too much about and so produce what might be called 'ho-hum' books—soonest read, soonest forgotten? Of course the question underlying these considerations is: do we respect children? Literature for children affects far too many people early in their impressionable years for adults to fail to give it their serious attention. This book is my attempt to encourage this attention.

I hope too that this study will serve as a useful guide for the many parents, teachers, and librarians who are called upon to buy books for children, all the more so since few Canadian children's books are the subject of serious book reviews.

Finally, my purpose in writing this work is to render due credit for some achievement. Canadian children's literature now constitutes a body of writing that deserves recognition and evaluation, and not merely from Canadians.

This last statement of purpose implies the likelihood of bias on my part. I was well aware from the outset that I ran a serious risk of partiality. Just as the Vancouver or Regina theatre critic is likely to find kind words for a local production simply because it is local, so have I doubtless been tempted to overvalue books simply because they are Canadian. A tendency to provincialism is particularly dangerous where children's books are concerned, for they least warrant being judged on the basis of national endeavour. Above all else, a children's book should simply interest children; the readers for whom it is intended will care not a whit about any other consideration.

I have therefore tried to resist any unconscious impulse to magnify the importance of the books under my purview. To achieve such objectivity (insofar as this is possible), I have sought to relate the contemporary Canadian books closely to the general body of literature and specifically to the children's books of other countries. If the scope of my book is exclusively national, my standards of judgement are not so. I have endeavoured to apply, first of all, general literary standards, those that would be accepted in judging writing for adults. Should children's books be rated in any lesser way? Secondly, I have tried to judge Canadian writing in comparison with the best modern writing, particularly from Great Britain and the United States.

This reasoning has dictated the structure of most chapters, which tend to follow a fairly consistent pattern. I usually begin with an examination of the main features of each type of writing. What goes into the creation of fantasy? What are the characteristics of the historical novel? What is the root of the Indian legend? Then, since the qualities of a type of literature can often best be understood by reference to the most successful examples in the genre anywhere, I refer to the outstanding children's books of other countries. The number of such citations and comparisons varies as the Canadian contributions demand. Thus the Indian legend and the realistic animal story, which are indigenous to Canada and form a rich literature, need few comparisons to make their quality plain, while fantasy—to me our least satisfactory literary product—requires numerous examples from English and American writing so that the Canadian failures can be more clearly understood.

Each chapter is followed by an annotated list of Canadian children's books. The list covers titles discussed in the subject essay and a selection of others (which are not necessarily recommended) and forms a convenient survey of the principal Canadian children's books for each subject or type. While all major contributions have certainly been noted, there has been no intention of including every book published since 1950. With two exceptions, books published after December 1965 have not been considered. (It is perhaps worth mentioning, however, that in examining the publications of 1966 and 1967, I found no reason to change any of the opinions offered in this study; in fact these recent books only strengthen them.) Some lists try to offer help to adults by specifying the reading level of the books in terms of the age or the school grade of the children for whom the books are presumed to be most suitable. Such an allocation of books to definite slots has its dangers as well as its obvious convenience. A good book has a remarkably wide range of appeal; a poor book is hardly worth recommending for any age group. (My attitude is perhaps best summarized by the present Chief Librarian of the Vancouver Public Library who, in discussing Roderick Haig-Brown's *The Whale People*, remarked: 'There has been some talk about whether this book is intended for children, for young adults, or adults. All I know is, that it's a book for me.') I have, upon occasion, acknowledged that a book is intended 'for young readers' (ages roughly six to eight). Here it seems sufficient to say that most books in the lists fall into a group that can be described as for 'the middle-aged child' (roughly ten to twelve years of age).

I take *Canadian* books to be those written by Canadians or by writers long resident in Canada. Most of these writers have based their books in Canada, so they are Canadian in content as well as in authorship. There are, of course, notable exceptions. N.B. Taylor's *The Aeneid of Virgil* is a memorable retelling of the Latin epic; William Stevenson's *The Bushbabies*, an outstanding book in every way, is set in modern East Africa. Though they deal with subjects of universal interest (would that there were more Canadian books like them in this respect), these achievements by two Canadians are part of our literature and must be considered with the books about Canada.

All of the works I discuss are in a broad sense creative literature

—that is to say, they are works in which *how* the author has said it affects *what* he has said. Within this wide tent may then be accommodated not only fiction in all its forms, but also history, biography, and legends. Each of these categories has its own chapter. Poetry and drama obviously belong here too, but the output has been so small, insignificant, and poorly written that these categories can be dismissed; that this evaluation has to be made, however, is of some significance. Books of information are excluded.

Even within these broad boundaries, it was not easy to decide whether certain books should be considered in this study, let alone in what literary category they should be classed. To begin with, no one knows better than I how hard it is to define a 'children's book'. In the true sense a children's book is simply one in which a child finds pleasure. Many a ten- or eleven-year-old can be found happily absorbed in anything from Blake's poetry to Golding's *Lord of the Flies*. The majority of the books discussed here were specifically written with children (young people up to the age of thirteen) in mind. Often, however, a great many children will take over a book not deliberately intended for them. This explains the inclusion in the present work of books by Seton and Roberts as well as such modern books as Farley Mowat's *The Dog Who Wouldn't Be* and Fred Bodsworth's *Last of the Curlews*. (It has often been said that a children's book can be judged by the extent to which it is enjoyed by adults, as they enjoy Kenneth Grahame's *The Wind in the Willows* and Joan Aiken's *The Wolves of Willoughby Chase*, among many other children's books. It would be interesting to find out how many adult Canadians read and enjoy the children's books of their own country.)

I have been made painfully aware that books cannot be categorized any more than people. A good book has many facets and it is not entirely fair to consider it under only one heading. For example, Edith Sharp's *Nkwala* and Roderick Haig-Brown's *The Whale People* could have been discussed in the chapter on the Indian legend, both for their myth-like quality and because they are genuinely rooted in early Indian life. They could have been discussed equally well in the section on the realistic adventure story, for adventurous they are. I have chosen to treat them where their basic literary form is most apparent—in the chapter on historical fiction. Some mediocre and poor books also defy classification, but for a very different reason. In the field of historical writing, for instance, it is sometimes difficult to discern the author's intention: did he set out to write history or fiction? In these cases, and in desperation, I have either guessed or depended upon the publisher's not-always-reliable blurb.

This study varies from most works of criticism—whether of children's books or of adult literature—in that it pays a good deal of attention to some obviously poor books. It has not been my intention to offer gratuitous advice to either writers or publishers. I have discussed and criticized failures because they can show us, in effect, when standards are lowered either deliberately or unintentionally. The body of Canadian children's literature, as yet rather small, cannot be adequately described without examining a fairly large percentage of the total output. Only by considering why the poor books are inadequate as well as why the good ones merit our praise can we arrive at the elusive definition of 'quality', which it is the purpose of this book to establish.

The most striking thing about Canadian children's books is their paucity. Since 1952 only some thirty or forty have been published each year, and in the years before there were far fewer. This is an infinitesimal number in comparison with the children's books of other English-speaking countries. Some 6,000 are published each year—3,000 in Great Britain and 3,000 in the United States. Canadian writers for children share all the problems that beset their colleagues in other fields of Canadian writing. They still have a fairly small market in Canada for their output and therefore small financial incentive for work. Often in choosing topics or a locale that would specially interest Canadians, our writers limit their sales potential outside Canada. A book on Captain Joseph Bernier, who claimed the Arctic for Canada, would not be read by many people in the United States, just as a recent children's book on the American President, James Polk, would not find its way into many Canadian libraries. But the potential readership for these books in their respective countries would vary considerably. Consider the difference in the two populations: 20 million* and 196 million. While both countries yield to regionalism in book purchasing, a book with a Florida setting would certainly have more readers in the United States than a book with a British Columbia or a Saskatchewan setting would have in Canada.

Moreover, Canada is still chiefly a book-importing country and there is the fierce competition for Canadian readership that American and British authors pose to their Canadian counterparts. This has not always worked to the disadvantage of the Canadian child. Children's libraries in Canada can be praised for their international flavour. With so few books of our own, we can and do bring the best of world literature to our children: our open approach to the world is one aspect of our identity. On the whole the competition from non-Canadian books has been a disadvantage to the publisher rather than to the writer or the reader. Writers have been known to comment on the reluctance of Canadian publishers to recognize their talent, but it is hard to imagine that a *good* Canadian book would not be accepted eagerly and sell reasonably well into the bargain.

There is no doubt that a slim output has influenced—or, more bluntly, lowered—standards of literary judgement and book selection in Canada. A widely held and not illogical view is that Canadian children's books—good, bad, or indifferent—must be supported for the sheer encouragement of writing and publishing in Canada. Most children's librarians with whom I have talked admitted that they operated on a double standard in the purchase of Canadian children's books, although many felt resentful at having to do so. While the support of the Canadian book trade was the chief reason given, there were two other important ones: the rising demands of the school curriculum for Canadian material at all levels of reading and the strong feeling that some effort should be made to counteract the number of books pouring into Canada from the United States (this feeling was not expressed towards British books). Such an attitude should not be taken entirely as an anti-American bias. It is more a sense of exasperation at the dependence on American material that can give rise to the

*Of whom some 6 million are French speaking.

anecdote—not apocryphal—about the Canadian child who came home from school and announced: 'George Washington is the father of my country.' If the child had just read *George Washington* by Ingri and Edgar P. d'Aulaire, the impression it made on him would be understandable, for this is an exceptional book. It is clearly a good thing that Canadian books face competition from the books of other countries, particularly the United States. There is a serious problem, however, in the lack of competition among Canadian books themselves. There can be no choice, for example, between a first-rate biography of David Thompson and an indifferent one—there *is* only one.

These enforced buying habits are frequently reversed in the matter of fiction. Here the majority opinion among librarians favours holding to excellent literary standards regardless of nationality or 'Canadian content'. Some, however, feel an obligation to purchase every Canadian novel, especially if it has an identifiable locale, the theory being that, even if a story is not well written, a child might learn, for instance, that Vancouver is on the west coast of Canada. Whether a novel should be valued as a teaching tool is something I discuss in the chapter on fiction.

It may come as a surprise that I have not sought to be guided by the popularity of the books considered, not even by the 'consumer reactions' of the child readers themselves. Anyone who has dealt with children and their books over a long period will realize that they are notoriously conservative in their reading. Newer and 'different' publications may take a very long time to make their way into the mainstream of acceptance. On the whole, children have not formed what could be called a common judgement about many of the books discussed here. Not many Canadian children's books from the past have endured, and it is too soon to say whether many recent books will last. Moreover, although some children are articulate about why they like or dislike a book, most are not. They will often give the answer that puts an end to the questioning with the greatest expedition. Even more than adults, children will answer questions about their likes and dislikes in books according to their reading habits. A child's opinion of *Alice in Wonderland*, say, will greatly depend upon his previous reading experience. If a child has read and enjoyed the nonsense of

Edward Lear, the wonders of the fairy tale, and the sophistication of Richard Hughes in *Don't Blame Me* or *The Spider's Palace*, his reaction to *Alice* is likely to be different from that of a child who has read only comic books and *The Bobbsey Twins*. Deliberately building in children an acquaintance with good books makes as much sense as taking them step by step through arithmetic.

Every book that a child reads comes to him only after a decision about it has been made by an adult, or, more exactly, by many adults: writer, publisher, bookseller, librarian, parent and/or teacher. Adults have to take the immediate responsibility for judging the quality of children's books and it is to the adults who care about children's books that I address this study. It is children, however, who make the final decision about what is lasting. Children have done this in the past and there is no reason to think they will abrogate their rights in the present or the future. The children of the next generation will show us whether we have been right about the books we favour now.

Literature
of the
Oral
Tradition

INTRODUCTION

To the French who sailed across the Atlantic in the sixteenth and seventeenth centuries, the land that was entered by the great Rivière du Canada appeared to hold limitless possibilities of fulfilling their imaginings and desires—gold for the taking, spices for the picking, and the Great Western Ocean and the Indies, which beckoned them forever onward in their travels like a mirage. There were wonderful tales to be heard, too. Marc Lescarbot recounts the following:

There is another strange thing worthy of record . . . It is that to southward, near Chaleur Bay, lies an isle where lives a dreadful monster called by the savages Gougou, which they told me, had a woman's shape, but very terrible, and so tall, said they, that the top of the masts of our vessel would not have reached her waist . . . and that she has often devoured, and still devours, many savages, whom she puts in a great pouch when she can catch them, and then eats them; and those who had escaped the peril of this unchancy beast said that this pouch was so large that she could have put our vessel in it. . . .*

Seventeenth-century Europeans found it difficult to separate fact from fiction in a land inhabited by 'savages', where anything could happen. Such stories were not recognized for what they were—indigenous myths, which in fact resembled the tales from Greek and Norse mythology to a remarkable degree. The Titans who could move mountains, the one-eyed Cyclops, Polyphemus who could swallow a man whole, the god Thor swinging his gigantic hammer, the goddess Artemis who demanded the sacrifice of a young girl—all these larger-than-life figures of myth could easily have fitted into the Indian material that Lescarbot recorded with such wonder. Only the names and cultural context were different.

Such a close correspondence of themes strongly suggests that the motivations and intentions involved in the creation of myths

*Marc Lescarbot, *The History of New France*, translated by W.L. Grant. Toronto, The Champlain Society, 1911. Vol. ii, p. 170.

must have been roughly similar for all primitive peoples. Just what those motivations and intentions were remains unknown, although there are theories aplenty to account for them. Plato, Vico, Frazer, Lévi-Strauss, Freud, Jung, and in our own time Mircea Eliade, Joseph Campbell, Northrop Frye, and Susanne Langer are only a few of those thinkers who have tried to explain the radical differences in world view between pre-literate and literate man. In most parts of the world mythologies have been analysed and separated out into various branches: myth proper (gods and heroes), folktale (stories about ordinary people whose lives are touched by magic—e.g. Cinderella, Rumpelstiltskin), and historical legend (Arthur, Roland). Whatever term is used to describe the various branches of myth, it is all material from the collective imagination of the race, passed down from generation to generation by word of mouth, given new life by each reteller and often interpreted anew by each generation.

Although the making of myths undoubtedly preceded the development of graphic symbols, myths became widely known and available only in written form. In the case of European myths, centuries of rewriting undoubtedly smoothed away the shapes and textures of the original narratives. Even more important, the development of writing froze or locked in ideas and traditions that were originally fluid and variable. Once the theme had been written down, few variations were possible.

There has been as yet no classification of Indian and Eskimo myths and we refer to them, often improperly, as legend. One fascinating feature of Canadian Eskimo and Indian myths is that they are the product of a *living* oral tradition that is still being transmitted and transmuted through the popular imagination. In a sense, however, the opportunity to witness myth-making in process may cloud rather than clarify interpretation. For example, the knowledge most of us have is based upon versions of Indian and Eskimo tales that we have read in children's books. It is possible that these retellings, effective though many of them are, do not begin to suggest the significance and hidden meanings the stories hold for the Indians and Eskimos themselves—the legends may be far richer than the versions we know. It is well to recall the classic warning of the famous anthropologist, Claude Lévi-

Strauss: 'A primitive people is not a backward or retarded people; indeed it may possess a genius for invention or action that leaves the achievements of civilized peoples far behind.'

Another frequent mistake is to remove myths from their original and still-living context as ritual. Among the West Coast Indians, for example, tales would be told and danced out for several evenings as part of the potlatch ceremony. For some Eskimo storytellers it was considered a triumph when the tale put the audience to sleep. In other instances the tale would be deliberately shortened to produce a kind of staccato effect for contrast, in which case it would more nearly represent the white man's equivalent of a joke than a 'story'. It is worth remembering, too, that many Indian legends were almost the property of a particular family. These stories became highly stylized and could be distinguished from other families' stock of tales by a sense of individuality and inheritance.

What Indian and Eskimo mythology needs, then, is its definitive *littérateurs* who can produce versions that are both faithful to the native cultural values and yet offer the literary and narrative power of their European counterparts. Unfortunately the Canadian equivalent of Grimm, Perrault, Jacobs, and Asbjornsen has not appeared.

In Canada the literature of the popular imagination is portioned out in inverse ratio to the size of the constituent elements in Canada's population. The tiny Eskimo community has a living and vivid mythology. The various Indian groups have accumulated a mass of stories subtly different from one another even in their trickster-heroes. French Canadians (about a third of the population) have managed to a considerable degree to clothe old tales from their homeland with Canadian trappings—and to create new legends out of their historical past (see Claude Aubry's *The Magic Fiddler*). English Canadians, the majority group, lacking an oral tradition of their own, have contented themselves with borrowing from other traditions in their production of books of folktales.

Canadian folklore illustrates the fact that Canada is culturally still a mixture, not a compound. Hugh MacLennan, the eminent Canadian novelist, referred to the separation of English- and

French-speaking Canadians as 'two solitudes'. He might well have said four, because in terms of legend and myth and popular imagination each of our founding ethnic groups seems to stand alone. There have been some borrowings and assimilation, of course, notably between Eskimo and Indian and Indian and French, but the differences are greater than the similarities. It might well be said that 'fabulae populares Canadenses sunt divisae in partes quattuor'.

1 indian
and
eskimo legends

INDIAN LEGENDS

The term Indian legend, like many other generalizations, is of course somewhat misleading, for it suggests a greater degree of homogeneity among the stories than is actually the case. The divisions among the North American Indians were numerous and each group was in many respects quite separate and different from its fellows. Still, the generalization is justified by more than convenience for there is in fact a genuine commonality to Indian legends. Contradictions are often more apparent than real and it can be said that these tales reflect an Indian outlook on life just as there existed a general Scandinavian outlook in Norse mythology.

Sharing a basic provenance with myths in other lands, the Indian legends often somewhat resemble them. Prometheus stole fire for the Greeks; Raven stole it for the West Coast Indians; Nanabozho for the Ojibway or Chippewas; and Glooscap for the East Coast Indians. The Canadian rabbit lost his tail as did rabbits around the world; and whereas Noah built an ark to escape a flood, the Indians built a raft or canoe.

Still, in balance the characteristics peculiar to Indian legends considerably outweigh the similarities that unite them to the mainstream of the primitive tale. These characteristics stem from the unique culture evolved by North American Indians in response to their environment. Henry Schoolcraft, the father of American ethnology and the first great compiler of Indian legends, explains it this way:

The style of narration, the cast of invention, the theory of thinking, are eminently peculiar to a people who wander about in woods and plains, who encounter wild beasts, believe in demons, and are subject to the vicissitudes of the seasons. The tales refer themselves to a people who are polytheists, not believers in one God or Great Spirit but in thousands of spirits; a people who live in fear, who wander in want. . . . —SCHOOLCRAFT's Indian Legends.

The Indians did not make the distinction between god and hero that is found in the Greek and Norse mythologies. They created a being whom the anthropologist describes as the 'culture-hero or transformer'. This being (who had various names in various parts of the country) bent the natural phenomena to his will and generally conferred favours upon his people, often forcing benefits upon them. The motivation of these heroes was not always purposeful, however. Much of the work they accomplished for mankind was through trickery and even mischief. Therefore Indian legends often lack the dignity that is found in other mythologies. The image of the Greek Titan, Prometheus, chained to a rock by Zeus as punishment for bringing fire to mankind, has the awesome and direct qualities of sacrifice and perpetual punishment. Indian versions of the same story lack both impact and simplicity because the theft has either a suggestion of futility or an air of the ridiculous. In one telling of this basic myth, Raven steals fire for the Indians, who are in a darkened world, and is asked by the chief of the Fire People, 'Why did you not *say* so at first and save us all this trouble and anxiety? Fire is the most plentiful thing in our kingdom and we hold it in no value.' (Cyrus Macmillan, 'How Raven Brought Fire to the Indians', *Canadian Fairy Tales*.) In another version, Raven, in the form of a deer, steals fire from the Snowy Owl and manages to set the woods on fire while carrying it. His people at first think little of his gift. (Robert Ayre, 'How Raven Brought the Fire', *Sketco the Raven*.)

It will readily be seen from these examples that, unlike the static, easily grasped personages of Western mythology, Indian heroes are volatile and inconsistent. They indulge in bewildering transformations, changing rapidly and seemingly at random from demi-god to human to animal. Many times there is indeed some uncertainty about whether the hero is appearing in his semi-divine, human, or animal nature.

The same elusive, quicksilver quality applies to the plots of the stories. Whereas European tradition has trained the reader to expect a tale with a beginning, a middle, and an end, with all parts neatly tied together, the Indian legend is full of loose ends. It is a mélange of anecdotes rather than a single unified narrative, patterned after dreams rather than following a conscious development. Some paragraphs from the raw material of the anthropologist may illustrate the point:

HOW THE BEAVER GOT HIS TAIL

When Gluskap was in Cape Breton, he obtained a canoe. He had such power that he took for this purpose a big stone which is now in St Peters, Cape Breton, and resembles a canoe with a person in the middle and a paddle alongside him. He went to the Bras d'Or Lakes. He saw a beaver and a muskrat. The muskrat had a tail like a paddle, the beaver had a poor round tail. Gluskap said to him, 'That tail does not suit you—it is too small.' He asked Muskrat, 'Will you exchange?' 'Yes.' Gluskap took the tail off Muskrat and gave the other tail to Beaver. 'This will make you strong.' He gave the tail to Muskrat: 'This will suit you. It is just your size.' Beaver had a wigwam in the water, and a little poplar tree about twenty yards from the water. Beaver started out with the tail he had gotten from Muskrat, went to the poplar, stood on two legs to bite it, and cut it down. He gnawed first high, then lower. The Big Tail he had procured held him up like a third leg. But Muskrat merely watches and dives quickly. Gluskap had so much power that he could do anything he wanted to do. (John Paul)—WILSON D. WALLIS *and* RUTH SAWTELL WALLIS, The Micmac Indians of Eastern Canada.

THE ORIGIN OF THE CANOE

Gluskap made the first canoe. He took as his model the breastbone of a bird. He procured a bird by killing it with a stone. From its flesh he had a good dinner. While he was picking the meat off the bird's breast, he thought, 'If something of this shape were made, it would float on the water.' He went into the woods to procure some bark. 'If I should kill anything in the water, I could go out for it in this, and would not have to swim.'

Gluskap was a Micmac. At Middle River, Cape Breton, he procured a beaver. About a hundred and fifty years ago the Indians found there the bone of a year-old beaver, one end of which bone fitted the hat of the finder. One end of the bone of the beaver's leg was as large as the man's head.—WILSON D. WALLIS *and* RUTH SAWTELL WALLIS, The Micmac Indians of Eastern Canada.

The rough-hewn quality of the above examples reflects the fact that they are the products of a stone-age unlettered people. The stories of the European oral tradition must originally have been equally crude in form. But over many centuries of literacy, the European myths and folktales were polished and refined. The Indian groups, though valuing eloquence, never had the opportunity to subject themselves to the discipline in communication imposed by the written word, and so their materials remain essentially unsifted.

The same artlessness that makes the Indian legend so loose in structure also makes for baldness in presentation. The embellishments and devices that have kept the stories from the European oral tradition alive and flourishing are quite lacking in their Indian counterparts. For example, the repetitive quality of an English folktale subtly builds the narrative to a climax. 'Be bold, be bold; be bold, be bold, but not too bold; be bold, be bold, but not too bold lest that your heart's blood should run cold'—so goes a famous example, and the tale gains in suspense and memorability with each restatement of the refrain. The Indian legends employ repetition too, but they express it in a highly monotonous manner; incidents and sentences are reiterated with a simple exactitude conducive to boredom. So too the cyclic pattern that binds together the incidents of a European hero story is seldom found in an Indian legend. The sub-tales do not reinforce each other and an Indian story is thus not only difficult to tell orally but is almost impossible to recall.

To these intrinsic deficiencies of artistry must be added the difficulty arising out of simple unfamiliarity. Indigenous though they are to Canada, Indian legends are culturally 'imported' and are no more native to Canadian children than an Ashanti lullaby. Hiawatha apart (and then only by virtue of Longfellow's anglicization of him), the Indian heroes are wholly remote figures. Tom Thumb and Robin Hood are part of the Canadian child's heritage and are effortlessly absorbed into his consciousness. Na-pe and Wisakedjak become known only by purposeful discovery.

Even the Indian landscape is somewhat alien to the Canadian reader. City-bred children do not quickly make themselves at home in dense forest or on sweeping plain and they certainly cannot easily accustom themselves to seeing the most common natural phenomena expressed in terms of the supernatural.

Neither, of course, can the writer of Indian legends. Like his audience he must, in most cases, lack an intimate acquaintance with 'Indian life', past or present. He must rely for his material on secondary sources, almost always of an unsatisfactory kind. Indian legends were collected primarily for ethnological and linguistic purposes, and the tales thus recorded are usually dreary, inconsequential, and halting, often downright incomprehensible to the non-anthropologist. One may even question their reliability, for the 'informant' himself almost never knew English and there is no guarantee that the translator's rendition was faithful, let alone fluent.

All this is to suggest that the making of a good book of Indian legends is no mere anthologizing labour. These legends demand scholarship to make them intelligible, craftsmanship to give them shape, and most of all creative artistry in communicating the freshness, sense of wonder, and directness that represent their greatest appeal to children. It is not easy to meet such demands. It is therefore a matter of some pride for Canada that a few writers have succeeded. A small but vigorous group of Canadian authors (mainly since 1960) have demonstrated the skills of selection and interpretation as well as a knowledge of Indian life and have attempted to make literature out of a large, unwieldy, diverse mass of oral tradition.

The potential for children's literature inherent in the Indian legends is most fully realized by Christie Harris in *Once Upon a Totem* (1963). Other collections may have more charm, or a more fluid style, but the legends chosen by Harris and her interpretation of them are outstanding in that they seek quietly to illuminate universal values. The stories are very much a part of early Indian life and very much a part of today.

The book contains five legends relating to the Indians of the North Pacific Coast, a people unusually rich in myth and legend. In their days of lordship, the abundance of the sea and forest gave them leisure to organize a highly complex social structure, to raise mighty and handsome cedar lodges, and to decorate them with symbols of their past and present greatness. Living above the level of the mere struggle for survival, they held sumptuous potlatches that became the heart of their tribal, social, and commercial life. They had time for song, time to dance—and time for the telling of tales.

Harris does not interpret the intricate character of the trickster-hero Raven but is concerned to present a group of separate stories, each of which has its own shape and development. Her task is therefore somewhat easier than that of those writers who have endeavoured to put some order into the cyclic Indian tales.

The first story in the collection, 'The One-Horned Mountain Goat', is a version of one of the most famous West Coast legends, not only because it has been the most frequently retold but because it reveals so dramatically the Indian concept of respect for animals. The people in the village had grown wasteful and careless, oblivious to the old laws that stated they should be kind to animals and kill only those they needed for food. When the hunters went to the mountain, Stekyawden, and killed goats wastefully and, as a final insult, brought home a kid for the village children to play with, the goats grew angry. Later, the people of the village were invited to a feast by a new tribe that lived on Stekyawden. The tribe, which was made up of mountain goats, fêted the villagers lavishly and then sent them tumbling down the mountain to their death. The only villager saved was the man who had been kind to the kid and protected it from the children. To this man the kid lent his coat and shoes to help him climb safely down the mountain.

This story has been retold for adults by Diamond Jenness in *The Corn Goddess* (1956), by Marius Barbeau in *The Downfall of Temlaham* (1928), and is the first story in *Men of Medeek* (1962) by Will Robinson. It has been retold for children by Hugh Weatherby in *Tales the Totems Tell* (1944), by Olive Fisher and Clara Tyner in *Totem, Tipi and Tumpline* (1955), and by an American, Fran Martin, in *Nine Tales of Raven* (1951). William Toye's version, *The Mountain Goats of Temlaham* (1969), in picture-book format, is by far the best for younger children.

Although the legend loses nothing in a simple retelling—such is its innate power—Christie Harris has enhanced it with detail and in so doing has added a new dimension, much as Walter de la Mare re-clothed the old folktales in his *Tales Told Again*. The hero, Du'as, is a boy rather than a young man or a chief. Harris has added a stern old grandfather, the proud chief Wi-ho-om, and the gay little sister, Katla. Du'as is torn between inner compulsion and training to honour the tribal taboos and his hero-worship of one who violates them. The author's style is simple and vivid, as when she is describing the vengeance of the goats, and one feels the rhythm of the archetypal legend:

He felt the hard earth quake, he heard it rumble deep in the rocks beneath him; he saw the feast house collapse, with its giant timbers. People and poles and flames moved out before him. They dropped in a hideous rockslide. Screams tore the air. Boulders tumbled and crashed and bounced off, thundering down toward the river valley.

Many Indian legends have a quality of anonymity. In their original form, characters may not even be identified, or their traits may be so little individualized as to make them types rather than people. But Harris, in her first sentence, brings her hero close to the reader: 'Long, long ago there lived an Indian boy, Du'as, who found one northern summer almost endless. It seemed to him that the golden tints of autumn would never brighten the aspen trees along the lower slopes of Stek-yaw-den.'

At the same time Harris does not sacrifice authenticity to literary values. The five stories retold in this collection are based on ethnological reports and on the author's direct experience of mingling with the Indians as much as possible in their homes and in their villages listening to the stories being told. Three stories have overtones of European folktales but stand sturdily on their own feet as indigenous products. The author tells us that the last tale—'Fly Again Proud Eagle'—is a historical adventure, based firmly on actual happenings. Be that as it may, it is also a portrayal of the longing, as old and as new as human experience, to recapture a lost homeland.

Most stories from the oral tradition are improved by pruning, honing, polishing, and refining until not a word seems out of place and the basic concept emerges with clarity, but with enough depth and mystery to allow readers to make their own interpretation. In Harris's recent collection, *Once More Upon a Totem* (1973), the considerable risk inherent in the embellishment of myth and legend is all too apparent. The first story, 'The Prince Who was Taken Away by the Salmon', is a famous Tsimshian tale, which, as recorded in Franz Boas' *Tsimshian Mythology*, has a definite mythological shape. In transferring it to the short-story or novelette form, Harris has destroyed its legend quality and, indeed, its basic pattern. Length becomes even more of a hazard in the second story, 'Raven Travelling', which is long and repetitious to the point of boredom; while the third one, 'Ghost Story', is so long and involved that it cheats the reader of the shivers promised by the title.

Alongside Harris's rather sophisticated talents, the older retellings seem now to be somewhat naïve, but they retain their charm and considerable popularity. The pioneer effort, and for many years the only retelling of Canadian Indian legends available, was Pauline Johnson's *Legends of Vancouver* (1911), which was not written specifically for children although it is read by them. The tales told by Pauline Johnson are unique in that she heard them directly from Chief Joe Capilano of Vancouver. Not understanding his language (she was a Mohawk), she listened to his halting English and then put them into 'literary' form. The hushed, intimate quality one associates with the beginning of a story that is told rather than read is an endearing characteristic of the book. Through the polished phrases the reader can indeed hear the old 'tyee' speak of a time when 'Indian law ruled the land. Indian customs prevailed. Indian beliefs were regarded. These were the

legend-making ages when great things occurred to make the traditions we repeat to our children today.'

Legends of Vancouver and Cyrus Macmillan's *Canadian Wonder Tales* (1918) and *Canadian Fairy Tales* (1922) were for many
years a child's only access to the world of the Canadian Indian.
The titles of the Macmillan books are significant. Professor Macmillan saw the Indian legends as an extension of the European
folk- and fairy-tale tradition and, although he actually heard the
tales (according to the prefaces), and had studied the originals, he
clothed them in the lighter form of the fairy tale. Those who knew
these books as children still feel a nostalgic reverence for them,
especially in their gift-edition form with the bold, mannered, romantic illustrations. This was the veritable stuff of fairy tales—
magic coats and wands, ogres, giants, and mermaids—put somewhat into a Canadian setting. Significantly, one story is called
'An Indian Cinderella', and a fair inference is that some of the
stories are actually white men's tales that have been adapted by
the Indians. All the stories in both of these books have been reissued in one volume under the title *Canadian Wonder Tales*
(1974), with illustrations by Elizabeth Cleaver. The stories about
Glooscap, the hero of the Micmacs, were undoubtedly the best,
and these were brought together and published as *Glooskap's
Country and Other Indian Tales* in 1955.

Another favourite from an older generation is Hilda Hooke's
Thunder in the Mountains, which was published in 1947. This
book has a definite pattern. It is divided into three parts—Indian
tales, stories about the coming of the white man, and stories with
a French-Canadian background—but pervading them all is a common mood, the feeling of doom that was linked in the Indian mind
with the coming of the white man.

These are good stories, told with an intimate quality. The little
asides directed at the reader—reminiscent of Hawthorne's approach in Greek tales—are particularly effective. Of larger consequence, more than any other book of Indian legends—indeed,
perhaps more than any other Canadian children's book—*Thunder
in the Mountains* gives a feeling of Canada. It is not just the plant-
ing of corn and pumpkin or the flash of red maple leaves or the
geographical names. It is Thunderbird swaggering across the sky

and causing a storm on Lake Superior; Whale puffing on the pipe that Glooscap gave him; the slender birches bowing to one another across the Ottawa River; the huckleberries as blue as the summer skies; the red logs of the cedars; the image of Nana Bijou, who can be seen as you look across the bay from Port Arthur—'He lies on Thunder Cape, his face turned to the sky, waiting for Gitche Manitou to wake him up.' Hilda Hooke presents a theme in each story—basically she is concerned with the struggle between good and evil—and the stories gain strength from a definite point of view.

A prime attribute of this collection is the underlying current of humour that is part of much of the world's heroic literature. It is well illustrated in the author's characterization of Paspaschao the Sapsucker as a bit of a tippler:

... [he indulged] until the stuff went to his head, and he hit himself against the trees because he couldn't fly straight. Which, of course, was a very foolish thing to do. . . . 'Good gracious!' said Paspaschao, rubbing his eyes, 'that sap must be getting rather strong. I suppose I shouldn't have taken so much before breakfast.'

Humour, a very distinctive kind of humour, is also the principal attraction in the several books that rework the ubiquitous theme of the 'culture-hero' or transformation-trickster. This type of hero was very dear to the heart of the Indian and appears in one form or another in the lore of almost every group. In the creation myth, the hero (Raven or Sketco or Nanabozho or Na-pe) typically does not himself create the Indian world all at once but rather shapes it to human use. He finds what is useful to men (the sun, the moon, stars, fire) and confers it upon them—or even forces it upon them, and not necessarily for the noblest of reasons. For, unlike the heroes of European mythology, the Indian hero is neither all good nor all evil; his powers are not absolute, nor does he always use them wisely. He may be a boaster and a trickster as well as a saviour, and he may betray man as often as he helps him.

The most adept use of such material is made in Robert Ayre's *Sketco the Raven* (1961), which provides a definitive approach to the great Raven cycle of legends. These were known and told among many Indian groups of the Northwest coast—the Tlingit, Haida, Tsimshian, and Kwakiutl—although they knew Raven under various names.

'Beyond the rim of the world, in the high North, in the North beyond the North, Sketco the Raven was born.' Ayre sometimes has a powerful eloquence suited to the Indian style. He gives unity to the cycle by consistently emphasizing Raven as the friend and benefactor of mankind, and has chosen the stories in which Raven uses his wits and his magic to bring comfort and hope to the Indians living in a darkened world. Raven steals fire from the great Snowy Owl, so that men may be warm; he releases the Sun that they may have light; and he brings game and moves the ocean to provide food from both the land and the sea. In these stories Raven is not only a magical being with power to transform himself into a Raven as well as other animals; he is also a small boy who grows to manhood determined to avenge the murder of his three brothers. Collectively the legends are a story of high adventure as well as a tale of the supernatural.

Ayre retains much of the sly fun of the original stories while avoiding their characteristic earthiness. Sketco jabs 'The Man who Sat on the Tide' with his harpoon first in the knees and then in the buttocks, and, as the giant yells and lunges at his tormentor, the sea pours down into a hole like the gurgling of the water going down the bathtub drain. There is also a capricious Poseidon called Fog Man, who makes fog by pulling his hat down over his head and provides comic relief in Sketco's odyssey of revenge.

The great Ojibway counterpart to Raven is the subject of Dorothy Reid's *Tales of Nanabozho* (1963), and the Micmac hero, Glooscap, is the focal point for Kay Hill's *Glooscap and His Magic* (1963). Both books emphasize the trickster qualities in their heroes, who, however, gradually change from buffoons to characters of dignity. Dorothy Reid keeps to the spirit of the originals by showing Nanabozho as foolish, capricious, and often cruel. In one story, when Nanabozho discovers that his secret hoard of silver is known to the white men, he and Thunder Bird cause a great storm. This in turn prevents his wife, Minnehaha, from getting fish for his supper. When the Great Man finds that his food is not ready, he explodes in a rage and turns his beloved wife into a stone. He himself is turned into stone for causing a storm to harm the white people, against the orders of the great spirit, Gitche Manitou—a quick ending. While deliberately conveying the unpatterned quality of the Indian tale, Reid has organized the material into an authentic-sounding, coherent life story—made up, of course, of self-contained tales. Her achievement is all the more noticeable in comparison with an American publication, Thomas B. Leekley's *The World of Manabozho* (1965). The number and diversity of these tales, and the resulting lack of cyclic continuity, make Leekley's Manabozho a far less memorable hero than Reid's.

Kay Hill's *Glooscap and His Magic* has more form and a more legendary or myth-like quality than Cyrus Macmillan's *Glooskap's Country*. Like Macmillan, Hill presents Glooscap as eternally benevolent. His tricks are good-natured and always serve to help someone in distress. However, here the similarities end. Macmillan's version tends to present Glooscap as almost a fairy-tale character. When Glooscap is making the birds, Macmillan has him wave a wand to achieve their transformation. Hill, more effectively, concentrates on the comic effect of the birds' vying for Glooscap's attention. Another great difference is in the style. Macmillan's is almost completely narrative while Hill makes effective use of conversation. She is also able to give considerable characterization to the animals who were Glooscap's friends. Her telling of how Ableegumooch, Glooscap's messenger, lost his tail is the most memorable of all the versions of this story. The book begins with the tales of organization and creation—Glooscap creates the world, then the animals, and then men; there is even a Cain and Abel theme—and ends with Glooscap's giving the game of lacrosse to his people.

Glooscap and His Magic has a robust and full-blooded tone reminiscent of the heroic European tradition. Many of the tales have in fact their almost exact counterpart in the oral literature of the world. There is the tale of the poor boy, Tabulech, who wins the chief's daughter by making her laugh—aided, of course, by a magic flute donated by Glooscap. The story of Oochigeas is the Indian's answer to Cinderella. Maltreated and abused by her older sisters, Oochigeas nevertheless triumphs over them in winning

Team, the invisible brave, who will appear only to the truthful. However, in spite of such parallelisms, the writer has successfully maintained in her retellings a flavour and a spirit that are distinctly Indian.

More Glooscap Stories (1970) shows a greater assurance with the material of legend than does Hill's first book. Everything is slightly sharpened—the style, the humour, the conciseness, and above all a sense of conviction that does not even need the precise use of Nova Scotian place-names to give the tales credibility.

For the Blackfoot Indians the 'Big Man' was Na-pe, the Old Man, and his story is told in Frances Fraser's simple and skilful *The Bear Who Stole the Chinook and Other Stories* (1959). Of all the Indian 'Big Men', Na-pe is the most consistently irascible. He alternately tricks the animals into helping him and then turns on them or is tricked by the animals. The stories about Na-pe himself are more anecdotal than the other tales in the book, and have a light-hearted humour. All the stories, however, have dignity and charm as well as a genuine Indian quality. The book proves that it is possible to write directly for children without over-simplification. Fraser gets her effect from the selection of her incidents rather than from condensing a mass of material. Again, even in these simply told tales, the resemblance to other folk literature is noticeable. 'The Ghost Pipe' is the Indian Orpheus and Eurydice; 'The Girl who Married the Morning Star' has echoes of the flood stories.

Diamond Jenness tells us in *The Indians of Canada* that the Blackfoot Indians were 'the strongest and most aggressive nation on the Canadian prairies in the middle of the eighteenth century . . . ' They fought with their neighbours, treated their women harshly, and certainly knew privation and starvation. These harsh realities are reflected in Frances Fraser's second book of Blackfoot tales, *The Wind Along the River* (1968), making it considerably different from the more humorous and lyrical *The Bear Who Stole the Chinook*. Four Na-pe stories apart, the remainder are obviously based on historical incidents from the not-so-distant past— stories of tribal wars, kidnappings, torture, and revenge. They display many characteristics of the Indian legend that trouble the non-Indian reader. They are anecdotal in character rather than full tales; they are unfinished and unpolished; they convey a sense of reportage rather than involvement on the author's part. They were indeed reported to Fraser 'by the elders of the tribe', and although they should no doubt be read and understood within the totality of the life and customs of the Blackfoot Indians of the time, this would not always be obvious to an uninformed reader, particularly a child reader. Though many of the themes and incidents appear in European myth, legend, and folktale, they are presented there within the framework of a universal moral order, ending in a confrontation between recognizable good and evil and expressed in a well-established conventional pattern. The stories in *The Wind Along the River*, with a few exceptions, exhibit a long-delayed concept of justice that is cold and chilling and alien to the child mind. They are first generation in that this appears to be their first appearance in printed form. A search in anthropological and ethnological literature did not reveal any prototypes. However, one story, 'The Blue End of the World', appeared as a Blackfoot tale called 'The Story of Scar Face' in Lewis Spence's *The Myths of the North American Indians* (1914), though the older version ends happily and the newer one ends in sudden and startling revenge. *The Wind Along the River* is an important collection, but for children it will not be as persuasive an introduction to Indian lore as the retellings by Ayre, Clutesi, Harris, Hill, and Reid, who have presented the Indian legend in a familiar rather than a distinctive pattern.

It is quite possible, of course, that the Indian legend's echoes and resemblances to European folk literature are illusory. They may actually derive more from the retellers than from the tales themselves—from the fact that the non-Indian authors, steeped in European traditions, have unconsciously imposed the patterns and flavour of the European tale upon the Indian material. The test of this hypothesis is in the making, for the newest and most important trend in the publication of Indian legends is the appearance of books by Indians themselves. Until the last decade, Pauline Johnson was the only Indian reteller of the legends of her people. The preservation and publication of the Indian oral tradition were left to the anthropologist and to non-Indian writers who had recognized its qualities and, in some fortunate cases, its appeal for children. Now, since 1968, Indians themselves have produced half a dozen books, and many more will no doubt follow.

The first such book, Norval Morriseau's *Legends of My People: The Great Ojibway* (1965), was *not* intended for children and the editor, Selwyn Dewdney, did not exercise a strong editorial hand. The material is therefore rather formless and in many respects is well beyond a child's capacity and interest. As the editor points out in his preface, the stories were 'poured out of Morriseau's mind and memory without regard for sequence, so that in their original form they comprised a fascinating but often confusing *pot-pourri* of legends, anecdotes, observations, reports and personal comments.' However, Morriseau writes with a feeling and a sense of conviction that are all too often lacking in the work of the non-Indian storytellers. There is also a very strong poetic flavour, which is apparently much more 'normal' for Indian speech than it is for our own. As Fraser Symington points out in *The Canadian Indian*: 'Indians used words in normal talk as poets of the literate societies used them in writing.' Even the formlessness is not without its effectiveness. The strong sense of structure that non-Indian authors have usually applied to Indian (and Eskimo) legends has resulted in tales that 'flow' well and 'build' to a dramatic point, but they lack the naturalness and authenticity of Morriseau's stories, which reveal a way of life and the living essence of a whole people.

Morriseau inspired and illustrated Herbert T. Schwarz's *Windigo and Other Tales of the Ojibway* (1969), a book that *should* interest children. The characters and incidents are standard in Ojibway lore— the windigo, the shaking tent, the thunderbird, whisky-jack—and the stories are briefly and dramatically told. Morriseau's illustrations depict both the fantasy and the inner reality of myth, having an impact similar to Charles Keeping's illustrations of Greek myth for Leon Garfield's and Edward Blishen's *The God Beneath the Sea*.

George Clutesi's *Son of Raven, Son of Deer: Fables of the Tse-shaht* (1967) has had the most dramatic success to date of Indian material related by an Indian. Clutesi reveals the essential point of his stories in his title. As his use of the word 'fable' implies, these are beast tales—the adventures of the foolhardy Son of

Deer and the greedy and thoughtless Son of Raven—used to teach the mores and morals of a society to children. With the exception of the first story, a moving and dignified version of the 'bringing of fire', each tale has that favourite Indian personage, the anti-hero, who struts and boasts until, in the end, the last trick is played on *him*. Clutesi's stories seem closer to *Aesop's Fables* than to the main body of Indian legend, but the author assures us that the stories were handed down in his family for at least 400 years (!), so there is no question of their authenticity and inde-pendent origin. The ease and polish of these fables are no doubt partly due to Clutesi's skill, partly to a long history of retelling; if they are not yet sharpened and honed to perfection it is perhaps because, for a folktale, even four hundred years is not a long time for the reworking of material.

Ko-ishin-mit loved to copy and imitate other people—especially the clever people. He would watch them doing their tasks, then he would go home and imitate them, no matter how hard it might be. He loved to go around visiting his neighbours at meal-time, look-ing for free meals. He would walk for miles for a feed. Oh, how Ko-ishin-mit loved to eat! Ko-ishin-mit would eat anything put before him, he was so greedy.

In some respects the introduction to *Son of Raven, Son of Deer* is as significant as the stories themselves. Clutesi tells us that the white man's nursery rhymes can be puzzling and disturbing to the Indian child. For example, he takes exception to 'Rock-a-bye Baby' on the grounds that 'The Indian child feels bewilderment with this type of nursery rhyme because there seems to be no concern or regard for a very apparent injury inflicted upon a little child.'* Similarly, he finds in 'Humpty Dumpty' evidence of the white man's callous disregard of suffering. If Indian children in general really view the white man's stories in this way, can it be that white children—or white adults, for that matter—are equally guilty of misinterpreting Indian legends? One begins to wonder uneasily

The Oxford Dictionary of Nursery Rhymes by Iona and Peter Opie says that the authorship of 'Rock-a-bye Baby' has been attributed to a Pilgrim youth who, arriving on the *Mayflower*, noticed the way the Indians hung their birchbark cradles, with baby inside, on the branch of a tree.

how much is really translatable from different cultures and literatures.

Other Indian authors seem to see themselves as pious recorders of a cultural heritage rather than as artistic tellers of tales. Their introductions invariably point out that the old people can still recall 'how it was' and that the tales were lifted from their memories and passed on as the ethnic life-blood of succeeding generations. When literary intent is present, the capacity for execution may not be. As Norval Morriseau has pointedly reminded us, 'Among the Indians, as among other nations, some people are born artists, but most are not.' Such recent publications as Patronella Johnston's *Tales of Nokomis* (1970), Alex Grisdale's *Wild Drums: Tales and Legends of the Plains Indians* (1972), and *Tales From the Longhouse* (1973) collected by Indian children in British Columbia, should thus be seen for what they are—unpretentious and, within their aims, successful attempts to bring together important stocks of legend, lore, and even history.

The memory of historical incidents is seen quite clearly in Grisdale's *Wild Drums*. A member of the Salteaux band in Manitoba, he recorded stories of tribal wars, kidnappings, and revenge. The events and characters are not all that dissimilar from the history of any other nation; the important difference is in the setting. The environment and the customs that form the background of the incidents add greatly to one's knowledge and understanding of the Canadian Indian. However, many of the stories, although short, have complicated plots and no more than pedestrian writing. In 'The Mystery Arrow' the young Indian hunter Lynx dreams about arrows, and the next day finds one sticking in his flesh. It kills his enemies, but misses a young deer. The chief puts the arrow in his lodge for safe-keeping, but the next day it is gone. Later the arrow is found sticking in the body of a baby.

The medicine man said, 'No one can keep this arrow. We will hang it at the edge of the woods where it can always be seen.'

So this was done and whenever a strange Indian came too near the village he was found dead, with the arrow in him. Men who tried to steal horses or young girls, died the same way. No one in this camp ever touched the arrow but Lynx, and he used it only when the hunt was poor and the people were hungry. The arrow was no use for killing animals unless the people were starving, then the chief would order Lynx to bring in fresh meat.

Lynx honoured the mystery arrow and before and after the hunt he always thanked the plum wood for its protection and goodness. But Lynx' wife was very jealous of the arrow and one day when he laid it on his drum before going on a hunt, she broke it in half and threw the arrow into the tepee-fire.

When Lynx asked her what had happened to his plum wood arrow she cried angrily, 'It was everything to you. All the people praised you and thought well of you when you used it to bring back buffalo and deer. You gave me no credit when I went with you on the hunt. It was bad medicine for everybody.'

Lynx was too sad to quarrel with his wife. He walked away from camp and into an island of poplar trees. In a little while the scouts at camp saw this bluff on fire. But it was too late to save Lynx, and many people said he wanted to die like the plum wood arrow.

The jealous wife told the chief and his councillors that Lynx had taken the mystery arrow with him. But none believed her, and no one pitied her in the wintertime when she had to do her own hunting because she did not have a man to do this any more.

In strong contrast as a narrative is the opening paragraph of Dorothy Reid's 'Nanabozho and the Wild Geese', a story posed in the framework of the European tradition.

Nanabozho lived with his grandmother in a small wigwam in the forest. He could swim better and run faster than any of the other boys, and he excelled them too in pranks. He loved to swim under water and jerk the fishermen's lines; he delighted in springing the women's rabbit snares.

One day, as he was wandering through the woods looking for mischief, he came to the shore of a small lake. He saw some bright red berries in the lake and tried to pick them, but all he got was a handful of chilling water that slipped through his fingers.—Tales of Nanabozho.

Tales of Nokomis by Patronella Johnston, an Ojibway, gives a rather gentle picture of Indian life. Her avowed intent was the transmission of nature myth and lore to Ojibway children. 'The First Water-Lily', 'The Burdock', and 'The Jewel Weed' have a certain homely charm. Unfortunately, by setting the stories in a transparently didactic framework—a grandmother teaches the stories to her grandchildren by a tedious conversational method reminiscent of nineteenth-century primers—the quality of unself-consciousness that surrounds, or should surround, the written products of the oral tradition has been lost.

Tales From the Longhouse has a more distinctive and effective approach. Indian children on Vancouver Island were asked to write their own tales and legends. Their first attempts were about television and movie 'Indians'. Then the elders stepped in to help. The results, couched in sparse prose, quite often project a feeling of authenticity and timelessness. As may be expected with this kind of group effort, there is considerable variation in the nature and quality of the material. Perhaps the best rendering occurs with the retelling of familiar stories—'In the Beginning' (the creation of the world by Nanabozho), 'The Legend of the Flood' (a version of the basic flood story), and 'A Legend of Spring Salmon' (a famous Tsimshian tale). Others are less-known local legends, while the remainder are snippets of lore and customs.

Relatively unpolished and little known as most of these publications are, they offer a fascinating view of folktales in the making, as it were. The same process of recall and assembly of tribal lore, of ordering and refining the material, and the same gradual shift in emphasis from ethnic to artistic values, must have occurred with the now-classic European stories. The development of the indigenous Canadian Indian tale will, no doubt, attain the same goal— a good story well told.

As yet, the stories that we have, whether by Indian or non-Indian, merely open the door on the fascinations of a world that is at once alien and strangely familiar. Although the differences between Indian legends and their European counterparts have been noted, the Indian legend does take its place in the world commonality of the oral tradition. The combination of familiarity and strangeness is an aspect of myths, hero stories, and folktales, and is their chief appeal to children. They reassure by their naïveté, enthral by their matchless story qualities, and stretch the child imaginatively and emotionally as he learns the fundamental qualities of the human race. Canadian writers have shown clearly that Nanabozho of the Ojibways, Sketco of the North Pacific Coast, Glooscap of the Micmacs, Wisakedjak of the Crees, Na-pe of the Blackfoot, and the hundreds of Indian chiefs and princesses and their animal friends—Bear, Rabbit, Turtle, Badger—belong as surely to children of the world as do their counterparts from other countries. The legends about them have a strong appeal for children because they reveal a world that is in many ways close to that of a child—a world in which 'every thunderclap came as a threat and every night as the last'. Furthermore, it is one in which imagination has free reign and society is colourful, independent, close to nature, and filled with animal lore. Many of the virtues the legends extol are universal: kindness to men and animals, courage and strength in the face of adversity, loyalty to family and tribe, unfailing devotion even unto death. The legends have special value for Canadians because they deal with a physical environment that is familiar to us: the mountains, rivers, and animals are ours, along with the frightening wilderness, the endless prairie, the swift-moving rivers, the fruits of earth and sea. Nor is the Indians' relationship with nature beyond our understanding: the struggle between man and his environment is still a dominant one in many parts of Canada.

Above all, these stories have humour—a quality that is conspicuously lacking in most Canadian children's books. It is sometimes sly and subtle, it is often rather unusual, but it is there, as witness this Cree tale, which was doubtless invented by some wag around the campfire after the white man came:

When Great One made mankind, he first made an earth oven. Then he modelled a man of clay and put him in to bake. He was not baked enough and came out white. Great One tried again, but this time he baked the man too long. He came out black. The third time Great One baked the man just the correct time, and he came out red. That is why different races have different colours.— KATHARINE B. JUDSON, Myths and Legends of British North America.

ESKIMO LEGENDS

The early Greeks conceived their world as arising out of a vaporous, formless mass; the Scandinavians saw theirs emerging from a chaos of fire and ice. In both mythologies man appears only after great primeval struggles with Titans and giants, with startling dramas played out in terror and trickery and battles, and in sacrifice and beauty. Such tales are the foundations of Western literature. In strong contrast, Eskimo creation myths seem simple, even naive:

It was in the time when there were no people on the earth plain. During four days the first man lay coiled up in the pod of a beachpea. On the fifth day he stretched out his feet and burst the pod, falling to the ground, where he stood up, a full-grown man. . . . When he looked up again he saw approaching, with a waving motion, a dark object which came on until just in front of him, when it stopped, and standing on the ground, looked at him. This was a raven, and, as soon as it stopped, it raised one of its wings, pushed up its beak, like a mask, to the top of its head, and changed at once into a man.*

This is part of the Raven cycle of legends, which is probably not indigenous to the Eskimo since Raven as creator and as bringer of light and fire was known also to the Northwest Coast Indians and the Northeast Asians. A Greenland tale, recorded by Rasmussen (in *Eskimo Folk-Tales,* 1921), is even less impressive. It simply states that the earth fell down from the sky and then, 'when the earth was made, came men'.

There is scarcely any region on earth that presents conditions more severe and inclement for man than the Arctic, for apart from the animal habitation, it is bare of all that is elsewhere considered necessary for life; and yet the Eskimo long ago came to terms with his environment and has successfully waged the struggle for existence. While doing this, he has given only the most fleeting thought to the phenomenon of man's creation. In some stories Raven is the sole creator; he also provides by stealth the sun, the

*J.W. Powell, *Eighteenth Annual Report of the Bureau of American Ethnology.* Part 1, 1899.

moon, and the stars. But there are other very brief stories of the spirits of a sister and a brother who, having quarrelled, become the sun and the moon. Variations in legends are, of course, accounted for by the differences among widely scattered tribes who rarely, if ever, came in contact with one another.

There is a matter-of-factness about the Eskimo's idea of his origin—a modesty, even an indifference that is unmatched in the myths of any other peoples. But man, and human achievement in the Eskimo context, forms the core of his world of legend.

The superior beings of the Eskimos may outdistance ordinary people, but they are human beings through and through, rarely supported by magic and witchcraft. When the supernatural does occur it is often tossed in as an aside: a young man suddenly appears to have the powers of a shaman or an angakok; an ordinary girl can throw up a mountain and turn a stream into a river. And so the supernatural seems in every way as normal as the everyday tangible world in which the stories are set. With the exception of Raven, animals are rarely mythologized—perhaps because they were the sole source of food and clothing. Certainly there is no animal figure to match Anansi, of African and West Indian legend, or Coyote of the southwestern United States and Mexico, or Monkey of Chinese legend. Animals are portrayed almost invariably in their natural actions and locations. (It is the animal tales that are most frequently retold for children.) Basically there is a whole-hearted reality to Eskimo legend in its succession of incidents probably based on historical events, especially the meeting of Eskimo and Indian. The protagonists are chiefly hunters, but the plots are liberally sprinkled with grandfathers and grandmothers and particularly orphans, a sharp reminder of the hazards of hunting.

Although it is Eskimo carvings and prints that have received the greatest popular acclaim, among Eskimos themselves their legends take pride of place. In the long Arctic nights the storytellers achieved the status of the bards and troubadours in early European culture and hold that position even today. The stories varied greatly in length. Some were mere anecdotes, while others took several nights to tell, with the storyteller feeling particularly successful if the audience fell asleep. The stories themselves seem to emerge from the environment, just as the igloos of the Eskimos are simply sculpted extensions of the snow and ice upon which they live. A young boy carves a snow bear in order to frighten a real bear; a girl flies by attaching to her arms the feathers of a snow goose; the Eskimos test their strength against the Indians. The brief Arctic summer has been praised for its beauty and lamented for its brevity, but it is interesting to note that most legends take little notice of it. Winter is generally the background, whether in the vast outdoors or in the close quarters of igloo or tent.

The struggle for existence has certainly induced a certain fear towards the environment—a combination of the healthy and the fatalistic. The Eskimo Aua expressed this fear to Rasmussen, the Danish explorer and ethnologist, in 1921:

We fear the weather spirit of earth, that we must fight against to wrest our food from land and sea. We fear Sila.

We fear death and hunger in the cold snow huts.

We fear Takanakapsaluk, the great woman who down at the bottom of the sea rules over all the beasts of the sea.

We fear the sickness that we meet with daily all around us; not death, but the suffering. We fear the evil spirits of life, those of the air, of the sea and earth, that can help wicked shamans to harm their fellow man.

*We fear the souls of dead human beings and of the animals we have killed.**

The most important and terrible figure in Eskimo lore is the spirit of Nuliajuk (or Takanakapsaluk, or Sedna), the mother of sea animals. She notices every little breach of a taboo, for she knows everything. Whenever people have been indifferent towards her, she hides all the animals and mankind has to starve. But the Nuliajak or Sedna legend, while it is the basic taboo legend, is only one of many that deal with the theme 'thou shalt not'. A good many stories are concerned with sudden killings and long-delayed vengeance. A mother lets her blind son starve; when he regains his sight years later he has her dragged into the water by a walrus. A girl who has been mistreated by her father turns into

*Knud Rasmussen, *Intellectual Culture of the Iglulik Eskimos*, 1929.

a bear and kills him. The losing team in a ball game resorts to magic to kill the winning team; a survivor plots punishment that takes a long time to accomplish.

Like folklore around the world, many of these tales give an idea of the Eskimos' moral code, and afford likewise a reflection of their feelings, of what they admire and what they despise and condemn. They love strength and fearlessness, helpfulness and kindliness. Cruelty not only hurts the person ill treated, but recoils upon the doer. Nothing is more certain than Nemesis.

Eskimo folklore does not lack robust fun and humour; Eskimos do not take themselves *too* seriously. Like much Indian folklore, Eskimo tales have an underlying earthiness that is smoothed out or omitted by the retellers for children. It is perhaps inevitable that these retellings are cast in the European mould, with a strong and decisive plot line. Such is not always the Eskimo way. As one Eskimo has stated:

It is not always that we want a point in our stories—if only they are amusing. It is only the white men that want a reason and an explanation for everything, and so our old men say that we should treat white men as children who always want their own way. If not, they become angry and scold.*

Many stories have obviously been embellished after the coming of the white man. A basic legend tells of the woman who married a dog who took on a man's shape. But her offspring were dogs. The mother set them adrift and they formed various tribes. The last of the brood stayed with the woman and became the ancestors of the Eskimo. (Franz Boas, *The Eskimo of Baffin Land and Hudson Bay*, 1901.) An obviously later version relates that four of the offspring were white men. 'The girl put the four white men in the sole of a boot and set it adrift in the sea. The men drifted down and produced all the white men that are now in the world.' (Helen Caswell, *Shadows from the Singing House: Eskimo Folk Tales*, 1968.)

There is a great wealth of Eskimo lore locked in anthropological and ethnological reports that have been available since the turn

---

*Knud Rasmussen, Intellectual Culture of the Copper Eskimos, 1931.

of the century. With all the difficulties inherent in translating in one leap an oral literature into a written literature into another language, it is still somewhat surprising that Canadian publishers have ignored this material for so long. Fortunately Americans have been more aware of its imaginative qualities and it is thanks to them that we have had such substantial collections as *Alaskan Igloo Tales* (1958) by Edward L. Keithahn, *Tundra Tales* (1967) by Nola W. Zobarskas, and an earlier book by Charles E. Gillham, *Beyond the Clapping Mountains* (1943). The reteller has two basic choices: to keep as close as possible to the original, whether it was recorded by anthropologists or taken down orally, trusting the reader to make his own link with an alien culture; or to retell the story with substantial modifications, keeping the basic spirit but adding an original and compelling creative quality, as Leon Garfield and Edwin Blishen did with their retellings of the Greek myths in *The God Beneath the Sea*. In general the Keithahn and Zobarskas collections respect Eskimo culture and endeavour to appeal to children through the stories selected for retelling rather than by imposing totally European patterns upon them. However, Gillham in *Beyond the Clapping Mountains* has softened the generally rather severe and realistic animal stories into sweet animal fantasies of the white man's tradition. This misapplication probably reflects the date of the book's publication; in the 1940s authors and publishers had not yet come to give full respect to preserving the authenticity of the native material—especially in books for children.

Ronald Melzack's *The Day Tuk Became a Hunter & Other Eskimo Stories* (1967) appears to be the first Canadian collection for children. It shares many of the characteristics of Helen Caswell's *Shadows from the Singing House* (1968), based in Alaskan Eskimo lore, which is of the same vintage. Both retellers used standard sources for their tales—Rasmussen, Boas, and Powers, as well as more recent collections such as the Keithahn—and both have cast their stories very much in the European mould. However, an interesting contrast develops in their retellings of the famous story of Sedna, the archetypal undersea figure who vigilantly and mercilessly takes care that all souls of both animals and man are shown the respect that ancient rules of life demand. The

Caswell book includes the starker details of the original. Sedna's father and/or brothers (depending upon the version), pursued by the girl's husband and in order to lighten the boat, throw her overboard. As she clutches at the edge of the boat they cut off the first joint of her finger, then the second, then the third, then the whole hand. Sedna becomes a sea goddess while the dismembered limbs turn into the animals that inhabit the sea—whales, walrus, and seals.

The rather gory details of the Caswell version are not all that prevalent in Eskimo stories. When they do occur they are no more shocking than such episodes in European folklore and have just as strong a mythic sense. However, Eskimo stories do lack the European tale's strong delineation of what is good and what is evil; a moral tone, however, might have been imposed by later generations in the stories' long cultural transmission.

Many Eskimo tales, of course, are neither as stark nor as distinctive as the Sedna legend. Some, such as 'Why the Raven Is Black' (Caswell) and 'How the Raven Brought Light to the World' (Melzack), are as much Indian as Eskimo, while others echo the standard plots of European folklore. 'Leealura and Maleyato' (Melzack), in which the great hunter Maleyato marries the girl 'whose needle makes no sound while she sews', is kin to the test story—Patient Griselda or Cinderella and her glass slipper. 'The Man and the Star' (Caswell) is a kind of 'Jack the Giant Killer' tale and the two children in 'The Witch' (Melzack) are as victorious as Hansel and Gretel.

In *Raven, Creator of the World* (1970), Ronald Melzack tells us frankly that 'it was necessary to retell the stories in a way that would appeal to children in our culture'. Appealing the book is, with its attractive format and large, bold, ice-blue pictures by Laszlo Gal. The rather soft writing style is calculated to make the stories palatable as an introduction to Eskimo legend for younger children and also marketable to adults. The stories have been pieced together from various anthropological sources to make a continuous cycle of the adventures of Raven. The treatment is somewhat similar to Robert Ayre's *Sketco the Raven*—about the trickster-hero of the West Coast Indians—but lacks its strength and rough humour. Indeed, the Melzack retellings fail to evoke the power and dignity of the bird itself in its own habitat.

The Melzack book begins gently: 'In the beginning there was only Raven and the falling snowflakes' and continues through Raven's rather mild adventures until he defeats a huge serpent; he then takes his leave, since '[he] knew what he had created was good'. Eskimo folklore in general reveals a more pragmatic outlook on life than deciding what is good in the world and what is bad. Melzack strives for authenticity, however. For example, in the story 'Raven Recovers Light for his People', the evil man who steals the sun and the moon and the stars is named Tupilak. A 'tupilak' is certainly an object in Eskimo lore; as recorded by Boas it is made by an enemy to injure another person, somewhat on the order of the African doll that, when stuck with pins, kills the person it resembles. But Melzack simply borrows the word for a proper name, ignoring its deep meaning. His retelling of 'Raven and the Goose' is close to 'Raven Takes a Wife' as told by the ethnologist J. W. Powell, but lacks its directness and matter-of-factness.

In his *Tales from the Igloo* (1972) Father Maurice Métayer allows the stories to speak for themselves; there is little modern embellishment. They were taken directly from the oral tradition since, as the preface tells us, they were 'first recorded on tape; each story was analysed to obtain an exact translation. This translation in turn served as the basis for French and English texts. On occasion the text as it appears here departs from the literal translation in the interests of adhering to the style of the English and French languages. Yet the smallest detail of Inuit thought has been faithfully respected.' (Father Métayer, who has lived with the Eskimos since 1939, has also written *Unipkat: Tradition esquimaude de Coppermine, Territoires-du-Nord-Ouest, Canada,* 3 vols, 1973.) Although *Tales from the Igloo* is mainly based on the culture of the Copper Eskimo, several of the stories, such as 'The Blind Boy and the Loon', are found in other Eskimo groups. The majority are animal stories but several are obviously based on historical events, especially 'Lost at Sea', which has the traditional plot of the Eskimo adrift on floating ice. In many of the stories, poetry is used as naturally and joyfully as it is used by the Eskimos themselves. The illustrations are very fine—bright in colour and active in line. They are by Agnes Nanogak, whose father was with Stefansson when he lived with the Copper Eskimos in 1910.

Herbert T. Schwarz, in *Elik and Other Stories of the MacKenzie Eskimos* (1970), also comes close to the living oral tradition. On a four-month storytelling hunt, Schwarz found exemplars of a still-vigorous tradition who told their stories in English or in Eskimo with on-the-spot translation. (Vignettes about these storytellers form an interesting appendix to the book.) As a doctor practising in the North, Schwarz joined that small group of professionals—explorers, missionaries, and administrators *et al.*—who have done the most to preserve and spread Eskimo culture.

Because the tales in *Elik* are rooted in one geographical location (the Mackenzie District) with an identifiable topography, and in everyday life rather than in a mysterious and primitive past, they therefore seem more immediate and modern than most Eskimo legends. Some are now standard: the story of the boy who was blinded by his stepmother (in other versions his mother), the story of Raven and the whale spirit (the spirit of the whale is always a beautiful girl). Others are less imaginative than informative: about the events that occur when Indian and Eskimo meet, the preparations and the hazards of the whale hunt, etc. Present in all the stories is respect for taboos and for the power of the medicine man, revealing a people who are cautious in the face of a harsh environment rather than superstitious in non-Eskimo terms. The work of the Eskimo illustrator, Mona Ohoveluk, is in the tradition of the lively, impressive graphic art that has become familiar in the last two decades through Eskimo prints and drawings.

If it were not for the descriptive passages, James Houston's *Kiviok's Magic Journey: An Eskimo Legend* (1973) might have stepped from the pages of the Brothers Grimm, with its theme of the beautiful girls whose cloaks of goose feathers are stolen while they bathe. Here the girls are snow geese, the thief who steals the feathers of one of them is Raven in his wicked manifestation, and the hero who travels far to recover his wife and children is Kiviok the Eskimo. The axe of a friendly giant flings out bright chips of ivory and Kiviok is carried beneath the frozen sea on the back of a sea trout. In calling the silvery fish he chants: 'Bubbles, bubbles/ End my troubles./Help me now,/Oh magic fish.' Here is evidence of the commonality of folklore: while plots and themes are similar, the details and perhaps an attitude to life can signify the country of origin. Russian folklore produces an image of vast plains and fleet horses, while German tales are usually played out in dark and mysterious forests. In the French version of 'The Sleeping Beauty' the prince kisses the princess awake, but in the Spanish version it is the prince who is asleep.

James Houston has long been known for his authentic legend-type stories of the Eskimo—spare narratives that in style, detail, and impact are honed to the essence. He has diverged from that style in *Kiviok's Magic Journey*, probably to interest quite young children for whom this picture-storybook is intended. His illustrations are softer than his usual severe, sculptured pictures based on Eskimo carvings; they swirl and dance. Like the text, they give the story a European atmosphere.

There is a vast pool of Eskimo material still lying undisturbed in the pages of anthropological studies, and probably much more residing untapped in the memories of the older living Eskimos. Neither source is easily reachable. The report literature is fragmented, and imbedded within the wider framework of Eskimo thought and culture. From all accounts the Eskimo are shy about revealing their tales. After all, myth, legend, and folktale should be shrouded in mystery, linked as they are to religion, ritual, and taboo. And, naturally enough, the Eskimo storyteller does not stop to explain things to his audience.

There are not many books of Eskimo legends for children, but those we have—whether they are in the European tradition of Melzack and Caswell or in the less polished but more authentic tradition of Schwarz and Métayer—have revealed a rich world of fact and fantasy that has irresistible appeal. It shows us not only the distinctive landscape of snow and ice, igloo and tent, walrus and polar bear, but the inner meaning of the life that the land imposes—the desperate struggle for survival, the kinship with animals, the reasons for Eskimo fear and laughter, for revenge and kindness. The world of the Eskimo and of his imagination has universal significance.

INDIAN LEGENDS

ALTON, E. (comp.). *Nanabozho and His Brother.* Illustrated by Doreen Foster. Toronto/Montreal, Holt, Rinehart and Winston, 1970. [64 pp.] ('A Language Patterns Book'.)

Several Nanabozho stories have been woven together, ending with the standard Indian flood and creation myth, which puts this composite story somewhat out of joint. The illustrations, in soft colours, cast a romantic glow and more than redeem the bald style of the text.

AYRE, ROBERT. *Sketco the Raven.* Illustrated by Philip Surrey. Toronto, Macmillan, 1961. 183 pp.

The complex Raven cycle of legends, known to the tribes of the North Pacific Coast, are here given shape and direction to make them comprehensible to the modern youthful reader, yet the author preserves the primitive quality of the tales and presents Sketco, the trickster-hero, in his bewildering transformations.

BEMISTER, MARGARET. *Thirty Indian Legends of Canada.* Illustrations by Douglas Tait. Vancouver, J. J. Douglas, 1973. 153 pp. (First published in 1912 by the Macmillan Company of Canada Ltd.)

The stories cover many different Indian groups—Cree, Ojibway, Ottawa, Shusway, Okanagan, and others—but all are very similar in tone and presentation. In their soft style and emphasis on magic they represent the outlook of their time—the endeavour to cast the Indian legend in the European folktale tradition.

CLARK, ELLA ELIZABETH. *Indian Legends of Canada.* Toronto, McClelland and Stewart, 1960. 177 pp.

In this anthology, which is not intended for children, the legends of many Indian groups are divided by type of story—creation myths, animal tales, etc. The brevity and simplicity of the retellings make this a useful reference source.

CLUTESI, GEORGE. *Son of Raven, Son of Deer: Fables of the Tse-shaht People.* Illustrated by the author. Sidney, B.C., Gray's Publishing, 1967. 126 pp.

The exploits of foolhardy Son of Deer and greedy and thoughtless Son of Raven are retold in brief, almost Aesop-like, fashion. These fables, which have been handed down in Clutesi's family for almost four hundred years, have an assurance and polish that are not often found in collections of Indian tales.

FISHER, OLIVE M. and CLARA L. TYNER. *Totem, Tipi and Tumpline: Stories of Canadian Indians.* Illustrated by Annora Brown. Toronto, Dent, 1955. 264 pp.

A 'reader-like' mixture of stories, plays, and bits of information on Indian life. It was obviously designed for the school curriculum in the lower grades, but it is doubtful if it would rouse children to a genuine interest in Indian lore or legend.

FRASER, FRANCES J. *The Bear Who Stole the Chinook and Other Stories.* Illustrated by Lewis Parker. Toronto, Macmillan, 1959. 72 pp.

These legends of the Blackfoot Indians are successfully retold for younger children. They vary from the jesting stories of Na-pe—the 'Big Man' of the prairie groups—to more lyrical tales that have European echoes.

FRASER, FRANCES J. *The Wind Along the River.* Illustrated by Lewis Parker. Toronto, Macmillan, 1968. 83 pp.

Na-pe returns in four stories similar to those in *The Bear Who Stole the Chinook* (above). The other thirteen are narrations of tribal events in the history of the Blackfoot Indians, 'recorded as they were narrated to [Frances Fraser] by the elders of the tribe'. They have a strong tonal and plot resemblance to Grisdale's *Wild Drums*, being anecdotal, rough-hewn, and filled with acts of violence and revenge—not cushioned, as in similar European tales, by a strong contrast between 'good' and 'evil'.

GOODERHAM, KENT (ed.). *I Am an Indian.* Toronto, Dent, 1969. 196 pp.

A collection of legends, poems, historical anecdotes, personal reminiscences that celebrates Indian life. Most of the material is taken from secondary sources, but some would not be available elsewhere. There are eight legends, stories of Son of Raven, Na-pe, and Wesakachak; the two most unusual are those that show the impingement of European culture upon the Indian—'Gluskap and the King of France' and 'Wolverine and the Great Serpent', a Huron version of the Faust legend. The book is marred by its 'reader-like' appearance and format.

GRISDALE, ALEX. *Wild Drums: Tales and Legends of the Plains Indians.* As told to Nan Shipley. Illustrations by Jim Ellis. Winnipeg, Peguis Publishers, 1972. 78 pp.

These tales, recorded by a Salteaux Indian, are based on obviously true incidents of the not-so-distant past and should be classed as historical anecdote rather than legend. They tell chiefly of warring tribes and brave deeds—especially those of women—and resulting acts of justice, cruelty, and revenge based on the tribal code. They also reveal much of the cycle of everyday life of the Prairie groups, an aspect of social history that is reinforced by the simple and explicit line drawings by a Chippewayan artist.

HARRIS, CHRISTIE L. *Once More Upon a Totem.* Illustrated by Douglas Tait. Toronto, McClelland and Stewart, 1973. 195 pp.

More than in her first book, *Once Upon a Totem*, Christie Harris aims, in style and tone, for the characteristics of the short story or the novelette rather than legend. However, in these three tales she does recreate the Indian world; notably the importance of the totemic symbols, the Indian view of life and death, and the sense of the power and goodness of nature.

HARRIS, CHRISTIE L. *Once Upon a Totem.* Illustrated by John Frazer Mills. New York, Atheneum, 1963. 148 pp.

The Indians of the North Pacific Coast were unusually rich in myth and legend. Five separate legends are retold in this collection with becoming dignity, yet with an intimate quality that brings the Indian world of old into the world of today.

HILL, KATHLEEN L. *Badger, the Mischief Maker.* Illustrated by John Hamberger. Toronto, McClelland and Stewart, 1965. 95 pp.

Badger, the Indian mischief-maker, who appears briefly in the author's earlier work, *Glooscap and His Magic*, has here a well-deserved book to himself. This is a light-hearted, amusing, and at times moving collection of legends.

HILL, KATHLEEN L. *Glooscap and His Magic: Legends of the Wabanaki Indians.* Illustrated by Robert Frankenberg. Toronto, McClelland and Stewart, 1963. 128 pp.

This is a stronger and more memorable retelling of the Glooscap stories than Cyrus Macmillan's *Glooskap's Country and Other Indian Tales* (see below). The conversational style and effective characterization give variation to a body of legend that is generally told in monotone narrative.

HILL, KATHLEEN L. *More Glooscap Stories: Legends of the Wabanaki Indians.* Illustrated by John Hamberger. Toronto/Montreal, McClelland and Stewart, 1970. 178 pp.

The eternally benevolent Glooscap, Lord of Men and Beasts, takes various forms to help his people out of trouble. Thus many of the stories are dependent upon a kind of soft magic for their climax. Others—and here Hill is at her best—have humour to the point of slapstick: 'The Rabbit Makes a Match', 'The Year Summer Was Stolen', 'Coolnajoo, the Foolish One'.

HOOKE, HILDA M. *Thunder in the Mountains: Legends of Canada.* Illustrated by Clare Bice. Toronto, Oxford, 1947. 217 pp.

A general collection of Indian legends and white men's tales. The author has a skilful, smooth-flowing narrative style. Her book could serve as an introduction to the more authentic works of Ayre, Harris, Hill, Reid, and Clutesi.

JOHNSON, EMILY PAULINE. *Legends of Vancouver.* Illustrated by Ben Lim. New ed. Toronto, McClelland and Stewart, 1961. 176 pp. (First published in 1911 in a privately printed edition.)

There is a nostalgic quality to these stories that sets them apart from other Indian legends. Pauline Johnson heard them mainly from a West Coast Indian chief, who, understandably, looked back with longing on the days when the land belonged to Indians alone.

JOHNSTON, PATRONELLA. *Tales of Nokomis.* Illustrations by Frances Kagige. Toronto, Musson, 1970. 64 pp.

Nokomis (grandmother) tells the nature tales of the Ojibway to her two grandchildren. The conversational teaching method, so prevalent in the nineteenth century, is used more gently here but is sufficient to mar the stories. Both the teller and the illustrator are Ojibway. The stylized illustrations glow with jewel-like colours.

MACMILLAN, CYRUS. *Canadian Wonder Tales.* Illustrated by Elizabeth Cleaver. London, Bodley Head, 1974. 288 pp.

This collection contains all the fifty-eight stories that appeared in Macmillan's *Canadian Wonder Tales* (1918) and *Canadian Fairy Tales* (1922). Cyrus Macmillan (1882–1953) claimed to have heard these stories from Indians and *habitants*, fishermen and sailors in 'various parts of Canada'. He retold them in the rather romantic style of a professor of English born before the turn of the century. Therefore the stories do not seem authentic, though as polished narratives they are very readable. The best of them—the Glooskap stories (see the entry below)—have lasting appeal.

MACMILLAN, CYRUS. *Glooskap's Country and Other Indian Tales.* Illustrated by John A. Hall. Toronto, Oxford, 1955. 273 pp.

Thirty-three stories reprinted from Cyrus Macmillan's *Canadian Wonder Tales* and *Canadian Fairy Tales* (see above). Though imbued with a soft, fairy-tale atmosphere, and having little dialogue, these smooth and romantic retellings are still appealing.

MORRISEAU, NORVAL. *Legends of My People: The Great Ojibway.* Edited by Selwyn Dewdney. Toronto, Ryerson, 1965. 130 pp.

This book was not intended for children and in many ways it is beyond their capacity and interest, but these revealing 'legends, anecdotes, observations, reports and personal comments' have many qualities that will attract the young person who seeks to experience something of the Indian imagination and way of life, for they, and the beautiful illustrations by a celebrated Ojibway artist, are authentic.

REID, DOROTHY M. *Tales of Nanabozho.* Illustrated by Donald Grant. Toronto, Oxford, 1963. 128 pp.

The hero of the Ojibway Indians was alternately foolish and wise, but in the main his exploits reveal the Indian delight in the ridiculous. Reid has captured the childlike simplicity of these legends, and skilfully reflects the newness and freshness of the Indian world before the white man came. This is a much more successful treatment of the Nanabozho tales than Thomas B. Leekley's *The World of Manabozho* (1965), an American publication.

SCHWARZ, HERBERT T. *Windigo and Other Tales of the Ojibways.* Illustrated by Norval Morriseau. Toronto/Montreal, McClelland and Stewart, 1969. 40 pp.

A group of Ojibway tales that, in no way pejoratively, can be described as standard fare—stories about the windigo, the shaking tent, the thunderbird, and whisky-jack. Schwarz, who heard the stories from Norval Morriseau, has not strived for the light, literary, and often conversational approach of Dorothy Reid in her Ojibway *Tales of Nanabozho*, but has kept to a plain, almost narrative style. It is the illustrations that lift the book into distinction. With fluid line and restrained colour (black, white, and sepia), Morriseau reveals the numinous nature of legend.

Tales From the Longhouse. By Indian children of British Columbia. Sidney, B.C., Gray's Publishing, 1973. 112 pp.
Indian children of Vancouver Island have here recorded legends, tales, and lore related to them by their elders. This is a fascinating mélange of well-known stories, such as a brief version of 'The Prince Who Was Taken Away by the Salmon', here called 'A Legend of the Spring Salmon', and highly regional and local tales, such as 'The Origin of the Vancouver Island Indians' and the story of why there is a red spot on Mount Tzouhalem when the sun goes down—'Shan-Tec's Cloak'.

TOYE, WILLIAM. *How Summer Came to Canada*. Pictures by Elizabeth Cleaver. Retold by William Toye. Toronto, Oxford, 1969. 32 pp.
This compelling Micmac nature myth has been retold from Cyrus Mac-millan's *Canadian Wonder Tales* (1918). Both its charm and its East Coast setting have been enhanced by Elizabeth Cleaver's colourful illustrations of a Canadian winter and summer, and of the times in-between.

TOYE, WILLIAM. *The Mountain Goats of Temlaham*. Pictures by Elizabeth Cleaver. Retold by William Toye. Toronto, Oxford, 1969. 32 pp.
Judging by the number of retellings, this is the most famous West Coast (Tsimshian) Indian legend. Its theme of 'kill only what is necessary for survival and respect the animal killed' is echoed in most Indian lore. Here it is retold with simplicity and dignity in probably the best story-telling version for younger children. With vivid, authentically designed collage illustrations by Elizabeth Cleaver, it is an effective picture-book.

WEATHERBY, HUGH. *Tales the Totems Tell*. Illustrated by the author. Toronto. Macmillan, 1944. 97 pp.
These stories of the Indians of British Columbia are retold for younger children. The inherent quality and interest of the tales are not completely destroyed by the author's over-simplification and pedestrian writing.

ESKIMO LEGENDS

CASWELL, HELEN. *Shadows from the Singing House: Eskimo Folk Tales*. Illustrations by Robert Mayokok. Edmonton, M. G. Hurtig, 1968. 108 pp.
Although these legends were collected in Alaska, they share a provenance with the recorded lore of other Eskimo groups in Canada. Such stories are 'Sedna, the Sea Goddess', 'How the Light Came', 'How the Fog Came', and 'The Girls Who Chose Strange Husbands'. The retellings keep the basic sturdiness and casualness of the originals, as recorded by the anthro-

pologists, and are sprinkled with Eskimo words to good effect. The small line illustrations, by an Eskimo artist, portray Eskimo life and artifacts.

HOUSTON, JAMES. *Kiviok's Magic Journey: An Eskimo Legend.* Illustrated by James Houston. Toronto, Longman, 1973. 40 pp.
The commonality of folklore is seen clearly in this Eskimo transformation tale. Raven, the evil one, steals the feather coat from a snow goose, which is left in its human form as a beautiful girl. Kiviok is the quest hero who, after arduous trials, releases his wife from a wicked spell. However, the setting and details are beautifully and uniquely Eskimo. The illustrations have a softness and fluidity that suit the magic of the tale. The integration of text and illustrations makes this a distinguished picture-storybook.

MELZACK, RONALD. *The Day Tuk Became a Hunter & Other Eskimo Stories.* Illustrated by Carol Jones. Toronto, McCelland and Stewart, 1967. 92 pp.
These are highly modified tales for younger children. Except perhaps for the basic Sedna Legend, the stories will not be alien to those accustomed to the European folktale. The full-page and double-page illustrations in black, white, and orange convey a feeling for the great lone land of the North more dramatically than do the tales.

MELZACK, RONALD. *Raven, Creator of the World: Eskimo Legends.* Illustrated by Laszlo Gal. Toronto/Montreal, McClelland and Stewart, 1970. 91 pp.
These tales of Raven have been culled from many sources, but together they form a pattern of the mythic origin of the people of the Western Arctic. Raven is presented here as a gentler, lonelier, less robust character than his Indian counterpart in Robert Ayre's *Sketco the Raven*. With its simple language, large type, attractive design, and vibrant full-page illustrations by Laszlo Gal, *Raven, Creator of the World* is an appealing introduction to Eskimo myth for younger children.

MÉTAYER, MAURICE. *Tales from the Igloo.* Edited and translated by Father Maurice Métayer. Foreword by Al Purdy. Illustrated by Agnes Nanogak. Edmonton, Hurtig Publishers, 1972. 127 pp.
Father Métayer recorded these tales of the Copper Eskimo directly on to tape and then transcribed them with a light editorial hand. This gives them rare immediacy and authenticity and also provides a direct look at Eskimo customs and beliefs. The stories range from actual events lifted into legend, such as 'Lost at Sea' and 'The Ball Players', to brief animal fables and a tale as familiar as 'The Blind Boy and the Loon'. The book was designed and illustrated in bold colour by Eskimo artists.

SCHWARZ, HERBERT T. *Elik and Other Stories of the MacKenzie Eskimos.* Illustrated by Mona Ohoveluk. Toronto/Montreal, McClelland and Stewart, 1970. 79 pp.
With the exception of the ubiquitous tale 'The Raven and the Whale', these stories appear to have been written down for the first time. The most

unusual are those that must have been based on true incidents—such as 'The Whale Hunt'—and those that stemmed from the traditional hostility between Indian and Eskimo—'Elik the Far Seeing One' and 'The Great Eskimo Rally at Fort McPherson'. Each story has a glossary of Eskimo words. In Part Two, Schwarz describes the Eskimo storytellers to whom he listened with obvious fascination. The line drawings by an Eskimo artist are deliberately realistic and representational.

2 | Folktales

'Once upon a time there was'—a king, a princess, a poor wood-cutter. Thus, with few variations, begin the folk and fairy tales that are a part of the world's heritage of traditional literature. Their origins by and large unknown, they survived by word of mouth until they were finally captured on the printed page. They are still, however, stories to be retold for every generation, to 'hold children from play and old men from the chimney-corners' as the storyteller begins to tell of the days when the world was young—when it was 'once upon a time'. These are the stories of 'Hop-o-My-Thumb' (England), 'Rapunzel' (Germany), 'The Baba Yaga' (Russia), 'The Boy Who Learned to Shudder' (Japan). Each country has its store of national tales, and the similarities among them from country to country are quite remarkable. No one knows if they spread outward from a common stock or if their themes were so universal—reflecting the love, fear, terror, and passion that dwell in the human heart—that each country in its more primitive era evolved much the same plots.

Since the folktale is thus, by strict definition, the product of a primitive, non-literate society, North Americans, other than the Indians and Eskimos, cannot really claim a native folktale literature. However, they could and did adapt and recreate the folktales deriving from their European or Asian or African origins. Rip Van Winkle and Paul Bunyan are not wholly American inventions, but the American flavour is so strong in the stories about them that it is quite proper to regard them as genuine American folk heroes. So, too, by virtue of their having been retold and rewritten by

Canadians or recast into a Canadian context, the stories that English and French settlers brought with them to Canada can be regarded as a part of Canadian literature.

The Golden Phoenix and Other French-Canadian Fairy Tales
(1958) is the best example we have of such foreign literature made
indigenous. The tales in *The Golden Phoenix* were collected by
Marius Barbeau, the noted ethnologist and anthropologist. These
are stories that were brought over from France three hundred
years ago by the colonists who settled along the lower St Lawrence
River. In their authentic texts they are now, Barbeau tells us, filed
away in collections of the National Museum of Canada. The
stories were rewritten by Michael Hornyansky, who has given
them a highly polished and literary form. In doing so he has acted
as a catalyst in presentation, as Perrault did for the French fairy
tales, Joseph Jacobs for the English, and Peter Christian Asbjörnsen for the Norse. However, the genius of Perrault, Jacobs,
and Asbjörnsen captured and preserved the national qualities, the
physical background, and often the social scene of their own
country. We look in vain for any distinctive French-Canadian
quality in Hornyansky's work. There is, of course, Petit-Jean, who
appears in two of the stories. He is the traditional hero of the
folktale in Quebec; like Jack of the English fairy tales, he is usually the youngest son—quick-witted, kind, and resourceful. While
these stories have not been absorbed into a French-Canadian
atmosphere or locale, they do have a French tone, close to the
witty and urbane style of the French poet and courtier, Perrault,
who gave classic form to the stories of Bluebeard, Cinderella, the
Sleeping Beauty, and other fairy tales. For his part Hornyansky
has written what could be considered touchstone versions of the
stories that are included in *The Golden Phoenix*. They are, moreover, excellent for telling as well as reading. They range in style
from the traditional 'fairyish' fairy tale, 'The Fairy Quite Contrary', to a rather naughty *fabliau*, 'Jacques the Woodcutter', the
plot of which was first made famous by Boccaccio.

The best story in the book is 'The Princess of Tomboso', which
recounts the familiar folklore theme of a vain and selfish princess
who eventually gets her come-uppance. An astute mixture of the
traditional and realistic, the story has a refreshingly tart ending

and a rhythm and lilt that bring out all its humour:

He took the bowl and shook it. A leather belt fell out. Written on it in letters of gold were these words:

PUT ME ON AND TELL ME WHERE:
QUICK AS LIGHTNING YOU'LL BE THERE.

Jacques lost no time. Clasping the belt around his waist, he wished himself into the castle. Whoosh!—and there he stood inside the castle. He wished himself back into the barn. Whoosh! There he was back again.

'Well, it works,' he said. 'Now I can travel cheap.'

Hornyansky can employ a wholly contemporary idiom yet convey the suggestion of other times, other places:

Once there was an old man whose wife had died. He wanted very much to marry again so that he would have someone to cook his porridge in the morning and fetch his slippers in the evening, but none of the women in the village would have anything to do with him because he never washed his beard. The old man blamed it all on his son, a young boy called Petit-Jean. Morning and evening, day after day, he beat Petit-Jean like a carpet. You would have wept to see him!

With its polish and craftsmanship, *The Golden Phoenix* could be described as a book of literary fairy tales rather than as a book of folklore. It is a work of distinction, alongside which other Canadian books in the same field seem rather lifeless. Of such competitors, the ones that come off best are James McNeill's two books, *The Sunken City* (1959) and *The Double Knights* (1964). No suggestion of Canadian interpretation is intended in these books, which are simply collections of folktales from around the world. The stories abound with the essential folktale characters—giants, hags, dragons, trolls, shepherds, kings, and princesses. They are pleasant and easy to read, and have the advantage of not being completely familiar. Unfortunately, they are also so uniform in style as to deny any relationship to a country of origin. Here, for example, is the beginning of the story that is meant to represent Ireland:

John Shea was a poor farmer who lived alone on a piece of scraggily land near the village of Banog in Munster. He had neither parents to love him nor a wife to care for him, and the overworked soil hardly yielded enough food to keep him alive, in spite of the long hours he toiled.

'To be sure,' he thought one day, 'I might as well be killed in a foreign land as die of starvation here.' So he put on his best shirt and trousers and his cap and set his feet on the road to the City of Cork.—'John Shea and the Fairy Treasure' in The Double Knights.

This is good plain writing, but the reader is not swept into Ireland as he reads. One cannot help but think of the unforgettable phrases of the great storyteller Joseph Jacobs, which provide a sad comparison. McNeill, a merely competent storyteller, lacks literary flair, a deep knowledge of folklore, and empathy with the 'folk' that traditional literature demands.

Admittedly the lack of local colour is not a crippling blow to a fairy tale. A story is a story after all. But just as the best in anything is a continual source of renewal, the best folktales offer something beyond the bare bones of the story. They should convey—indirectly to be sure—the spirit and ways of the country and people that underlie the events. A great folktale is not just the product of a people; it also represents them.

The Lucky Coin and Other Folk Tales Canadians Tell (1972) by Leslie Quinton (pseud.) includes stories from the homelands of some of the ethnic cultures that make up the Canadian population —Norwegian, Finnish, Sikh, *et al.*—along with stories that are Indian, Eskimo, English, and French in origin. The sources they are taken from are standard ones, but only in one case is an acknowledgement given. An appendix consists of ethnic notes on the cultures represented that are so over-simplified as to be condescending, if not misleading and sometimes comic. Some sample statements: 'Ukrainians crave freedom' (as if no one else does) and 'Among the twenty thousand people of Spanish descent in Canada, few are fishermen.'

Closely allied to the folktale is the 'tall tale', which is also of unknown origin, though it is associated not with the remote past but with the more recent past. The greatest number of these stories has developed around the figure of Paul Bunyan, the mighty logger. This is not the place to indulge in the academic argument over whether 'Ole Paul' originated in Canada or the United States. Some say Maine, some say New Brunswick. Harold Felton, who has made a study of the Paul Bunyan legends and has also studied their origins, says that 'the best authorities agree that the Irish and French lumberjacks of the Lake States started the stories of Paul Bunyan and Babe the Blue Ox in the woods'. (*Legends of Paul Bunyan.*)

There is just one Canadian contribution to these legends (compared with a vast body of literature from the United States): *Logging with Paul Bunyan* (1957) by the late John D. Robins. Robins was a magnificent storyteller and his easy, make-it-up-as-you-go-along style sets his book apart even from the most distinguished American versions. It is based on stories Robins told originally on radio broadcasts and was edited after his death by the folksong specialist, Edith Fowke. The author relates these stories as if he himself were a friend of Paul Bunyan's and this sense of immediacy gives his book a complete authenticity, no matter how great the extravagance of the fantasy:

> *Well, boys, it's just like I'm tellin' you. Paul stood there an' chawed at that little pine—it wasn't more'n eight inches through —he chawed at that little pine all forenoon an' mighty nigh half the afternoon. He didn't move only when he'd sink in too deep with standin' too long in one place. I knowed by the look of him he was doin' some mighty hard thinkin' so I didn't say nothin' to him. I knowed better. Well, 'long about four o'clock, nigh as I can remember, all of a sudden Paul slaps the legs of his corduroys, an' he gives 'em a slap that knocked everythin' down off the shelves in the office an' busted a keg of ink.*
>
> *Then he says to me, he says, 'Ed, send the tote teamster out to the Soo first in the mornin'. An' I want you to foller with Babe.'*

When we recall the engaging and convincing backwoodsman's drawl with which Robins acted out the stories, their great success as broadcasts is easily understood. In written form, however, a steady diet of unlettered speech becomes wearisome after a while.

The outstanding American versions—those by Wallace Wadsworth, Esther Shepard, Dell J. McCormick, James Stevens, and others—manage to give the impression of rough backwoods talk without consistently indulging in it.

Lorrie McLaughlin's *Shogomoc Sam* (1972) has been almost unnoticed, both as an interesting book in itself but more importantly as an advance in the development of regional folklore (which the author might have continued if she had not died). Shogomoc Sam arrived in children's literature out of the logging background of New Brunswick as the young helper of a Bunyan-type hero called Main John Glazier, and indeed there are some larger-than-life episodes in the story. But it departs from the 'tall tale' tradition in having some characteristics of the modern psychological novel. Sam, who is an orphan, tries to find out what his 'real' name is and where he came from, but finally discovers that this is not important to him. 'My name is Shogomoc Sam!' he shouts. While conveying a powerful feeling for New Brunswick, McLaughlin manages to tell what may be an indigenous folktale and to clothe it in modern dress. She put more into the tale than it could hold, but it is a good example of regional fiction that has universal interest.

Depressingly, there is no evidence that Canada will match the continuing American interest in the writing of tall tales. The American past, particularly the expansion westward, appears to be able to inspire an unending series of legends and tales. There are stories of Davy Crockett, Daniel Boone, and Johnny Appleseed. John Henry represents, in exaggerated form, the working Negro; Old Stormalong is whaler, cowboy, and farmer who challenges the great white whale, Mocha Dick. Southern plantation life produced the Uncle Remus stories, and the 'Jack' tales, borrowed from English folklore, have the background and speech of the depressed Appalachian country. In the meantime, Canadians who are just as colourful—Radisson, Tonty, Riel, Dumont, the men who built the CPR, the Mounties—go unsung.

Almost every European country, and the United States, has produced versions of the Latin and Greek myths, and here again Canada is sparsely represented. N. B. Taylor, who taught medicine at the University of Toronto, has created in *The Aeneid of Virgil*

(1961) a retelling of the great Latin epic that is both graceful and scholarly and that shows respect for the young reader. *Four Ages of Man: The Classical Myths* (1962), by the poet Jay Macpherson, is in many ways an excellent book. It is comprehensive, well organized, and useful, but it is hardly more distinctive or memorable than a handbook of plot digests. An opportunity lost.

Folklore comes in many guises, from non-verbal ones like embroidery and dances to songs and games. In *The Lore and Language of School Children*, Iona and Peter Opie quote Dr Arbuthnot, the eighteenth-century physician and writer: 'Nowhere was tradition preserved pure and uncorrupt "but amongst School-boys whose Games and Plays are delivered down invariably from one generation to another." ' That Canadian children are still carrying on their own traditions in songs, rhymes, and games (the standard nursery rhymes are transmitted by adults) can be seen in Edith Fowke's delightful *Sally Go Round the Sun* (1969) in which she has brought together and discussed at the back three hundred songs, rhymes, and games of Canadian children. Although they are not all exclusively Canadian, some old rhymes have acquired a Canadian reference: 'Oh, I don't want no more of army life / Gee, Mom, I wanta go / Back to On-ta-rio-o!' As the Opies' books have shown us, children creatively invent and unselfconsciously perpetuate jokes and rhymes and games without any interference from adults. 'Roses are red, violets are green / My face is funny, but yours is a scream' may not be great literature, but it shows that the tradition is alive and doing well in Canada. Fowke's Canadian contribution to the lore in this field is a fine one—as appealing to adults as to young people, though in different ways—and a feast for the eyes, with colourful illustrations by Carlos Marchiori. He has kept to a folk-art motif in his decorative drawings and brilliant primary colours.

Once again a chapter must end with the now-familiar complaint about the relative dearth of imaginative literature. With folk and fairy tales, myths, and tall tales, as with legends, fantasy, and poetry, the output has been small and the achievement meagre. Michael Hornyansky believes that the reason lies in the fact that the Canadian writer has had 'the problem of being dwarfed by two big brothers who speak the same language'. ('In Search of the

Phoenix', *Horn Book*, August 1960.) Perhaps so; at any rate it would appear that, some notable exceptions apart, Canadian children will have to continue to look to England and the United States for the books that stir and do not merely tell.

BARBEAU, MARIUS. *The Golden Phoenix and Other French-Canadian Fairy Tales*. Retold by Michael Hornyansky. Illustrated by Arthur Price. Toronto, Oxford, 1958. 144 pp.
Eight French-Canadian folktales that originated in the Old World are given here a highly polished literary modern treatment with modern overtones in the style. An outstanding book.

FOWKE, EDITH (comp.). *Sally Go Round the Sun: 300 Songs, Rhymes and Games of Canadian Children*. Musical arrangements by Keith MacMillan. Illustrated by Carlos Marchiori. Designed by Frank Newfeld and Don Fernley. Toronto/Montreal, McClelland and Stewart, 1969. 160 pp.
These songs, rhymes, and games are not all Canadian in origin, but 'every item in [the book] has been chanted by Canadian children'. A colourfully attractive, entertaining, informative book. With its notes and comments (unobtrusively placed at the back), Fowke presents the kind of research that one associates with the distinguished Iona and Peter Opie.

MCLAUGHLIN, LORRIE. *Shogomoc Sam*. Illustrated by Randy Jones. Toronto, Macmillan, 1970. 61 pp.
Here we read how down in New Brunswick they talk of Main John Glazier (a literary kin of Paul Bunyan) and his young helper Shogomoc Sam. This humorous and sensitive 'tall tale' about them, which has some modern touches, has lively drawings that convey a sense of the locale.

MCNEILL, JAMES. *The Double Knights: More Tales from Round the World*. Illustrated by Theo Dimson. Toronto. Oxford, 1964. 128 pp.
This is a companion volume to the author's *The Sunken City*. The illustrations and decorations add a distinctive note to a fairly ordinary text.

MCNEILL, JAMES. *The Sunken City and Other Tales from Round the World*. Illustrated by Theo Dimson. Toronto, Oxford, 1959. 160 pp.
Here are both familiar and unfamiliar tales, retold simply and directly and presented in an attractive format.

MACPHERSON, JAY. *Four Ages of Man: The Classical Myths*. Toronto, Macmillan, 1962. 205 pp.
A comprehensive and organized retelling of the Greek myths. While there are many more attractive versions for children, this would be of particular value to a youthful scholar for its introduction, chronology, and notes.

QUINTON, LESLIE (pseud.). *The Lucky Coin and Other Folk Tales Canadians Tell.* Illustrated by David Shaw. Toronto, McClelland and Stewart, 1972. 128 pp.

This collection brings together well-known tales—including Indian, Eskimo, and French-Canadian—from the many nationalities that make up the 'Canadian mosaic'. Only in one case is the source of the story noted, though all the stories are available in standard collections. There was no attempt to find an unusual one. This can be considered proof that a good book cannot be produced by a committee. The pen-name 'Leslie Quinton' was used by Lyn Harrington, Madeline A. Freeman, and Audrey McKim.

ROBINS, JOHN D. *Logging with Paul Bunyan.* Edited by Edith Fowke. Illustrated by Adrian Dingle. Toronto, Ryerson, 1957. 97 pp.

A zest in the telling and an informality of style give these 'tongue-in-cheek' stories of the mighty logger an air of innocence and authenticity. A genuine Canadian contribution to the literature on Paul Bunyan.

TAYLOR, N. B. *The Aeneid of Virgil.* Illustrated by Joan Kiddell-Monroe. London, Oxford, 1961. 242 pp.

This prose retelling is soldily based on the original and retains its fire and vigour. It is for older children than the standard softer version by the English writer Alfred J. Church, whose *The Aeneid for Boys and Girls* was first published in 1908 and has remained a steady favourite. As an introduction to Virgil, the Church may have to yield to the Taylor version, not only in respect of adherence to detail but because Taylor manages to preserve in prose something of the quality of the epic measure.

Fiction

3 | Fantasy

The dragon had the trade-mark Of Faërie
written plain upon him. In whatever world he
had his being it was an Other-world. Fantasy,
the making or glimpsing of Other-worlds, was
the heart of the desire of Faërie. I desired
dragons with a profound desire.—
J.R.R. TOLKIEN, Tree and Leaf.

Faërie, Folktale, Fairy Tale, Fantasy—all these terms are closely linked; indeed, they are often used interchangeably. All tell of worlds—Tolkien's Other-worlds—whose inhabitants and laws are different from our own. These are the worlds of fire-breathing dragons and talking cats; worlds in which Cinderella must leave the ball at midnight and only a certain prince can break the spell that binds the Sleeping Beauty.

The folktale and its sister, the fairy tale, were developed by the unlettered imagination of an unknown people and travelled down the centuries through oral tradition before being written down. Fantasy—books like *Alice in Wonderland* and *The Wind in the Willows*—is a much more modern type of literature. It is invariably the product of a known master artist who can impose a sense of design upon invention and can give substance and credibility to what in other hands would be considered gossamer materials.

While the old and new forms have much in common—in fact the word Faërie could encompass both in a generic sense—fantasy has its own rules and now its own traditions. It is different from the folktale in intent, complexity, and sophistication.

Fantasy is probably the most sophisticated form of fiction being written today. Not only must it conform to and meet all the standards of good novel writing; it must also use the fantastic, wholly or partially, directly or indirectly, to express what cannot be expressed in any other way. Fantasy carries the reader into a universe beyond everyday reality, where the restraints of time, gravity, and mortality no longer operate. But the strange world projected by fantasy is not a disorderly one. Its conditions are as practical and as consistent as our own. It begins with its own unique set of premises, but within this framework it follows the dictates of sequence and causality. Whether sustained at the level of high seriousness (as in George MacDonald's *At the Back of the North Wind*) or of delightful nonsense (as in Richard Hughes' *The Spider's Palace*), fantasy chooses its material logically, not at random.

For the purpose of fantasy is not to escape reality but to illuminate it: to transport us to a world different from the real world, while demonstrating certain immutable truths that persist even there—and in every possible world. In Tolkien's *The Hobbit*, for example, no other world exists but the eerie, often magical universe of Middle Earth. Yet central to the story is a familiar code of values. The hobbit is faced with a challenge to his courage and resolution: he must change either for better or for worse. His response to the challenge is a proper one in any world. What really happens is that the old universe is seen through new eyes.

In illuminating reality, fantasy often heightens and intensifies it. Sometimes a truth can be more forcefully expressed through fantasy than through a plainer tale—expressed so that it is not only understood but felt. In *Charlotte's Web*, E. B. White is able to make death comprehensible and acceptable to children. Charlotte's death is neither sentimental nor overwhelmingly sad. Because the experience is presented in a fantastic world, at one remove from ordinary life, the emotion can be kept within bearable limits. Because the whole story has made Charlotte vividly real, her death is a genuine sorrow; but because the story has also shown her to be always a spider, her death can be accepted as part of the inevitable order of the universe.

Such truths may well be beyond the capacity of some readers

to grasp. A fantasy may often be read on two levels. It may be only an adventure story for some children; others will have—at once, or on later reflection—the richer experience of sensing the inner truths beneath the exciting and entertaining tale. For this reason fantasy has the longest life with children and the greatest appeal for adults. Fantasies may be for children but they are not childish.

The fact is that the writers of the finest fantasies are invariably writers of superior rank: John Ruskin, Lewis Carroll, T. H. White, James Thurber, Kenneth Grahame, Rumer Godden, Richard Hughes, to name but a few. They chose fantasy because they had something they wanted to express and found a children's story the most appropriate way to express it. Thus C. S. Lewis was basically a philosopher who used his Narnia cycle to embody his religious and moral concepts. On the surface, these are simple stories of enchantment. However, the values revealed in one world apply to the circumstances of the other. Thus Scrubb, cowardly spoiled schoolboy in *The Voyage of the Dawn Treader*, returns from his adventures in the land of Narnia with a new outlook that enables him to cope with the trials of British public-school life. Similarly in *Tom's Midnight Garden* by Philippa Pearce a restless, lonely boy finds in another world the hope that gives his life value and meaning.

And because the great fantasists are masters of method as well as 'message', such values are presented obliquely and delicately, not blatantly. The morals are implicit; fantasy does not preach. The didactic tale is simply a prelude to a 'lesson' and seeks only to inculcate; fantasy opens doors to morals of a universal order, but the reader must find them for himself, and in the search he makes them more lastingly his own.

The subject is, of course, quite beyond the rather bald definition attempted here so far. The power of fantasy is in how much it evokes, not what it denotes, and to that extent no simple listing of traits can quite characterize what is involved in the creation of a book of fantasy.

The best clues to the nature of fantasy come from the great practitioners themselves. For Walter de la Mare, fantasy must have that 'compelling inward ring . . . the inner consistency of reality'. The latest and perhaps the last word comes from Tolkien, whose *The Hobbit* and *The Lord of the Rings* have epitomized fantasy for our own generation. He sees it as the creation of a Sub-World or a Secondary World that is 'not a lower, but a higher form of Art, indeed the most nearly pure form and so (when achieved) the most potent'. Fantasy is for him, then, much more than mere fancifulness or strangeness or ingenious imagination. Any inventive mind can picture the sun as green. Only imagination and artistic discipline can create the circumstances that make it seem natural and right for the sun to be green.

In view of these rigorous artistic requirements, it is not surprising that there is no important body of Canadian fantasy. Apart from the fact that superior talent is scarce in any country at any time, Canada lacks most of the requisites that would provide a hospitable context for the production of fantasy. For one thing, there is no tradition of 'faërie' comparable to the oral literature of the older countries. Canadian writers in general have hardly sniffed at the fumes of fancy or the nonsensical. Where in Canadian literature is there any counterpart to Hudson's *Green Mansions*, Garnett's *Lady into Fox*, T. H. White's *The Sword in the Stone*, or the weird tales of Isak Dinesen? Since writing for children tends to follow and not lead writing for adults, the scarcity of books dependent upon highly individualistic creation may be regretted, but it should not be misunderstood. Fantasy, of all forms of children's literature, depends least on purely local interest. The props of history and geography, accuracy and pedagogy —the modest goals of unimaginative writers—are simply not pertinent to the writing of fantasy.

A Canadian setting, however, has inspired most of the few books in this area. The wilderness of British Columbia forms the background for all of Catherine Anthony Clark's books, for *A Walk Out of the World* by Ruth Nichols, and for *Secret in the Stlalakum Wild* by Christie Harris. A Cape Breton stream is the birthplace of Mel Thistle's *Peter the Sea Trout*; the Georgian Bay area of Ontario is lovingly and imaginatively described in Ruth Nichols' *The Marrow of the World*; and the inner city of Toronto and the lakefront take on a slight aura of mystery in Janet Lunn's *Double Spell*. In *The Magical Miss Mittens* by Lynn Cook there is a journey into Canada's past.

Catherine Anthony Clark, of British Columbia, is Canada's first serious writer of fantasy and the only one who has produced a substantial body of work. Her first book, *The Golden Pine Cone*, was published in 1950. She followed this with *The Sun Horse* (1951), *The One-Winged Dragon* (1955), *The Silver Man* (1958), *The Diamond Feather* (1962), and *The Hunter and the Medicine Man* (1966).

Clark's books are set in the mountainous land of British Columbia. Those who know the province well take delight in pinpointing some of the places she describes. Her great strength is in her settings and in her ability to people the snowy peaks, the forests, the lonely paths by the lakes with a peculiarly Canadian kind of spirit-folk—the Rock Puck, the Ice Folk, the Head Canada Goose, the Lake Snake, and prospectors who live on the borderline between the real world and the world of fantasy.

On the periphery of her plots are the symbols of some of the ancient myths and legends of the Indian tribes of British Columbia. There is the Raven, the Thunderbird, the Magic Woman, the Killer Whale. These are not central to the plot, but they succeed in creating atmosphere. Alongside them are numerous witches, sprites, and enchanted animals. More symbolic are the Indian chiefs and princesses—shining personages who rule the spirit lands with justice.

The children in these books are at one with their setting. They are not, like Alice in Wonderland, aliens in a card game, or in a looking-glass world. They are not wrenched, as are the children in C.S. Lewis's *The Lion, The Witch and The Wardrobe*, from English school holiday life to a wholly unrecognizable land. Clark's children drink sparingly from the magic potion. They are exposed to events that seem only somewhat larger than life and to a land that remains familiar to them.

All six of Clark's books have somewhat the same plot. This is by no means a fault, however, as each book after the first brings a pleasing sense of the familiar. All are quest stories. The children, a boy and a girl in each story, go in search of a person or set out to return an object they have found—a golden earring in the shape of a pine cone in *The Golden Pine Cone*; a diamond feather in *The Diamond Feather*; a luck stone in *The One-Winged Dragon*; a piece of glass in *The Silver Man*. Except for Bren and Lucy in *The Golden Pine Cone*, all the children are rather unhappy. Mark in *The Sun Horse* is an orphan; Michael in *The One-Winged Dragon* does not believe that his father loves him; Jon and Firelei in *The Diamond Feather* are orphans; the young hero in *The Silver Man* has recently lost his father. The fact that they are unhappy and rather at odds with the world around them makes us ready to accept their gentle break with the real world.

Clark's style of writing varies tremendously—and within one book. She can be harsh, jarring, and plain, sometimes in a compelling way. Unfortunately she can also be lush and overripe, especially when she tries to write for 'effect'. Cumulative flamboyance makes the reader feel he is thrashing through a tropical forest.

There are two major flaws in Clark's work apart from her uneven style: a general overstructuring of plot and the introduction of a welter of minor characters who have little or no relationship to the story as a whole. There is enough plot material in every book to make three stories and enough characters to call for an index. As a result, each book lacks a strong and simple story line and no character is ever fully developed. Perhaps her most memorable creation is the clownish Rock Puck in *The Diamond Feather*. But his place in the book resembles his gait—he hops in and out of the story and is in no way necessary to it. His presence lends a welcome note of humour, but only at the cost of distraction from the main theme. In spite of the standards set by John Masefield in *The Midnight Folk* and by Mary Norton in *The Borrowers*, Clark has not yet learned how to weld minor characters to the narrative and make each one a structural part of the whole.

The power of imagination also falters. Clark seems doubtful about her own medium and is seldom willing to take more than two steps into the world of fantasy. Thus in some books, notably *The Silver Man*, the reader is quite uncertain when a spell of enchantment has been cast. For example, the boy Gil enters into magical adventures and is transported to a different part of his familiar world by means of a talisman, while the girl in the story appears to be living her 'normal' life even though she takes part in the strange events. Clark's gentle transitions from the reasonably familiar to the fantastic do not demand from the reader the same effort at belief as do the somewhat similar stories by the English writer Elizabeth Goudge, but neither do they ever produce the same conviction. As a result, Clark's strength as a fantasist lies, paradoxically, not so much in the allure of the strange as in the homely charm of the realistic. When the children in *The Sun Horse* try to help a wounded swan, they use a very practical method. 'They decided to carry it in Mark's T-shirt which Giselle made into a bag with a safety-pin which closed up the neck.' When Jenni in *The One-Winged Dragon* dropped an egg on the floor, her reaction was quick and simple. 'So Ruggles, the bushy, white, foxy dog was called in and made to lick the egg off the linoleum.' Firelei in *The Diamond Feather* decided to do some baking for the old man who was keeping her and her brother prisoners, and with a few realistic touches the reader is made to share her dilemma and her triumph. 'She broke the eggs into a bowl and beat them with a fork, but they looked very flat. If only she had the egg-beater from home that made a big yellow foam. Perhaps more baking powder would make a fizz.'

The same kind of modest no-nonsense is applied to morality. Clark is a moralist through and through. In every one of her stories the underlying theme is the search for happiness and the way in which children can find it for themselves and for adults. Early in *The Sun Horse*, Giselle is established as a child of great sense:

> Giselle was a girl who liked to listen; she was quiet and peaceful and like a little woman in some ways. She washed her blue slacks and white blouses herself and had a red ribbon always tied neatly round her black hair. She would not linger playing if there was work to be done at home.

And at the end of *The Diamond Feather*, when the children have won through, the great and mystical Chief Raven says to them:

*'Jon and Firelei, children from the Outer World, we have re-
spect for you. Against your own wills, you came here to us, showing kindness, truth and courage beyond the common.'*

But the purpose, though explicit, is accomplished through the
stories themselves and not through extraneous incidents. There
is no overt teaching or preaching, but there is not much drama
either. There is never a gigantic struggle between good and evil—
a theme that is at the root of many fantasies, such as Lewis's
Narnia books, *The Tree That Sat Down* by Beverley Nichols, *The
Doll's House* by Rumer Godden, and a host of others. It is the edge
of darkness that gives the best fantasy much of its depth, meaning, and value. Children do not want to meet a dragon face to face;
they want their world to be safe and secure. But they thirst for the
kind of imaginary world that contains a dragon that can be confronted and overcome. As Tolkien points out, 'For the heart is
hard enough though the body be soft.' Only in Clark's *The Silver
Man* and in her latest book, *The Hunter and the Medicine Man*,
are the lines of battle clearly drawn, and in this respect they are
her most successful stories. Yet *The Hunter and the Medicine Man*
is a disappointment. From the first few pages it is all too evident
that Clark's formula is as firmly fixed as the mountains of British
Columbia. Her signature is also present in the usual delightful
details and characterizations of minor characters—here the pale,
sad lake spirits and the energetic and spirited Mrs Buck, who helps
the children in a practical sense. But although familiarity is a comforting ingredient, it is sad to see no development at all in a writer
of so much 'sense and sensibility'.

Writing twenty years after the publication of *The Golden Pine
Cone* in 1950, Christie Harris in *Secret in the Stlalakum Wild*
(1972) seemed to confirm the pattern of fantasy set by Catherine
Anthony Clark—a real and identifiable setting, the use of Indian
lore for theme and atmosphere, and, most strikingly of all, a hesi-
tant step into the supernatural. Canadian fantasy, it appears, offers
only a slight impingement of a fantasy world upon the real one;
it eschews the creation of a new and different world, with its own
compelling force and internal consistency.

In *Secret in the Stlalakum Wild* the young heroine Morann,

rather pettishly unhappy with her family role, is sidetracked from her search for recognition into an understanding of nature and conservation. On the wild, mountainous terrain of northern British Columbia she is visited by the 'Stlalakum sprites' who 'get into you the way light gets into water. The way an electric current gets into a motor. They make you do things you hadn't thought of doing.' Through them she sees a vision of the way the land was preserved by the Indians of old, confronts a symbol of the destruction of that preservation in the double-headed Lake Snake, and finally, like Gluck in *The King of the Golden River*, comes to learn that healthy green and golden nature is more valuable than the green or gold in man's pockets. Thus Harris gives us a substantial ecology theme in the tradition of Ruskin, Kingsley, and Tolkien.

The great difference between Clark and Harris is in tone and style. Though Clark is gentle and uncommitted in her attempts to contrast the everyday world with the fantastic, her books yet have an aroma of 'faërie' that gradually steals upon the imagination. Harris's brief entries into the realm of fantasy in the 'Stlalakum Wild' are jerky and stagey and finally almost spoil her overt purpose, which is to teach her youthful readers the importance of conservation. Morann is probably the most bouncy and outgoing heroine since L.M. Montgomery's Anne—a strong contrast to children in most fantasies, who tend to be somewhat lonesome and alienated from their everyday surroundings. Morann is healthy, open, and modern, a very ordinary girl who is almost dragged into an adventure for the common good. The opening paragraph sets the tone of practicality:

> *Life seemed only too predictable to Morann on the blistering hot day her father's sister Sarah was due to arrive. So much so that she took steps to start things off in a new direction. Determined to be somebody's favourite for a change, she went at the day head on. She brushed her hair hard, and she reeked of perfume when she finally emerged from the bathroom.*

The rather hearty manner of the opening is not entirely typical of the style. It ranges from some fine descriptive passages to 'modern' conversations riddled with schoolgirl and schoolboy colloquialisms. If a break in high style is considered a fault in fantasy, it should be remembered that the same criticism has been levelled against C.S. Lewis in his Narnia Chronicles—but with far less justification.

Harris has a deep and demonstrable knowledge of West Coast Indian myth. Her books of Indian legends have been justly acknowledged as important contributions to the literature. She also has a deep feeling for the landscape of British Columbia; but it is her self-conscious concern for it that brings us to another point and a new problem.

Although it is perhaps an issue that has recently received more comment than it deserves,* the concern for the influence of landscape on Canadian literature seems especially relevant to Canadian fantasy. The establishment and manipulation of landscape is an especially important characteristic of all great serious fantasy. The limning of a detailed and authentic 'other world' (often complete with maps) helps to distinguish fantasy from folk and fairy tale, for the events occur not just somewhere or someplace, but in well-described Narnia, or Middle Earth or Wonderland. (Only the sophisticated fantasists, such as Roald Dahl in *James and the Giant Peach* and Justin Norton in *The Phantom Toll Booth*, have ignored the fabric of a tangible and memorable setting; however, although their books have achieved a certain popularity, they are not deeply felt or remembered.) The place may be real—like Alan Garner's Alderley; or imagined—like Ursula Le Guin's Earthsea. Only part of it may be recreated, like the home of the dolls in Rumer Godden's *The Doll's House* or the garden in Philippa Pearce's *Tom's Midnight Garden.* Or the real landscape may be wrenched apart by the intrusion of the supernatural, as in William Mayne's *Earthfasts* or Alan Garner's *The Owl Service.* But in all cases the shift in the landscape, when well done, immediately sets up a tension between the real and the fantastic and creates an atmosphere that is familiar yet strange—one of the hallmarks of fantasy.

---

*See Margaret Atwood, *Survival: A Thematic Guide to Canadian Literature,* Toronto, Anansi, 1972; and Lawrence R. Ricou, *Vertical Man Horizontal World: Man and Landscape in Canadian Prairie Fiction,* Vancouver, University of British Columbia Press, 1973.

It is this shift, with its implication of re-creation, that Canadian fantasists seem unable or unwilling to confront. Much can be blamed on the land itself; perhaps there is simply so much geographical space that the Canadian imagination cannot embrace it, reorder it—or escape it. The land also lacks traditional associations. Build a fantasy on King Arthur and place-names abound— from Mount Badon to Tintagel. Take a house that is centuries old, like Lucy Boston's 'Green Knowe', and a mystery immediately becomes plausible. Without such aids the Canadian landscape seems inhospitable or even inimical to fantasy, and so it all too often remains a framework for, rather than a participant in, the story; that is, it does not help to shape the events. The feeling of immensity and coldness that is generated is almost an antithesis to the nature of fantasy. In Canada, writers of fantasy have to make new things familiar.

In this light (and if these premises have any validity) the achievements of our newest and youngest major fantasist are all the more remarkable. Ruth Nichols was only eighteen when she wrote her first fantasy, *A Walk Out of the World*, which was published in 1969. Her second, *The Marrow of the World* (1972), brought her equal acclaim at home and abroad. She comes closer than anyone who has written fantasy in Canada to creating a believable 'sub-world' or 'secondary world' in the great tradition of fantasy, one that is set in a recognizable but modified landscape.

A Walk Out of the World begins with the simplicity of a folk-tale.

> *Once there were a brother and sister who lived in an apartment house in the middle of the city. It was the sort of building that is not a home and does not become one no matter how long you may live there.*

Because of the forest, the sea, and the mountains that surround it, and because of its 'newness', the city that Ruth Nichols describes is undoubtedly Vancouver. But the actual city is transformed into an Everycity, devoid of nature, and the adjacent light wilderness becomes the secret, enchanted wood of the faërie-tale realm, or what D.H. Lawrence called the 'dark forest of the soul'. Nichols' forest exists in opposition to the city world and is being destroyed by it. (The effect of the destruction of nature upon the imagination, however, is left to the reader's interpretation.) The story moves swiftly on.

For the children, Judith and Tobit, the forest is taboo because it still holds a world that is unknown; but they enter it willingly (Judith in particular) because they need to escape from the unbearable reality of the world about them—a world that threatens to close them in and swallow them up. They are claustrophobic and unhappy, 'not really themselves'. Judith says, 'I want to run . . . but it's as if we're shut up in a box and can't breathe.' Charles Kingsley and George MacDonald created their imaginary worlds for the children of the Victorian age, whose familiar world they recognized to be oppressive and industrially alienating. Ruth Nichols does much the same thing for the modern reader. 'A delicate world of wandlike trunks surrounded them, and pale twilight like the ghost of some forgotten day'—this is the bridge to 'a walk out of the world', and once over it the children succumb to the laws of an ancient archetypal kingdom poised for battle against a usurping king after hundreds of years, and awaiting only a decisive sign, which is the arrival of Judith. In this ritual quest the scenes move from the edge of our civilization (the Lake House that is built on pilings of weathered unpainted logs) to a more primeval world: the Red Forest (with its underground dwellers), the Whispering Plain (open and free); then to farmlands and villages (the beginnings of civilization again) to the White City (the apotheosis of civilization), built on a hill, where the great battle between the forces of good and evil is joined.

As the settings change, the children are subtly transformed. Judith feels a 'deep, obscure joy' as she wakes on her first day in the magic world. They gradually take their places as adults in the epic struggle, much as the children in Lewis's Narnia Chronicles rule as kings and queens in the enchanted land but are ordinary school children in their own.

A similar formula works in *The Marrow of the World*. The end of summer, a setting of 'autumn magic', is closely related to an actual setting—that of the Georgian Bay area in Ontario. But it becomes an imaginary landscape too: the underwater domain of the Mer-people, the dark kingdom of the dwarfs, the forest with a traditional, noble 'woodsman', a land that does not exist under our stars:

Philip reared back, searching the sky. The stars still shone white and cold above him, and gradually a pattern blended into awareness in his mind. From horizon to horizon a great constellation filled the sky, looped and jagged like a rope of diamonds. All round it the darkness was powdered with lesser stars, faint and glittering as mica-dust, whose light seemed worlds and centuries remote from the place where he and Linda lay. And low over the trees shone a great green star, translucent as a jewel. Of Jupiter, whose cold brilliance he was used to seeing in the autumn sky, he could find no trace.

The novels are basically similar in plot, although *The Marrow of the World* shows more maturity than *A Walk Out of the World*; indeed it has a depth and subtlety that is unusual in children's fantasies and brings to mind the complexities of George Mac-Donald's adult fantasies, *Lilith* and *Phantastes*. As an adopted child, Linda has not yet come to terms with her new life. She is haunted by dim, troublesome dreams—Jung's race memories—that come to fruition in the fantasy world, which also may be a world of her own imagining. In the real world the death of a moth can summon dim recollections and in the fantasy world the appearance of a great grey wolf is equally and frighteningly familiar:

A low cry broke from Linda: half animal, a wordless sound of recognition. Philip knew, for she had told him, that she had seen this creature in dreams fifty times before.

Like Judith and Tobit, she has a link with this 'other world' and is summoned into it by forces beyond herself. But her quest for the 'Marrow of the World' is determined by the will of her witch half-sister, Ygerna, and involves the making of a choice under threat and coercion. And so the final struggle is not only the universal one of good versus evil, but between the opposing sides of Linda's own nature. And, like Judith, she finally discovers that, although she has completed her search for identity in the Magic World, the knowledge she has acquired is really only applicable in the real. For all the children 'a walk out of the world' is really a step further into it.

These novels are also similar in style and tone: they are mannered and formal, with a rather curious coldness that may derive from the anonymity of the landscape:

Yet Philip could see that the land had begun to rise. Three days out from Lake Evaine, the forest ended and the barrenlands began. Philip and Linda turned back to look one last time at the wall of pine trunks and blue-green needles; then they rode forward. The road could still be followed, though now and then it faded into the grass, and they had to search before rediscovering it some way further on.—The Marrow of the World.

The children are truly Canadian, however. They move through immense distances and attendant perils with an assurance born of knowledge and experience:

Linda squinted dubiously at the swift-flowing clouds. 'Do you think it's going to rain?'

Anxiety sharpened Philip's voice. 'With the country you grew up in, you don't know the look of a snow cloud when you see one? It won't rain.'

'We'd best find somewhere sheltered to camp then.'

Ruth Nichols' fantasy worlds have been described as 'eclectic', and this criticism is apt. Quite a satisfactory game can be played identifying the links with other fantasies. For example, in both books the boys play a loving protective role towards the girls, as does Sam Gamgee towards Frodo in Tolkien's *The Lord of the Rings*. But hers is a rich eclecticism, derived, as with Malcolm Lowry, from the assimilation of a vast store of literature. Of course fantasy itself is a derivative genre rooted in myth and legend and in conventional, primitive patterns that must be played out again and again. In any case Ruth Nichols has added her own originality—the importation of dwarfs to the Canadian wilderness; the almost unbearable tensions between the real world and the fantasy world; and, most compelling of all, the creation of a great primeval substance, the 'Marrow of the World', which brings to its possessor eternal life.

Some writers have chosen to move animals rather than humans through a natural landscape. In many respects animal fantasy might be considered a 'natural' for Canadian writers, given the available knowledge of animals, their importance in our indigenous myths of the Indian and the Eskimo, and the great success of the realistic animal story. Our animal fantasies, however, have proved to be an almost unbroken succession of failures.

Perhaps the major point to make about animal fantasy is that it is such a difficult form. Animal stories are difficult enough to write for children; it is more difficult to write good fantasy and most difficult of all to write great animal fantasy. For it is here that our capacities to suspend disbelief are put to their greatest test. Unless the author is a fine literary craftsman, his characters quickly become obvious wooden symbols of humans, with no integrity of their own; or, less frequently, they become too naturalistic and remain merely animals who perform actions that we simply cannot credit.

Animal fantasy has its own special laws, which are almost inexplicable. They can be deduced only by examining the works of the few outstanding animal fantasists—Beatrix Potter, Kenneth Grahame, Walter de la Mare, Rudyard Kipling, E.B. White, as well as Robert O'Brien in *Mrs. Frisby and the Rats of Nimh* and Richard Adams in *Watership Down*. These writers have taken animal characteristics that tend to reflect the characteristics of a certain type of human and reversed them to produce a mirror image of human behaviour. *The Wind in the Willows* shows an extraordinary insight into the human comedy, into human individuality, into Kenneth Grahame himself, yet it preserves the integrity of the characters as animals. Ratty remains a rat, Mole always a mole, and Toad is an effective example of the danger of denying one's innate nature. Canadian writers seem to feel that all they have to do to create successful animal fantasy is to make an animal talk.

One wonders why Mazo de la Roche's *The Song of Lambert* (1955) and Fred Lindsay's *Mouse Mountain* (1964) were published at all. These books fail because they are counterfeits: rather than insights into either animals or humans, they offer only gimmicks. In *The Song of Lambert* Mazo de la Roche equates fantasy with

fanciful incidents and allegorical names—the butcher is called Mr
Blood and the dyspeptic millionaire Mr Van Grunt. The author so
fails to arouse any sympathy for Lambert (a lamb, of course) that
the reader longs for him to be divested of his human characteristics and converted into chops. Lindsay's *Mouse Mountain*—set in
British Columbia—has cartoon-like animal characters and the
kind of writing associated with comic-strip balloons. Coleridge
pointed out that the reader of fantasy must be brought to 'a willing
suspension of disbelief', and Tolkien's famous amendment, apropos another fantasy failure, is very apt here: 'Disbelief has not so
much to be suspended as hung, drawn and quartered.'

Not even Margaret Laurence could meet the rigorous demands
of animal fantasy. In fact her widely acclaimed success as a novelist makes her one book of fantasy for children, *Jason's Quest*
(1970), the most disappointing book in Canadian children's literature.

Jason, a young mole, sets off on a quest to find a cure for the
strange sickness that is plaguing the ancient underground city of
Molanium. He is accompanied by two cats, intent on doing noble
deeds, and by an owl in search of wisdom. In the city of London
(England) they make friends, defeat a gang of rats engaged in the
protectionist racket, and win their hearts' desires: noble deeds are
accomplished, the owl learns wisdom, and Jason discovers the
secret of Molanium's illness (boredom) and wins a wife besides.
The bald recounting of a plot is often both deceptive and unfair
to a writer. However, the faults in *Jason's Quest* lie both in the
writing and in a misconception of animal fantasy. There seems to
be no reason for a cast of animal rather than human characters.
Margaret Laurence works through a simplistic transference of
human externals to the animal world. Glitter La Fay, the mole
singer, plays at the Mousedrome rather than the Hippodrome;
paws are clapped rather than hands; and 'appearance is only fur-
deep'. Topaz the cat goes into a cat 'boo-teek':

*Madame Amina was sorting through a counter full of bells and
bangles. She came back with a miniature silver bell on a silver
chain and slipped it around Topaz's neck. She then stood back to
admire the effect, and held up a large round mirror so Topaz could
see herself.*

'Ah,' Madame Amina cried. 'Simply perfect! With your coloring, it blends so beautifully. It's you, modom!'

Anthropomorphism is virtually complete. And neither plot nor style (nor the animals themselves) is enhanced by the tiresome and thinly disguised moral lessons.

On the other hand, Mel Thistle in *Peter the Sea Trout* (1954) and W. Towrie Cutt in *Message from Arkmae* (1972) have chosen a wiser—though no doubt an easier—path by making their animals' actions and surroundings natural. Fantasy is used lightly, as a kind of catalyst, to increase the reader's perception, rather than as a full-bodied ingredient.

Peter the Sea Trout conveys to the young reader the life-cycle of the sea trout—although not as graphically or as knowledgeably as Roderick Haig-Brown describes that of the salmon in his *Silver*. Still, Mel Thistle's biology is considerably better than his fantasy. Having gone to great lengths to establish the piscine characteristics of Peter, who is on a quest for wisdom, Thistle then asks too much of the reader when he expects his fish to be accepted as moralist, philosopher, and religious leader. The moral is not a clear-cut one, nor even an understandable one, being muddied with Peter's visions and voices and with the laws of preservation and conservation. The actual story-line in *Peter the Sea Trout* is as broken, complex, and confused as its morality. It has some compelling passages, however. Here is the hero in his boundless natural setting:

Out in the great Atlantic, Peter knew for the first time the spell of isolation, the grey magic of distance. Days of swimming lay behind him and weeks of swimming lay ahead, the nearest land was half a mile below him. Unknown, a feeling grew inside him, till suddenly he became aware of the joy of swimming in a world of water cradled in immensity. The ocean-mood gripped him and there were no boundaries anywhere, inside or out. The chemistry of thought suffused him, changing his body, and he leaped for joy.

Both Margaret Laurence and Mel Thistle fall into the dialect trap. Perhaps recognizing their failure to distinguish between their animal characters as animals, they seek to distinguish them by speech: Laurence's Australian cat speaks 'strine' and the one from the West Indies uses 'man' in every sentence. Similarly Mel Thistle uses a rough dialect; for example, Jimmy Sculpin says: 'Oh, 'im! Thass ony Edgar the' Cod, as stoopid a fish as ever I seed.'

A surer grasp of both the world of reality and the world of fantasy is demonstrated by W. Towrie Cutt in *Message from Arkmae*. Its 'message', an ecological one, is much more didactically presented than that of Christie Harris in *Secret in the Stlalakum Wild*, but the fantasy is more hauntingly and delicately original. It may be, of course, that the theme of the protection of animals can generate more emotion than that of the conservation of land.

The setting is Sanday, one of the Orkney Islands, and the waters that surround it, where the seals are pursued by hunters for profit and by scientists who would keep them penned for observation and experimentation. The boys in the story are Selkie Wards, members of the Ward family reputed to have seal blood, and it is to them that the seals utter their desperate cry for help. In an underwater cave the boys meet the Finman, the last survivor of a legendary race, and hear his awesome warning:

> *When all are swallowed—*
> *Bird, fish and land beast*
> *Man, red in tooth and maw—*
> *Man will eat man.*

With its touches of rich Scottish dialect, its feeling of mystical communion between the boys and the singing seals, and with the creation of the memorable and highly original Finman, *Message from Arkmae* is one of the few books in any genre where the message is expertly and palatably worked into the story. But as a fantasy it just misses success—probably because of the message. (Fantasy can implicitly suggest a message but it should not have to deliver it.)

So does *Swann & Daphne* (1960), by the poet Anne Wilkinson, who died not long after it was published. The story has the undertones of a Greek myth and is intended as a satire on the conformity of modern society. Two children appear one day in the combined back gardens of Mr and Mrs White and Mr and Mrs Green.

Neither couple has been blessed with children. The Whites take the boy and name him Swann because of the soft feathers that cover his head instead of hair; the Greens take the girl whose hair is made of green leaves, and she is named Daphne. All goes well with the children until their parents are forced to send them to school. First they are persecuted, then overly admired, then exploited, until they are forced to depart. The brief story ends when Daphne is turned into a birch tree and Swann into a swan.

Wilkinson wrote with a poet's sensitivity, a delicate humour, and a knife-like precision that cuts at prejudice towards anyone different from ourselves, at the pettiness of minor officialdom, and at the greed of men willing to exploit the helpless for profit. But *Swann & Daphne* fails as a fantasy, for it is more allegory than narrative. Swift and Bunyan had similar motives, but almost in spite of themselves they told so good a story that children were entranced. Wilkinson worked at cross purposes. She used the children's-book format for social outcry, and few children will be deceived or charmed into thinking *Swann & Daphne* is really for them.

If Anne Wilkinson set up a half-real situation for her social comment, Pierre Berton has manufactured an entirely ersatz world based on comic books for his. On the surface *The Secret World of Og* (1961) has all the right ingredients for success: a miniature fantasy world (highly reminiscent of Mary Norton's *The Borrowers*), which some enterprising children enter quite naturally; a touch of danger; even a dog and a cat. But the fantasy does not do what it must do: grip and convince. Berton is so busy with side issues—satirizing the mass media, preaching against racial discrimination, moralizing about the aimlessness of an imitative society and about fearing the unknown—that his plot drizzles into a meagre sermon without effective climax or conclusion.

It is impossible for Pierre Berton to be dull, however. The liveliness that characterizes his writings in other fields is also evident here, particularly in respect of pace. Although the humour and satire are strained and more often slickly adult than simply childlike, they are indisputably present, and one should be grateful for at least these two qualities in Canadian fantasy.

In an unselfconscious way both Anne Wilkinson and Pierre

Berton used an urban setting as a springboard for their fantasies. This is not usual. Only recently have such fantasists as William Mayne in *Earthfasts* and *A Game of Dark* and Alan Garner in *Elidor* made use of English county and industrial towns as settings that are visited by beings from 'the other world'. Janet Lunn is the first writer to use a Canadian city in the same way. Toronto becomes her setting in the classic sense. In *Double Spell* (1968)— more appropriately entitled *Twin Spell* in the paperback edition— the twins, Elizabeth and Jane, are strangely compelled to buy a valuable old doll in a Yonge Street antique shop whose proprietor, in turn, is strangely compelled to sell it to them for a pittance. Its possession seems to change their lives. Their family acquires a lakefront house where another pair of twins in the past have suffered at the hands of their cousin, Hester. Hester's hatred breaks forth into the present and Elizabeth and Jane are saved from it only by that indefinable bond that exists between twins.

This bald recital of events in no way does justice to Janet Lunn's skilful manipulation of the fantastic versus the real or to her unfolding of the past, which turns out to be a bit of family history. In an extraordinary twist she has one of the twins sucked into the ghostly world, and it is only in retrospect that we realize how the girls' personalities became interchanged. However, as in so many Canadian fantasies, a good idea is not completely worked out: the link between the past and the present is arbitrary and not consistent; the doll has too tenuous a place in the plot; and the story as a whole is too slight a vehicle for the dark events that erupt so suddenly at the end. However, this is Lunn's first book and it is to be hoped that her considerable talent will blossom in another.

Is there something about the Canadian experience that makes writers contrived and stilted? This thought comes to mind because of two good writers who passed through Canada, as it were, and left us with two rather similar books of fantasy, both of them much below their normal standard of achievement. John Buchan wrote *Lake of Gold* in 1941 when he was Governor General of Canada. A time fantasy, it compares obviously and unfavourably with Alison Uttley's *A Traveller in Time* in which a modern girl finds herself back in the time of Mary Queen of Scots and is caught up in the plans of the Babington family to help the young queen escape. There is not a jarring note in the book, whether one is in time present or time past. In *Lake of Gold*, however, the bridge between the two worlds creaks and indeed begins to give way as one steps from the present to the past. It is also a rather heavily written book; gone is the fast and light pace of *Greenmantle* and *The Thirty-Nine Steps*. It is hard to believe that the author of *Lake of Gold* could have forgotten the craftsmanship and tempo that suffused the adventures of Richard Hannay.

Eva-Lis Wuorio, who lived in Canada as a child, also tried her hand at a Canadian time fantasy. *Return of the Viking* (1955), like *Lake of Gold*, has no continuing plot; it is a series of episodes about children who go into Canada's past and meet some important people there. In the first story we encounter Leif Ericsson, who tells the children about his voyages and then goes off to northern Muskoka to learn to be a commando with the Norwegians training in Canada. He eventually returns to fight for Canada and for Norway and in time becomes one of the heroes of the war. The children also meet Champlain and Hébert, get involved in an episode during the days of William Lyon Mackenzie, and finally make the acquaintance of Prince Rupert, the founder of the Hudson's Bay Company. However, the fantasy is so patently used as a device to teach history that the reader never really feels a part of the past. Since leaving Canada Wuorio has written slight but charming stories about other parts of the world; their spontaneity and light touch are completely lacking in her Canadian productions. We can only wonder, wistfully, why this is so.

Lyn Cook also shows a strong predilection to teach in *The Magical Miss Mittens* (1970). From the Nova Scotia village of Granville Ferry, three children go back in time and see such varied persons and places as King John at Runnymede, Socrates in prison, Poutrincourt at Port Royal, among others, and are able to use their first-hand knowledge to get A-pluses in their school history projects. They also learn history from an uncle-like figure, Mr Spinney. For the most part the facts learned are those that might be found in any history textbook and the children's involvement in past events is as confusing and tedious as the magic bridge into the past that is personified by 'Miss Mittens'.

The children in Edith Nesbit's time fantasies, *The Phoenix and the Carpet* and *The Story of the Amulet*, and Dan and Una in Kipling's *Puck of Pook's Hill*, away from adults, bring magic about by themselves. The resulting adventures have lightness and humour, as in Nesbit, or a movingly deep sense of history as in Kipling. Lyn Cook's children are carefully guarded, guided, and supervised. With its 'nice' adult cardboard figures (both real and historical), its lack of cohesion (history is uncomfortably mixed with treasure in the present), and its tedious length, *The Magical Miss Mittens* is about as heavy-handed a fantasy as can be found.

The past within the present is the theme of John Latimer's *The Last Pharaoh* (1970). In 1879 three explorers, in search of living dinosaurs, are captured on a trip to Africa and live as slaves in a remnant of Egyptian civilization—'a living civilization cut off from its source three thousand years—but living'. This type of story is perhaps better described as high adventure or reverse science fiction rather than as fantasy; in any case it is a type of literature made famous by Conan Doyle's *Lost Worlds*, Jules Verne's *Journey to the Centre of the Earth*, and Rider Haggard's *King Solomon's Mines*. Calling to mind the romantic flavour of these classics, *The Last Pharaoh* has a comfortable familiarity that eases the 'willing suspension of disbelief' beyond the author's capability to do this on his own. Doyle and Verne remain convincing chiefly because of their unhurried approach to their plots and their mannered and leisurely style. Latimer, in 128 pages of fairly ordinary prose, cannot match them. Yet the plot is well worked out; it moves at a fast pace and reaches a satisfactory climax. Latimer should be commended at least for producing an agreeable extravaganza. Romance is by no means a Canadian speciality.

Fantasy for English-speaking children has been enriched by the writing of a French Canadian, Claude Aubry, whose two books, *The King of the Thousand Islands* (1963) and *The Christmas Wolf* (1965), have been ably translated into English by Alice Kane. *The King of the Thousand Islands* tells the story of how Maha Maha II, King of the Yellow Ants, early in Canada's history constructed the Thousand Islands to please a siren brought from the sea for his amusement. *The Christmas Wolf* is a slight story—an animal tale that is perhaps closer to legend than fantasy. Its credibility can be swallowed only with a large gulp; but then, on a snowy Christmas Eve in a Quebec village, when the parishioners are gathered for midnight mass, we are quite ready to expect miracles, even the conversion of an old starving wolf who has come down in life. The moral is as plain as that in the fables of Aesop and La Fontaine—and just as beguiling. Aubry writes with lightness, charm, and skill; his books exemplify the irony and grace that are so much prized in French writing and that are of course equally welcome in English.

Children as authors and illustrators have always had a great attraction for adults—more than they seem to have for other children. Children's art and children's poetry have been presented in numerous books, notably *Miracles* edited by Richard Lewis. In Canada there has been an upsurge of such publishing, mostly by schools or small publishers and supported by grants from the Canada Council. However, William Robson, who was nine years old when he wrote his fantasy trilogy—*The Magic Mailbox*; *The Boronian War*; *Trouble Underground* (1970)—is probably our first child novelist, or at least the first to be published by a commercial press. His stories have both the charm and the lack of expertise children show when they recount a story orally, often emphasizing points that would not occur to an adult. William Robson's children escape from an orphanage—not exactly a ubiquitous institution in modern Canada—in our earth to Earth 2, where they have wildly dangerous adventures obviously inspired by TV cartoons. In spite of a fair amount of publicity (young Robson was written up in *Maclean's*), these little books never became popular with children or adults. The publishers, perhaps caught up by the cuteness, apparently did not offer the editorial help they would have extended to an adult author and corrected neither spelling nor punctuation; thus they worked against the effectiveness of the stories. The illustrations are childlike scrawls, less artistically appealing than the work of Kendall James Mac-Donald and Joey Hildes, two young author/illustrators in the picturebook field (see page 276).

With the exception of Ruth Nichols, Canadian fantasists have ignored E.M. Forster's dictum that readers of fantasy have to 'pay a little extra'; that is, they have to look beyond the sense memories that ordinary fiction requires for shared experience and make their own creative effort through imagination—they must participate. Canadian writers do not ask enough of their readers. By keeping them so firmly in the here and now, by locking them in a landscape that is totally familiar to them, or by allowing the world of the supernatural to break only slightly into the real world, they prevent their audience from doing what it wants to do—to believe, like the Red Queen, six impossible things before breakfast, or, on a more serious level, to experience reality through spiritual intuition.

Our writers may well sense the inherent difficulties in writing in this genre. Less than a dozen fantasies have been published in the last eight years, a period that coincides with a renaissance in Great Britain. Writers such as Alan Garner, William Mayne, Joy Chant, and Richard Adams have brought a generation since Tolkien to a more subtle appreciation of fantasy's power. In the United States the Ballantine Publishing Company has reprinted many worthwhile adult fantasies and has encouraged new works, so that the whole development of fantasy is laid before us.

Throughout the long period of its existence, fantasy has changed little compared with other types of children's literature. Building their own internalized world, the writers of fantasy are less subject to influences outside their own fertile imaginations. Still, imagination develops from external stimulus, and Canadian fantasy of recent years has shown evidence of a desire to reveal the power and beauty of the Canadian landscape. The books of Catherine Anthony Clark, Christie Harris, Ruth Nichols, and Janet Lunn, while belonging to the general stream of fantasy, do not simply mimic standard models. Fresh and original, as is all good fantasy of any period, these works as a group emerge as uniquely Canadian. Even in a type of literature that is less concerned with national boundaries than any other, these writers have grasped that Canada is neither Great Britain nor the United States.

AUBRY, CLAUDE. *The Christmas Wolf.* Translated from the French by Alice Kane. Illustrated by Edouard Perret. Toronto, McClelland and Stewart, 1965. 42 pp.

An unusual Christmas legend set in the Laurentians. The style shows a combination of strength and delicacy, like the old wolf himself.

AUBRY, CLAUDE. *The King of the Thousand Islands: A Canadian Fairy Tale.* Translated from the French by Alice Kane. Illustrated by Edouard Perret. Toronto, McClelland and Stewart, 1963. 53 pp.

The story of how the Thousand Islands came to be has a considerable measure of originality, charm, and humour. While it could be described as 'slight', in translation it adds considerable strength to the body of Canadian fantasy in English.

BERTON, PIERRE. *The Secret World of Og.* Illustrated by William Winter. Toronto, McClelland and Stewart, 1961. 146 pp.

A family of children find their way to Og, the land of the little green men. This is an amusing attempt at relating some modern, even universal, problems to a child's comprehension, but because of its facile adult cleverness, it is not a complete success as a children's book. It has been reissued in paperback with new illustrations—many of them in colour—by Patsy Berton (Toronto, McClelland and Stewart, 1974. 159 pp.). The spirited drawings, in the comic-book tradition, suit the story, but their abundance leaves very little to the imagination.

BUCHAN, JOHN. *Lake of Gold.* Illustrated by S. Levenson. Toronto, Musson, 1941. 190 pp.

This look at Canada's past through the medium of fantasy is better history than it is fiction, but the overall combination results in dryness.

CLARK, CATHERINE ANTHONY. *The Diamond Feather; or, The Door in the Mountain, A Magic Tale for Children.* Illustrated by Clare Bice. Toronto, Macmillan, 1962. 224 pp.

After many difficulties, two orphan children bring happiness to a prospector by releasing his wife and children from a magic spell. The charm of the book lies in some of its minor characters, who clearly belong to the mountains of British Columbia.

CLARK, CATHERINE ANTHONY. *The Golden Pine Cone.* Illustrated by Clare Bice. Toronto, Macmillan, 1950. 182 pp.

All Clark's fantasies are set in British Columbia. Bren and Lucy return the golden pine cone to Tekontha, who rules the lands of lakes and forests, and in so doing have numerous magical adventures. This is mild, but nonetheless genuine, Canadian fantasy.

CLARK, CATHERINE ANTHONY. *The Hunter and the Medicine Man.* Illustrated by Clare Bice. Toronto. Macmillan, 1966. 183 pp.

Clark here offers the comfort of familiarity rather than the novelty of a departure from her usual style and pattern. Two children help an Indian boy release his mother from the spell of the Medicine Man. They are assisted by the courage of the Hunter, by the rough practicality of Mrs Buck, a trapper's wife, and by beneficient spirits, all of whom seem a natural part of the forests and waters of British Columbia.

CLARK, CATHERINE ANTHONY. *The One-Winged Dragon*. Illustrated by Clare Bice. Toronto, Macmillan, 1955. 278 pp.
Chinese and Indian magic and myth are mingled convincingly in the story of two children who, with the aid of a dragon, go on a quest to seek the daughter of an old Chinese farmer, and in so doing find their own happiness. This is a fantasy that gives an understanding picture of the Indians of British Columbia.

CLARK, CATHERINE ANTHONY. *The Silver Man*. Illustrated by Clare Bice. Toronto, Macmillan, 1958, 231 pp.
A rock crystal of great beauty in a setting of ancient Indian workmanship is the talisman by which ten-year-old Gil enters a new and strange world. This has a stronger, less complicated plot than Clark's other fantasies, as well as deeper characterization and considerably more suspense.

CLARK, CATHERINE ANTHONY. *The Sun Horse*. Illustrated by Clare Bice. Toronto, Macmillan, 1951. 209 pp.
The 'Sun Horse' has lured Giselle's father into Forgetful Canyon and she and her friend Mark try to find him. West Coast Indian legends and symbols are woven into the story in a rather complicated and strained manner.

COOK, LYN. *The Magical Miss Mittens*. Illustrated by Mary Davies. Toronto, Macmillan, 1970. 233 pp.
Through doors in a mysterious house that is inhabited by a mysterious woman (Miss Mittens), three children enter various historical periods related to history projects at school and escape again through the magic in a pair of mittens. The portrayal of everyday child life in Granville Ferry, N.S., has some merit, but the many time journeys are dull and confusing, and the story's intention is too obviously didactic.

CUTT, W. TOWRIE. *Message from Arkmae*. Toronto, Collins, 1972. 96 pp.
When all are swallowed—/ Bird, fish and land beast/ Man, red in tooth and maw—/ Man will eat man./ This is the warning of the Finman, survivor of a legendary race, as the seals off the Orkney Islands are hunted with guns or captured for observation and experiment. Although obviously written for its ecological message, the author manages to sustain an aura of fantasy and adventure.

DE LA ROCHE, MAZO. *The Song of Lambert*. Illustrated by Eileen Soper. Toronto, Macmillan, 1955. 51 pp.

Lambert is a lamb that is the personification of 'cuteness'. It is hard to believe that this pathetic attempt at fantasy is from the pen of the writer of the Jalna series.

HARRIS, CHRISTIE. *Secret in the Stlalakum Wild*. Illustrated by Douglas Tait. Toronto/Montreal, McClelland and Stewart, 1972. 182 pp.

A young girl is persuaded by the Indian spirits of British Columbia's mountains, lakes, and forests—the 'Stlalakum'—to join the battle for conservation, and in the process finds herself and her role within her family. Harris's style is as modern as her theme and her heroine, but as a journey into the unknown her story lacks the holding power of the more traditional fantasies of Ruth Nichols.

LATIMER, JOHN. *The Last Pharaoh*. Camden, N.J./Toronto, Thomas Nelson & Sons, 1970. 128 pp.

In 1879, in the heart of Equatorial Africa, three explorers are captured and taken to an inaccessible valley where they live as slaves in a pocket of Egyptian civilization that has not changed for 3,000 years. Although the events are exciting enough, the story is too short and is told in too ordinary a style to make the imaginary world as convicing as the settings of *The Lost World* by Conan Doyle or *The Journey to the Centre of the Earth* by Jules Verne.

LAURENCE, MARGARET. *Jason's Quest*. Illustrated by Staffan Torell. Toronto/ Montreal, McClelland and Stewart, 1970. 211 pp.

Jason, the young mole, and his companions, two cats and an owl, set out on a quest to find a cure for a mysterious illness that plagues the underground city of Molanium. The scenes are played out in London (England) in a manufactured, modern slapstick comedy that has little relationship to genuine animal fantasy.

LINDSAY, FRED. *Mouse Mountain*. Illustrated by Florence Lindsay. Toronto, McClelland and Stewart, 1963. 96 pp.

An animal fantasy set in British Columbia in which the animals are only clumsy caricatures of humans.

LUNN, JANET. *Double Spell*. Illustrated by A.M. Calder. Toronto, Peter Martin Associates, 1968. 134 pp. (Also published in paperback as *Twin Spell*. Pictures by Emily McCully. New York, Dell Publishing, 1969. 158 pp. A Dell Yearling Book.)

The twins, puzzled by the effects upon them of an antique doll they have purchased, search Toronto for a clue to the past. This is a slight, somewhat flawed fantasy for younger children, yet it touches the nerve of darkness and terror and is a significant step in the development of Canadian fantasy.

MARTEL, SUZANNE. *The City Underground*. Translated from the French by Norah Smaridge. Illustrated by Don Sibley. New York, Viking, 1964. 157 pp.

After atomic devastation, a highly technical, rather arid civilization develops under the city that was once Montreal, while a more primitive society that keeps its spiritual values struggles on earth. A better-than-average science-fiction story from French Canada.

NICHOLS, RUTH. *The Marrow of the World*. Illustrated by Trina Schart Hyman. Toronto, Macmillan, 1972. 168 pp.
Linda is sent on a long and difficult journey to recover a portion of a primeval substance, the 'Marrow of the World', for her wicked half-sister, Ygerna. The depths of Georgian Bay and the rugged country surrounding it make a memorable setting for this dark and haunting tale. With this book, her second, Ruth Nichols became Canada's most compelling creator of fantasy.

NICHOLS, RUTH. *A Walk Out of the World*. Illustrated by Trina Schart Hyman. Toronto, Longman, 1969. 129 pp.
A walk in the forest on an eerie day takes Judith and Tobit into an 'Other World' where they play their roles as adults in an epic and traditional quest—the restoration to a kingdom of its rightful heir. The landscape of British Columbia is subtly transformed to create a believable world for a succession of majestic events.

RILEY, LOUISE. *Train for Tiger Lily*. Illustrated by Christine Price. Toronto, Macmillan, 1954. 186 pp.
Crossing the Canadian prairies in a train, a group of children find adventure with a Grade B magician. This insipid and contrived fantasy has a sequel: *A Spell at Scoggin's Crossing*, illustrated by David Knight. (Toronto, Abelard-Schuman, 1960. 175 pp.)

ROBSON, WILLIAM. *The Magic Mailbox; The Boronian War; Trouble Underground*. Illustrated by the author. Toronto, New Press, 1970. 56, 52, 53 pp.
A group of children escape from an orphanage to Earth 2, where they have much excitement and many adventures. The author, who was nine years old when he wrote these stories, has a great knowledge of weaponry and reveals his exposure to TV culture. But despite some excellent turns of phrase and a genuine inventiveness, adult writers of fantasy can take heart. In this case a little child shall not lead them.

THISTLE, MEL. *Peter the Sea Trout*. Illustrated by Jean Donald Gow. Toronto, Ryerson, 1954. 177 pp.
The denizens of the Atlantic are presented as talking fish and Peter the hero is on a search for truth, happiness, and beauty. Although this has an original idea and a fairly interesting story line that incorporates considerable natural history, it is not successful fantasy.

WILKINSON, ANNE. *Swann & Daphne*. Illustrated by Leo Rampen. Toronto, Oxford, 1960. 48 pp.
The sophisticated combination of myth and fancy, with its commentary on some adverse aspects of modern society, has perhaps made a book for

adults rather than children, but this story has memorable qualities and should not be lost to either.

WUORIO, EVA-LIS. *Return of the Viking*. Illustrated by William Winter. Toronto, Clarke, Irwin, 1955. 208 pp.

Similar in idea and mechanism to John Buchan's *Lake of Gold*, this return to Canada's past has livelier writing but less credibility.

YOUNG, DELBERT A. *The Ghost Ship*. Illustrated by William Taylor. Toronto/Vancouver, Clarke, Irwin, 1972. 191 pp.

Two boys exchange places in the sixteenth and twentieth centuries through a crude fantasy device (both are knocked on the head at the same time). But since the action takes place almost entirely in the past aboard Drake's *The Golden Hind*, the story becomes historical fiction—accurate but dull.

4 | historical fiction

It is a wry commentary on the state of Canadian historical fiction for children that a consideration of the subject must begin with a question: are these books really historical fiction?

Historical fiction is surely nothing less than the imaginative re-creation of the past. The good historical novel involves the reader in a bygone era, dramatically and emotionally. The reader, and especially the young reader, must be made to identify with the past, to live it in his mind rather than to study it.

'Living the past' depends squarely and solely on the writer's evocative skill. The parcelling out of so much history and so much fiction cannot create the conviction that a successful historical novel must have. It could be said that Hope Muntz's *The Golden Warrior*, a story of the Battle of Hastings, is all history because the characters were actual people, from William and Harold to Eyestein Gorock, fleetingly mentioned as betrothed to Harald Sigurdson's daughter. Zoé Oldenbourg's *The Cornerstone* might conceivably be classified as mostly fiction because it has a huge cast of invented characters. Yet both are historical novels because Hope Muntz has created the personalities of history for another generation and Zoé Oldenbourg sweeps us back into a huge tapestry of thirteenth-century France.

No matter what the design of the framework—firm as in *The Golden Warrior* or loose as in *The Cornerstone*—the historical novelist is primarily writing fiction. The adjective merely particularizes the noun, as does 'science' in science fiction and 'detective' in detective fiction.

This scale of priorities allows the creator of historical fiction considerable freedom in the treatment of his material. He may expand events or telescope them; he may interpret a fact or ignore it as not pertinent to his artistic aim. He may even enjoy the liberty, denied to the historian, of going beyond the bounds of historical evidence. But this must be done warily. The adjectival novel depends in part for its effectiveness on the facts that it embodies and the writer must respect them. Put vegetation on the moon and the credibility of science fiction is destroyed. Costume drama must get the costumes right and the detective story should not cheat on clues. Accuracy is an asset; plausibility is essential.

Between the contending pulls of imagination and authenticity, the historical novelist must take a firm stand. It is all too easy to lean in one direction and be drawn to the most readily attainable goal. Authenticity, which costs hours of work, is within the reach of almost any writer with a flair for research, but imagination is something that effort alone cannot purchase. The dual nature of historical fiction, then, often lends itself to misinterpretation of goals. Many writers rely on the supposition that all one needs is a historical period with plot attached. Or, one step higher but not high enough, they become so embroiled in maintaining historical accuracy that the imaginative content of the story is submerged in an accumulation of detail.

The artistic problems inherent in the historical novel are increased in books for children. Here events must be more closely winnowed and sifted; character more clearly delineated, but without condescension or over-simplification. The child must be moved rather quickly into the consciousness of another time and his imagination immediately stirred to it. Because the child has greater need than the adult for self-identification with a hero, the hero of the past must have some immediacy for the young reader of the present. Perhaps the greatest contribution the historical novelist can make to a child's reading is to show him that an event in the past did not happen in isolation but was part of a continuous series of events that have influenced and given meaning to his own time.

Writers for children have at their disposal one convention that has been tried frequently and successfully: the introduction of an invented boy or girl character (pluralized, if desired) who represents the reader in the past. A variation of this approach makes the hero or heroine an actual historical figure, but at an age level close enough to the reader's to make identification possible—young Richard the Fearless in Charlotte Yonge's *The Little Duke* or seven-year-old Queen Isabella in Hilda Lewis's *The Gentle Falcon*.

Whatever the plot device, the best novels are those in which child calls to child across the years. The English author, Rosemary Sutcliff, perhaps the greatest living writer of historical novels for the young, writes chiefly of prehistoric and Roman days in Britain. Her main characters are always children or young people, who are chiefly engaged in heroic deeds and adventures. Her books exhibit a powerful and intuitive imagination combined with exhaustive research that is never intrusive. Her books, crowded with excitement, danger, and action, have almost an epic quality. Her people's struggles to remain free and unconquered become a universal struggle—an echo of the struggles of mankind that have gone before and a foreshadowing of all those yet to come. The events may be in the past, but the courage, hope, generosity, and friendship that her characters express are immutable in each generation.

The American Esther Forbes shows what can be done with tightly knit history presented in a more conventional, less imaginative manner. Her *Johnny Tremain* is a story of the American Revolution, complete with the Boston Tea Party and Paul Revere's Ride. The young hero is just as real—perhaps even more so to children—than the historical hero, Paul Revere. The personal events in Johnny's life have a meaning of their own. Certain things happen because he is Johnny and no one else. Other things happen because he is involved in great events. The end result, however, is that a child will feel, if not that he has fought in the Revolution, at least that 'he was there'.

Muntz, Oldenbourg, Sutcliff, Forbes—whether writing for child or adult, and however different their approach to the historical novel—have two attributes in common. They are the masters rather than the slaves of their historical material, so steeped in their period that their imagination can be released. They are also gifted writers. It is against the standards of historical fiction exemplified by these novelists that Canadian achievements must be measured. Unfortunately, only a misplaced patriotism could take comfort from the comparison.

By and large, Canadian historical fiction for children is a succession of failures. Its virtues have been in the reporting of history, its failings have been literary. Canadian writers may claim full marks for the conscientious and accurate assemblage of dates, names, and events. But on the whole the plots are manipulated and the characters invented are *papier-mâché*. Even the historical personages have a rubbed-out appearance. These books do recount an aspect of the past but they seldom recreate it. In paraphrasing Canada's history, our writers fill their pages with irrelevancies and snippets of lore. They decide to parcel out so much history and so much narrative, and in doing so they usually weigh the parcel in favour of history. And how they love to teach it! Gratuitous dates and place-names abound, along with 'how-to-do-it' information: how to prepare pemmican, to make candles, to tan a deer hide, to construct a Red River cart—all interesting in themselves but misplaced in the pages of a novel.

Olive Knox's *The Young Surveyor* (1956) is typical of the pedagogical approach. It is based on the Jarvis survey for the Canadian Pacific Railway in British Columbia in 1874 and 1875. A seventeen-year-old boy accompanies E.W. Jarvis and learns surveying from him. The reader perforce learns it too, since the first two chapters consist of little more than questions and answers on the subject. Christie Harris's *Forbidden Frontier* (1968) has more of a story line than most Canadian historical novels for children. But even Harris, experienced writer that she is, falls into the didactic trap.

> *Alison was excited about going to Kamloops. Once it had been the connecting link between the Company's two vast areas of operation west of the Rockies: New Caledonia that reached north to Alaska, and the Columbia District that stretched south to California. It had maintained two thousand horses for the Brigades that wound south to the Columbia River through the easy, open Okanagan Valley.*

Alison is nine years old, hardly of an age to grasp the full significance of going to Kamloops from Fort Alexandria, even in the 1860s. Imparting information while pretending to tell a story is a literary device that used to be regularly perpetrated in eighteenth- and nineteenth-century England, when children penalized such gaucheries by ignoring them in favour of real stories when they came along. It should not be presumed that Canadian children of the present willingly do otherwise.

The Young Surveyor represents most of the faults to which the genre is liable. Dismiss it, then, as an isolated mistake? Alas, no. For sales appeal is not synonymous with intrinsic merit. Diluted history as it is presented in books like *The Young Surveyor* and *Forbidden Frontier* has its market (presumably among educators) and thus its own *raison d'être*.

Any market is best exploited by a standardized product. Under- standably, then, many an attempt has been made to apply the theory to writing, especially writing for children. Such books are commissioned by a publisher, written to a formula, and designed to form part of a series. Not that the series link is in itself neces- sarily damaging. Arthur Ransome's 'Swallows and Amazons', Edith Nesbit's 'The Bastable Children', the Narnia books of C.S. Lewis, the 'Eagle of the Ninth' group by Rosemary Sutcliff—all these author series show that their creators had so much to say that their joy in their subjects and characters could not be con- tained in one book. Canadian publisher-series books, however— the 'Buckskin Books' and the 'Frontier Books'—read as if specific data had been fed into a computer. Each book is by a different author, but the similarity of approach is clearly reflected in the results. The formula seems to call for the following requirements: history must be deadly accurate; history must take precedence over fiction; don't narrate—just report event after event after event; don't worry about style or characterization; limit the vocab- ulary to the number of words specified by educationalists as normal for the age group.

The 'Buckskin Books', we are told by the publisher, are 'excit- ing stories for younger readers—tales of action and adventure set against the background of rousing events in Canadian history. They are books full of lively incident that provide children with a wide and wonderful variety of good reading.' Against these claims may be placed the following analysis. Each book consists of no more than 122 pages and no fewer than 113. The vocabulary is stringently limited: except for the proper names, the words are those derived from the textbooks produced for the age group. In each book (more than ten have been published since 1961), the story line is a thin thread of Canadian pseudo-history, with fiction lying uneasily amid the facts. The books have been prepared for children from eight to ten years of age, presumably on the assumption that fairy tales and fantasy are no longer proper fare.

Two of the early 'Buckskin Books' have themes familiar in North American children's literature. In *The Great Canoe* (1962), by Adelaide Leitch, a little Indian boy attaches himself to a famed explorer; in *Father Gabriel's Cloak* (1962), by Beulah Garland Swayze, a white girl is captured by Indians. Most 'Buckskin Books' have young heroes with whom the reader can identify, and authentic settings and special information as in *The Great Canoe*, which has descriptions of Indian tribal beliefs, customs, and rituals. They are less successful in style and characterization.

The best of the series are those books that show little or no attempt to establish a definite period in history, such as Catherine Anthony Clark's *The Man With Yellow Eyes* (1963), which concentrates on a boy's race to record his father's mine, and Leslie and Lois Benham's *The Heroine of Long Point* (1963), the story of a rescue on the Great Lakes. But the overall impression of the series remains that these books were designed for an uncritical market and have little else to recommend them than their 'Canadian content'.

No one denies the need for Canadian historical fiction, particularly in the schools, but the question is whether Canadian history, Canadian literature, or Canadian children are well served by such baldly commercial products. It must be said in favour of the 'Buckskin Books' that there are few better historical novels for younger children against which to compare them. Historical fiction for the eight-to-ten age group is admittedly difficult to write. However, there are enough good non-Canadian examples to show that it can be done: *The Emperor and the Drummer Boy* by Ruth Robbins; *The Matchlock Gun* by Walter Edmonds; *Otto of the Silver Hand* by Howard Pyle. These books take a single incident and tell it simply but dramatically. They are thrilling and even chilling, sufficiently so to carry the unusual word along with the simple ones. They are beautifully produced with superb illustrations. Unfortunately they cost three times as much as the 'Buckskin Books'.

The 'Frontier Books' exemplify the deficiencies of the formula story at the older age level. Described by the publisher as historical novels, they are completely based on history and no fictional characters of any consequence appear in them. Typical of this series is *John Rowand, Fur-Trader* (1963) by Iris Allan. It is the story of an actual fur-trader who left his home in Montreal as a boy of fourteen to spend his days with the North West Company. We follow his rather uneventful life until he dies at the age of sixty-two. The outstanding happening is the amalgamation of the North West Company with the Hudson's Bay Company. John W. Chalmers' *Horseman in Sacrlet* (1961), which recounts the career of the famous Sam Steel of the North West Mounted Police, is a mere refurbishing of facts.

The series format may inhibit creativity, but it cannot be blamed for all a writer's deficiencies. A change of publisher, and an escape from the series format, did not help Iris Allan with *White Sioux: The Story of Major Walsh of the Mounted Police* (1969). Described as a 'biographical novel', it is little more than a record of the historical events surrounding Major Walsh's career. Its very dedication to fact raises questions about its tone. Were the officers of the Mounted Police really as indifferent to, and uncomprehending of, the Indians' situation as this book shows? And did that great friend of 'Sitting Bull', Major Walsh, really address him as 'Bull'? With all its accurate research, this is a case where the writer's interpretation of character and events needs a note of explanation.

Their dullness aside, novels that are mainly intended to present factual information raise doubts about their creative qualities. Perhaps it is fairer to look at them simply as an attempt to make history more palatable, just as the rules of arithmetic may be more easily learned when set to some rhyme. The 'Frontier Books' seem to declare, in effect, that a child would not be interested in reading a purely factual account of, say, La Salle's life, but might be in-

duced to swallow the intellectual pill of history or biography
when it is sweetened by a light coating of fiction.

Historical fiction, much more than history, allows the writer
and so the reader the fun of 'taking sides'. Geoffrey Trease in *The
Grey Adventurer* can turn our sympathies from the gay cavaliers
to the more prosaic Roundheads, as can Rosemary Sutcliff in
Simon. Alison Uttley in *A Traveller in Time* manages to convince
us, until the end of the book, that the Babington Plot to help
Mary, Queen of Scots, escape will indeed succeed. But Canadian
writers appear to have a self-imposed limitation in respect of
pitch. There is no reason to believe that Canadian children are
uniquely appreciative of the virtues of restraint, but those who
write for them prefer gentility over gusto. Even so competent a
novelist as John Hayes almost never exploited the conflict inherent
in his well-chosen subjects. His *Land Divided* (1951), for example,
is about the Acadians, tragic victims of a war that settled the fate
of empires. But emotion or the taking of sides was shunned. Give
the young hero a father who is an English army officer and a
mother who is Acadian. Have Michael's Acadian cousin Pierre
help in the search for Michael's father when the latter is captured
by the French. In turn, of course, Michael's father will kindly and
courteously help his Acadian relatives to settle in the foreign town
to which they have been banished; this succeeds so well that the
impression is given that they will be far better off there anyway.
Michael's mother presents no dramatic problem either; she takes
the oath of loyalty to King George. Why in the world did Longfellow become so emotional about Evangeline?

Even in Hayes' *Treason at York* (1949), blandness and impar-
tiality set the prevailing tone. The issues would seem to force a
choice—after all, Canada was *invaded* in the War of 1812—but
Hayes somehow enables hero and reader to escape involvement.
Various circumstances ensure that the hero shall bear little or no
sense of enmity to the American adversary. In many ways the
book is a plea against fighting with one's neighbour. This is admirable morality but does not satisfy the claims of either entertainment or historical truth. Arthur Lower, in *Canadians in the
Making*, points out that the defence of Canada in the War of 1812
helped forge this nation and 'goes to the roots of Canadian life'.

Hayes assuages feelings when it would have been more valid and dramatically effective to strengthen them.

Hayes does come round to committing a hero in *Rebels Ride at Night* (1953), on the Rebellion of 1837. The protagonist takes sides with Mackenzie, though more for personal than political reasons. This definite identification makes it perhaps the most satisfactory of Hayes' books and certainly far better than the other two novels on the same subject, Emily Weaver's *The Only Girl* (1925) and Lyn Cook's *Rebel on the Trail* (1953), in which the Rebellion is seen from the periphery by young heroines. While both their families are alarmed by the mild attachment of the elder son for Mackenzie's cause, the Rebellion itself is treated as a pointless scheme of a foolish few. It is implied that a little more patience and equanimity would have obviated the whole incident. Although this is the view of current historians, there seems to be considerable evidence that the Rebellion followed and indeed was caused by a period of strong tension. This is well shown in James Reaney's *The Boy with an R in His Hand* (1965). The year is 1826 and two orphan boys come to 'muddy York' to be under the protection of a proud and greedy uncle who seems to have stepped out of an old fairy tale. He represents the arrogance and ritualistic attitude of the ruling class that came to be known as the Family Compact. A picture of the society of the time emerges clearly, even though the book is short (101 pages); we read about a hanging for cow-stealing, a girl who has been branded as a thief without evidence, an apprentice system that secures a boy from childhood to twenty, how a man's livelihood is destroyed while the authorities look on, and a fight for a free press. It is difficult to say whether Reaney deliberately chose to tell the story in the stereotyped convention of Victorian children's books—that is, with the characters either all black or all white. If he did, the manner doesn't quite come off, but the book has undoubted charm and impact. It comes as a surprise at the end of the story to remember that the Rebellion is still ten years off.

In the light of the foregoing discussion it is not at all strange that Canadian historical fiction gingerly sidesteps the greatest issue in Canadian history: the conflict between French and English. The few books available to children dealing with the events culminating in the Battle of the Plains of Abraham are all by British or American authors: G.A. Henty's *With Wolfe in Canada* (British—1886), Ronald Welch's *Mohawk Valley* (British—1958), Virginia Watson's *Flags Over Quebec* (American—1941), Allan Dwight's *Guns at Quebec* (American—1962), Wilma Pitchford Hays' *Drummer Boy for Montcalm* (American—1959). It seems as though the emotional implications of this theme for Canadians can hardly be toned down, and hence had best be avoided altogether. However, the scarcity of material on the age of exploration and the French and Indian wars seems beyond explanation. Only a few Canadian writers of fiction (e.g. Fred Swayze in *Tonty of the Iron Hand* and *Iroquois War Trail*, Adelaide Leitch in *The Great Canoe*, and Beulah Garland Swayze in *Father Gabriel's Cloak*) have dealt with this earlier period. Even the story of that heroine beloved by the textbook writers, Madeleine de Verchères, has been left to our American compatriots, in such books as *Madeleine Takes Command* by Ethel C. Brill and *Outpost of Peril* by Alida Malkus.

The overall impression that Canadian writers withdraw from the emotional impact of historical fact is strengthened when one examines two outstanding historical novels for children. Both of them—Roderick Haig-Brown's *The Whale People* (1962) and Edith Sharp's *Nkwala* (1958)—avoid the great debates of Canadian history. Indeed, they might more properly be described as anthropological or ethnological novels rather than as historical fiction. They deal not with recorded events nor with personages from history but with a social setting no more specifically defined in time and place than British Columbia 'before the white man came'. This is not to say that the narratives are not based on solid historical research: the historicity is evident but never obtrusive; fact underlies every fictional event but never dictates its design. Both authors have a firm belief in the truth of their stories and the power to engage the belief of their readers.

A description of their plots will suggest that these books are more similar than is actually the case, for their differences are basic. In dealing with the ethos of a race, *The Whale People* has a simple strength, dignity, and even starkness that are akin to the great northern myths, while *Nkwala* has a softer, more precious cast that is close to being romantic. The Hotsath tribe of the west coast of Vancouver Island are 'the whale people'. They hunt the whale from dugout canoes with weapons of wood and bone and horn. Atlin, a boy of the tribe and the son of its chief, receives both practical and spiritual training to prepare him to take his father's place as the whale chief. Upon his father's death he subjects himself to severer discipline in order to receive the spiritual insight—the appearance of his 'tumanos' or particular spirit—that will confirm his leadership. As a chief he is able to lead his tribe back to prosperity, wisely avoiding war with the neighbouring Tsitikat tribe and winning the chief's daughter for his wife. The style is simple and is almost unadorned by descriptive adjectives:

The whale was travelling very slowly now, tail flukes sweeping wearily from side to side in a narrow arc, his body heaved and rolling on the following swells. The canoe drew close, pitching and sliding, now threatening to crash against the whale's bulk, now falling off to a distance of ten or fifteen feet. Nothing was still or steady even for a moment and Atlin wondered how anyone could hope to make a killing thrust. Then the canoe lifted on a swell and, through a moment of terror, seemed to hover over the whale's back. In that moment Nit-gass jumped and the ready paddles backed and swung the canoe clear of danger. Atlin saw his father slip once, recover his balance and run forward along the whale's back as far as the little flipper that showed when he rolled. There Nit-gass made two swift and fearful thrusts. The whale shuddered, drove with his tail and forced his body half out of the water.

Nkwala is a Salish Indian boy of the Spokan tribe. At twelve years of age, as prescribed by Salish law, he seeks a dream, a song, or any spiritual happening that will reveal to him his protecting guardian spirit and give him a man's name. 'Ahead were days and nights of trial, when the boy went alone into the mountains to search for his guardian spirit, his song and his name. This was as his father, his father's father and father's father before him, had done. He went alone, but always and forever with him went the law.' But Nkwala's dream is withheld from him. Then, forced by hunger, the Spokans enter the land of the Okanagan tribe. The Spokan chief remembers that Spokan and Okanagan were once the same blood and hopes to establish the Spokans' 'blood right' to the Okanagans' root-digging grounds before battle is joined. The story, quietly begun and quietly told, moves to a swift and dramatic climax as Nkwala risks his life for a moment of speech between Spokan and Okanagan.

It is surely one of the attributes of the historical novel that in revealing the past it speaks to the present. Both *The Whale People* and *Nkwala* do this in great measure and they do it mainly through the fictional events and the characters of the two boys. The authors' research tells us what Indian society was like at that time; their creative imaginations make us part of man's long quest, first to find himself and then to find his place in the world around him.

Nkwala and *The Whale People* also offer some useful lessons in design. Both employ a short time span—*Nkwala* a few months and *The Whale People* about two years. By contrast, most other novels, with an other-directed structure imposed by history book or publisher, simply attempt to cover too long a period. Fred Swayze's *Tonty of the Iron Hand* (1957) chronicles twenty-six years of Tonty's experiences; Olive Knox's *Black Falcon* (1955), twenty years of a white boy's life with the Indians. And most others not much less.

The insensitivity to the need for dramatic unity is also manifested in the pervasive tendency to complicate plots and proliferate details. The typical historical novelist is likely to march his hero from fort to fort, from battle to battle, in such a confusing itinerary that parts of the book must often be re-read in order to determine what is actually taking place. Even so good a novel as Thomas Raddall's *Son of the Hawk* (1950) could do with some pruning because it lacks a strong focus. Its impact is dissipated by a welter of episodes.

Simplicity goes with artistic integrity. *Nkwala* and *The Whale People* show this clearly. So does John Craig's *The Long Return* (1959). This is the story of a white boy captured by Ojibways. He lives with them for several years and becomes fond of them. When he makes his escape, he does so almost with reluctance.

The plot is exciting but it is also simple. And there is not a date in the book, so that Craig has ample opportunity to concentrate on character and style and the development of credibility. So too does John Hayes in *The Dangerous Cove* (1957). The Fishing Admirals, on their yearly trip to the fishing banks of Newfoundland, put into force their charter to drive the settlers away from the coast. The two heroes help to oppose and ultimately defeat them. A simple and credible plot (although here watered down by a sub-plot) and the sharp focus produced by a short time span and a fast-paced narration combine to achieve a successful integration of history and invention.

In Cliff Faulknor's *The White Calf* (1965) and Christie Harris's *West with the White Chiefs* (1965) we can see two interesting and opposite techniques in the writing of historical fiction. *The White Calf* conveys a sense of period without the crutches of dates, place-names, and famous historical events. Faulknor's knowledge of the Indian groups that roamed the Canadian prairies in the middle of the nineteenth century is considerable; and he is able to let his knowledge inform his readers naturally. The weakness in the book lies in the imaginative quality of the writing. The plot rises at times to exciting episodes, but it is too loosely constructed to have artistic unity. The young hero, Eagle Child, is a rather colourless boy who soon has to yield the stage to his older brother, the dashing Tailfeathers. Indeed, the adult characters—Tailfeathers, the Medicine Man, and Eagle Child's father—steal whatever 'show' there is to be stolen. The style is pedestrian: it is hard to believe that any reader will turn the pages with breathless interest. Yet in emphasizing story quality above the recording of events, *The White Calf* helps to keep the chief purpose of historical fiction clearly before us.

While books such as *The Long Return*, *The Dangerous Cove*, and *The White Calf* have their strength in plot, Christie Harris in *West with the White Chiefs* shows what can be done in a novel for children that maintains a relatively strict adherence to historical fact. All the characters actually lived and operated in the situations Harris describes. The book is firmly based on the journal of Dr John Cheadle; he and his companion, Viscount Milton, have been called the first trans-Canadian tourists. Harris concentrates on their first trip across the Rockies in 1863. They survived because of the resourcefulness of their Indian guide, Louis Battenotte. With vivid descriptions of precarious river crossings and treacherous mountain climbs, Harris reveals the historical period and portrays the grandeur of the setting. The fictional aspects are so minimal that they need hardly be discussed except to mention that they are the weakest parts of the book. All comes from the journal, and the strength of the book is in Harris's ability to select the telling incidents and to describe them in enough detail to make them memorable. The characters, Cheadle, Lord Milton, and the comically pedantic and parasitic Mr Felix O'Byrne, who latched on to the party, pale beside Dr Cheadle's own descriptions but are still lively for a Canadian children's book. The Indian child, the guide's son, is perhaps the only real disappointment. He frets about his father's problems a little too much to be believable and, although the amount of space devoted to him is considerable, he is colourless in comparison with the adult characters. As he is only occasionally referred to in the Cheadle journal, it seems that Harris's inventive powers failed when she had to move from fact to creative fiction.

Harris also demonstrates the primacy of her feelings for Indians as human beings rather than as representatives of a racial group. Her plea, however, for the ultimate achievement of a meeting ground between Indian and white man, based on their common humanity, is gratuitous—Dr Cheadle in his journal seems to have taken this for granted. It is hard to say why *West with the White Chiefs* is not an outstanding book. We have to go back to the writing, which is easy to read, sprightly, but in no way memorable.

Perhaps we should not despair for historical fiction in Canada when it can produce as subtle and sly a view of history as is offered in James McNamee's *My Uncle Joe* (1962). The protagonist only remembers Riel as a dinner guest in his father's home; the Rebellion is never actually encountered. Yet both the man and his movement are fully realized. A wealth of meaning is conveyed in brief compass (63 pages), and a door is opened on the privacy of history.

For the group as a whole the claims must be much more modest, but they are not negligible. Canadian children will learn some history from these novels. They will find considerable variety in the settings. In their overall range, from the Newfoundland of *The Dangerous Cove* to the British Columbia of *The Young Surveyor*, these books well portray how 'the east-west dream does mock the north-south fact'. They give some sense of the vastness of Canada and its varied scenes. They succeed often enough to give the lie to the premise that Canadian history is dull.

In the final analysis, there are only a few books that represent the typical virtues while not at the same time being weighed down by the typical faults. What we ask for are a theme of interest, the selection from history of such characters and facts as will carry a story forward without letting it bog down, sound research, able characterization, and passable writing. These are the virtues of John Hayes' *The Dangerous Cove*, Marion Greene's *Canal Boy*, Cliff Faulknor's *The White Calf*, and Christie Harris's *West with the White Chiefs*.

Admittedly Canadian writers have a harder task in dealing with history as material for fiction than do their counterparts in Great Britain, France, or the United States. Canada lacks revolutions, civil wars, medieval pageantry, an 'age of kings'. Perhaps this land of compromise has had a history too complex, too subtle to provide the conflicts that form the basis for a good rousing tale. Yet, however valid these excuses, the range of historical topics represented in Canadian children's literature still seems extraordinarily narrow and the treatment of them unnecessarily bland. The choice of themes, for example, is almost invariably obvious: either the subjects that the textbooks label as 'important' or those that have their colour already built in, such as life with the Indians, the fur trade, the Rebellion of 1837, the Cariboo Gold Rush, which appear in books over and over again. Only a very few stories show the fresh material that can be revealed by the exercise of ingenuity and originality: John Hayes' tales of the Selkirk settlers and of the Fishing Admirals of Newfoundland; Thomas Raddall's *Son of the Hawk*, based on an attempted revolt in Nova Scotia in 1776; Marion Greene's effective use of the turbulent Ottawa of the 1820s as a setting for her *Canal Boy*.

The rest is almost silence, and of events after the Riel Rebellion there is very little in our fiction for children. Many episodes in

Canadian history, both great and small, have been ignored. Where are the books based on such themes as our flood of immigration in the nineteenth century, the Fenian raids, the collapse of the Quebec Bridge, the sinking of the *Empress of Ireland*, the *Bluenose*, John Booth's lumber camps? What about a book about a boy sailing with Captain Vancouver or a girl sailing (in different circumstances) with Mrs Simcoe? The incidents or themes that have influenced our history and that are uniquely Canadian, and stirring, are innumerable: the building of the CPR, the opening up of the North by bush pilots, the peopling of the prairies, the Doukhobor riots, the Winnipeg General Strike.

Canadian history is not easy to dramatize. If it is deficient in mythological events and figures, bloodshed and victories, dynamic personalities and eccentrics, its interpreters in fiction have perhaps the burden of developing new forms. But even so, adventure may appear in many guises: a well-told story can be exciting whether it is about a battle between knights in armour or a skirmish in the forest, a boy adrift on the Sargasso Sea or Lake Superior. Good Canadian historical fiction must do more than impart the distinctive flavour of Canada's historical development. It must give history a universal meaning. Writers for children such as Rosemary Sutcliff (*Outcast*), Hans Baumann (*Sons of the Steppe*), Ronald Welch (*Knight Crusader*), Alfred Powers (*Hannibal's Elephants*) do not merely record history in fictional form; they bring it alive through the power of the creative imagination and in so doing reveal man's hopes and aspirations. The major revelation of historical fiction for children may well be the unfolding of man's steady march to law and order and the good life. Surely Canadian history has this to offer its children, and to children everywhere.

These statements are perhaps unfair to a few more recent writers who have achieved a quality of freshness, but in these cases one or two sparks do not kindle a fire. The themes remain static and constant: of the twenty-six books published since 1965, sixteen are concerned with Indians, two with the Loyalists, and the others with the search for the Northwest Passage, the building of the Canadian Pacific Railway, town life in Ontario in the 1830s, the life of John Cabot. The best one, however, has a non-Canadian background: King Alfred's England.

Two welcome books are about women—Pearl Packard's *The Reluctant Pioneer* (1968) and Elizabeth Clutton-Brock's *Woman of the Paddle Song* (1972)—but these were not specifically written for children and unfortunately the wearisome, repetitive details, with a slight veneer of fiction, will attract only students researching a paper on pioneer women. In style they represent the continuing trend: they simply fictionalize history, as do Christie Harris's *Raven's Cry* (1966), Lyn Harrington's *The Luck of the La Vérendryes* (1967), Fred Swayze's *Fire Over Huronia* (1968), and Delbert Young's *Last Voyage of the Unicorn* (1970). Other books make a slight plot completely dependent upon historical events: Doris Andersen's *Blood Brothers* (1968), W. Towrie Cutt's *On the Trail of Long Tom* (1970), and John Hayes' *On Loyalist Trails* (1971) and *The Steel Ribbon* (1967), set in a work camp of the CPR.

If the historicity of these books is praiseworthy, the storytelling fails, along with the sense of conviction. Fortunately several British authors of historical fiction continually demonstrate that both can be maintained. Hester Burton's *Castors Away*, set in the Napoleonic era, is about a family whose members, through an extraordinary effort, bring a soldier back to life. Almost unwittingly they enter the wider world of an England that is rallying against the French in the devastating naval battle of Trafalgar. The day after a storm that has wrecked a troopship on the shore of the little village where the Henchman family is staying, twelve-year-old Betsy awakens to find her little brother gone and goes down to the seashore to look for him:

'There he is!' she shouted.
And both girls ran stumbling across the beach towards him.
It was not a bundle of clothes that Martin was riding. It was a soldier of the 28th.
The two girls stared at him, wide-eyed with horror. His face was a waxen white, and his lids were closed lightly over his eyes, as though in a sleep.
'He's a silly man, Betsy,' said Martin. 'He won't wake up.'
Betsy snatched up the child and held him in her arms.
'It's the dead man they left on the wreck,' whispered Nell.

'I'll take him home,' gulped Betsy, burying her face in Martin's chestnut curls.

But Martin did not want to go home. He struggled and turned his head so that he could look again at the soldier lying on the beach below him, his sister kneeling white-faced by his side. Suddenly frightened, he began to sob.

'But he ought to wake up,' he cried. 'The silly man ought to wake up.'

Because of Hester Burton's superb sense of narrative and her vision of a reality that lies beyond historical fact, she can describe a five-year-old boy's first physical contact with death in terms that child readers will understand, but without shock and horror. She does not soften either truth or realism when it is within the context of history. Outside of a short passage in Hardy's *The Trumpet Major*, there have been no word pictures of the return of the ships from Trafalgar comparable to those of Hester Burton. This part of the book embraces the tragedy of Nelson's death; the disembarkations of the wounded after five weeks and more of the journey home; the dazed prisoners with gangrenous limbs and suppurating wounds, maddened by constant pain. Accuracy, realism, clear narrative and characterization are all combined, even in details of everyday life as it is being lived in the midst of great events; the state of medicine in 1805 and the position of women, for instance, are skilfully made to be a natural part of the story. Canadian writers of historical fiction, lacking the kind of sensibility that can bring a whole world of people and places to life, seem blind to anything that does not directly contribute to the progression of the historical narrative, and so they become dull and monotonous—and their books are thin.

Kay Hill's *And Tomorrow the Stars: The Story of John Cabot* (1968) almost symbolizes the limited approach to historical fiction many Canadian writers have taken. It was first conceived as 'a straight biography', but finding that there was only enough 'properly documented and indisputably accurate material' for a single chapter, the author chose to flesh out the meagre bones of Cabot's story 'with imagination'. The result is neither fictionalized biography nor historical fiction, but this is far less important than the fact that, though the author might be well steeped in the material of her period, she was not able to select from it artistically in order to make an absorbing and clear life story. It is a long book—343 pages of fairly dense type—that is packed with historical points that are not easy even for a history buff to decipher. She writes that Fra Andrea 'was one of the new breed of churchmen allowed by tolerant superiors to propagate the New Learning even though it began with the study of men rather than the mysteries of God.' She is probably referring to humanism, but what, to a child, is 'new' (to say nothing of 'old') learning? Again: 'There were many holidays in Venice, fortunately, enlivened by elaborate and colorful parades. It was one way for the Senate to keep a populace happy and unaware of their essential lack of freedom.' What did the lack of freedom consist of? Was any other society of the time more free? These are not isolated examples of presuming on a young reader's knowledge. Some other criticisms may seem picayune, but they too reflect an approach to writing that is that of a researcher rather than a novelist. John Cabot's name changes with the bewildering frequency associated with a Russian novel: the reader meets him as Giovanni Caboto, Zuan Caboto, Vanni, John Cabot. With all the burdensome detail contained in the book, it ends rather coyly and unhistorically: 'He took a last look at the sky—laughed, and turned to meet the storm . . . ' One point of fact is that Cabot did not return from this voyage.

Mary Alice and John Downie in *Honor Bound* (1971) and Herbert Tait in *Redwulf the Outlander* (1972) display some feeling for story as well as for history. Although *Honor Bound* has the conventional subject matter of a Loyalist family's flight from the American War of Independence, their hardships, and the building of a new life in a new land, it also has some very natural children, a bit of a mystery, and an ingratiating pair of villains. Its childlike quality is rare in Canadian fiction for children and it succeeds in illuminating the past rather than simply providing extra-curricular material for the junior historian.

Redwulf the Outlander is one of our few historical novels to have a setting outside Canada (the books of 'John Redmayne' are the others). This story of a young Viking, his forced departure from his home, and his eventual involvement in King Alfred's ninth-century Wessex is a sweeping narrative that is not hindered by the author's scrupulous attention to detail, although there are too many events and characters. Unfortunately at the end it becomes so self-consciously historical that the story loses its emotional centre.

So does Christie Harris's *Raven's Cry* (1966), which relates the history of the white man's impact upon the Haida from 1791 to the present. But on this broad canvas, the effect of the central theme—the white man's cruelty, stupidity, and indifference towards the Indians—is dissipated. In presenting the Haida as completely noble (although also weak, mistaken, and indecisive), the author ignores their own brand of sophistication: the slave society, the dark side of the potlatches, and their own divisive wars. A less partisan look at this particular era would have revealed more clearly the internal forces that destroyed the Haida, as well as the external ones: the organization of the European political and commercial empires and their technology.

If literary faults result from dedicated but narrow historical research divorced from a creative and imaginative vision of history, other problems are created by no research at all. Hester Burton once stated that 'readers of a historical novel have some right to know how much of what they read is history and how much fiction'. Bryan Buchan's novelette, *Copper Sunrise* (1972), deserves to be examined in this connection. It could be described and simply dismissed as a historical romance if it were not for its tragic and shocking ending. It is set loosely in time and place—vaguely identified as the late-eighteenth century (?) and the east coast of Canada (the place-names are apparently invented). Buchan leads the reader into a kind of forest idyll, typified by the friendship between a white boy and an Indian boy, which ends in the savage butchery of a few Indians by a group of white men infuriated by some petty thefts. The blood stirs; but if this climactic episode is a symbolic portrayal of man's inhumanity to man rather than a historical incident, the reader, and particularly the child reader, should be told. A child is not apt to have a historical perspective and so the difference between what did happen and what *might* have happened should be made clear.

Copper Sunrise is for younger children, as were the 'Buckskin'

books of a few years ago, and suffers from the same problems of a lack of incisiveness in incident and style. Were it not for the success of James Houston's *Eagle Mask* (1966) and *Ghost Paddle* (1972), it might seem that Canadian historical fiction for this age group was foredoomed to failure. It is true that in these tales of West Coast Indian life Houston has not had to concern himself with recording historical fact, but out of a wealth of available evidence he has been able to choose exactly those details of Indian life that give meaning to the background and that advance an original story. Within sixty-four pages, highly illustrated, he has produced two gems, although *Ghost Paddle* is more tautly contrived and exciting than *Eagle Mask*. *Ghost Paddle*, the story of a young prince of the Raven Clan who accompanies his father on a peace mission to a neighbouring tribe and saves the mission by his courage, moves swiftly to a climax but preserves a mythic quality. Both books could serve as an introduction to *The Whale People* by Roderick L. Haig-Brown and *Nkwala* by Edith Lambert Sharp, which are set in the same time and place.

Yet the greatest triumph of the last decade may well belong to the French-Canadian writer, Claude Aubry, with *Agouhanna* (1972). Although it was written in French, it was first published in English—unfortunately in a flawed translation. But even this cannot mar Aubry's skill as a storyteller. It takes genuine imagination to conjure up a young boy of a fierce Iroquois tribe, who shrinks from hunting and killing and fears pain and loneliness, and to match him with a young girl who feels the opposite and yet likes and admires Agouhanna. It takes even greater talent to make us believe in these characters—which Aubry does. In *Indians of Canada* Diamond Jenness points out that we know the Iroquois historically only through their involvement in the wars between the French and the English and that we know little of their lives before such intrusions—which is the time of which Aubry writes. Within this context, he quite legitimately disdains the stereotyped image.

The high incidence of books on early Indian life seems to call for some comment. Do Canadian authors of historical fiction constantly turn to this topic simply 'because it is there'? It may be that the Indians represent one of our few national themes (along with the building of the CPR and the Mounties) about which interest and feeling can quickly be aroused. It can be assumed that a novel based on Dollard of the Long Sault, Captain George Vancouver or Joseph Howe would not command the same attention, given Canada's instilled parochialism. Indians, whose similarities from group to group were greater than their differences, are immediately and obviously recognizable in all parts of the country. They need as little explanation as the Cavaliers and Roundheads in England or the Yanks and Rebs south of the border—figures that are part of the consciousness of a nation, as are the Indians of Canada. An emotional sympathy with them is predetermined. Material about them is not very complex; it is fairly accessible and can be used without laborious research. (Herbert Tait spent five years on the research for *Redwulf the Outlander*.) The books of the last eight years may well represent catharsis—a form of expiation for the way native peoples have been treated, a search in the past for an explanation and a solution. (It is worth noting that books written today by the Indians themselves, with the exception of legends, deal with life in the present.) There may also be a metaphorical explanation—a flight from the blighted wilderness to an absorption in a primitive vision of the world. Indians (and to a lesser extent Eskimos) are generally seen as having been at one with their environment, a state to which modern man at times longs to return. As William Reid reminds us in *Out of the Silence*: 'In a few weeks, men could gather enough salmon to last a year. Shellfish grew thick on the rocks and sandy bottoms, halibut carpeted the shelf floor; berries were plentiful on the hillsides.' The social aspects of Indian life have also had a romantic attraction for the young, as is reflected in some attempts at communal and group living, a return to a society that 'knew no law beyond custom, no history beyond legend, no political unit larger than the family, no government beyond an informal meeting of family heads, plus the tacit acceptance of the superiority of the ranking chiefs.'

Whatever the reasons, novels about the Indians of long ago are much more numerous than those about more recent events in history. It is therefore all the more distressing that they do not succeed in their appointed tasks. No recent writer has matched

Roderick Haig-Brown's *The Whale People* or Edith Lambert Sharp's *Nkwala* in their evocation of the mythic qualities of Indian culture. Doris Andersen in *Slave of the Haida* (1974) tells an interesting tale but never manages to involve the reader in the Indian world of the far-distant past. Those writers who have chosen the later periods seem to move uneasily within their material, seeking solutions rather than unfolding a way of life. At the end of Doris Andersen's *Blood Brothers*, the Indian agent, speaking of the boy Qwata, says:

His grandfather is teaching him the old law and legends, but he wants him taught the new ways, too. I hope they'll send him to your school when you get it built. If he goes to a white man's school, he'll grow up to understand the need to adapt himself to a new life and he'll teach his people what he's learned.

The head of the Hudson's Bay post in *The Reluctant Pioneer* has this to say:

I hope someday this country will appreciate them. They will make good citizens if properly handled.

A weakness for falling back on a conventional textbook approach to history, rather than using an imaginative literary one, has demonstrably reduced the readership for Canadian historical fiction.

ALLAN, IRIS. *John Rowand, Fur Trader: A Story of the Old Northwest.* Illustrated by Doug Sneyd. Toronto, Gage, 1963. 205 pp. ('Frontier Books'.)
The life of John Rowand (1787–1854) spanned over sixty years of important developments in the fur trade. This book about him is fictionalized history rather than historical fiction.

ALLAN, IRIS. *White Sioux: The Story of Major Walsh of the Mounted Police.* Sidney, B.C., Gray's Publishing, 1969. 203 pp.
A slightly fictionalized biography of an officer in the newly organized North West Mounted Police who dealt firmly with the Indians under the treaty arrangements and in particular with 'Sitting Bull'. Although accurate in detail, it does not deal with the larger sweep of history and does not interpret the events it describes. It is also plagued with a cold and graceless style.

ANDERSEN, DORIS. *Blood Brothers*. Illustrated by David Craig. Toronto, Macmillan, 1967. 136 pp.

A Minnesota Norwegian community takes up free farming land near Bella
Coola, B.C., and meets the resentment of the Indians towards the white
men who usurp their land and are ignorant of their customs. The friendship between a white boy and an Indian boy provides the rather tenuous
plot. The background has the ring of authenticity, as do the characters,
but the book as a whole does not come alive.

ANDERSEN, DORIS. *Slave of the Haida*. Toronto, Macmillan, 1974. 166 pp.

To be a slave of the Haida is a terrible indignity for a captured young
prince of the Salish who has had his own personal slave. Only Christie
Harris in *Once More Upon a Totem* has so far revealed this aspect of West
Coast Indian life for children. Set in the same unrecorded time of Haig-
Brown's *The Whale People* and Edith Sharp's *Nkwala*, *Slave of the Haida*
has neither the grandeur of the former nor the poetry of the latter. But it
is a fast-moving, plainly told tale, with striking details of Indian life, that
should appeal to young children.

AUBRY, CLAUDE. *Agouhanna*. Translated from the French by Harvey Swados.
Illustrated by Julie Brinckloe. Toronto, Doubleday, 1972. 89 pp.

An unusual story of a pacifist Iroquois boy and a war-loving little girl that
is richly steeped in Indian family affairs, the training of the young, and
totemic endurance tests. The story is told against a background of the
Canadian forest—beautiful, yet filled with hidden dangers. The style is
frequently marred by awkward translation.

BALLANTYNE, LAREINE. *The Scout Who Led an Army*. Illustrated by Lee Clif-
ton. Toronto, Macmillan, 1963. 113 pp. ('Buckskin Books'.)

In 1813 nineteen-year-old Billy Green led General Vincent's army from
Burlington Heights through the woods for a surprise attack on the American forces at Stoney Creek. A simulation of historical fiction for younger
readers, this book has some facts but not much else.

BASSETT, JOHN. *The Canal Builders: The Building of the First Welland Canal*.
Illustrated by Leslie Callan. Toronto, Allen, 1964. 99 pp. ('The Young
Adventurers Series'.)

The building of the first Welland Canal, 1824-8, by a private company,
was a great feat of perseverance as well as engineering. Here two boys help
to save the canal from sabotage. An unusual theme and a clear-cut fictional
plot give this story some merit, but because of flaws in the creation of
atmosphere and character it rarely gets 'off the page'.

BASSETT, JOHN. *Frontier in Flames*. Illustrated by Leslie Callan. Toronto, Allen,
1965. 110 pp. ('The Young Adventurers Series'.)

An interesting and unusual subject—the Fenian Raids—is stifled by an
emphasis on fact rather than on fiction, resulting in a weak plot and lack
of characterization.

BEMISTER, MARGARET. *The Arrow Sash: A Novel of New France for Young Adults.* Illustrated by Hans Zander. Toronto, Musson, 1965. 168 pp.
The heroine of this book is one of Louis XIV's famous 'King's Girls' and the hero a handsome and mysterious *coureur-de-bois*. Although using all the ploys of the stereotyped romantic novel, it portrays some aspects of daily life in Quebec in 1669, including Indian life, with fair authenticity.

BENHAM, LESLIE and LOIS BENHAM. *The Heroine of Long Point.* Illustrated by Vernon Mould. Toronto, Macmillan, 1963. 113 pp. ('Buckskin Books'.)
About a shipwreck on Lake Erie and a brave woman who helps save seven men. Based on a true episode, the story lacks the dignity and drama in the telling that it deserves. This, however, is one of the more satisfactory 'Buckskin Books'.

BRAMWELL, BARBARA and HEATHER BRAMWELL. *Adventure at the Mill.* Illustrated by William Lytle. Toronto, Macmillan, 1963. 113 pp. ('Buckskin Books'.)
An Ontario family living close to the border feels the impact of the War of 1812. In trying to write simply for younger children, the authors denude the story of any quality beyond ease of reading.

BREMNER, LOIS. *The Lodge of Omal.* Toronto, Ryerson, 1965. 84 pp.
The Kwakiutl tribe of British Columbia meet the late-eighteenth-century European explorers and barter for sturdy axes and knives. The slight story is unconvincing, and it is doubtful if it would fulfil its obvious intention of interesting younger readers in Indian life and customs.

BUCHAN, BRYAN. *Copper Sunrise.* New York/Toronto, Scholastic Book Services [1972]. 111 pp.
If it were not for the terrible and tragic ending, this little book might well be described as a historical romance. Vaguely set in time and place, it presents the concept of 'the noble savage' living in peace and innocence close to nature. Lack of historical evidence defeats the author's intent—to show the cruelty of the white men—while the nondescript style fails to draw the reader into his forest idyll.

CHALMERS, JOHN W. *Horseman in Scarlet: Sam Steele of the Mounties.* Illustrated by Lex Bell. Toronto, Gage, 1961. 165 pp. ('Frontier Books'.)
The work of the North West Mounted Police is well described, but Sam Steele as an individual never rises from the pages. It is difficult to see why this is described as a historical novel, since the fictional element appears to consist only of invented conversations.

CLARK, CATHERINE ANTHONY. *The Man with Yellow Eyes.* Illustrated by Gordon Rayner. Toronto, Macmillan, 1963. 122 pp. ('Buckskin Books'.)
A boy on horseback races a stagecoach to record his father's claim to a mine and so foils the villain. One of the more palatable books in this series for younger readers because the writer tells a good story.

CLUTTON-BROCK, ELIZABETH. *Woman of the Paddle Song.* Toronto, Copp Clark, 1972. 176 pp.

Charlotte Small was the daughter of a Scottish father and a Cree mother who married David Thompson when she was thirteen years old and accompanied the great explorer on many of his famous journeys, including the crossing of the Rockies in 1807. Based on available Thompson material, the story is cast in a slightly fictional form. Charlotte is the first-person narrator, but even this device does not bring her to life as a personality. For older readers.

COOK, LYN. *Rebel on the Trail.* Illustrated by Ruth M. Collins. Toronto, Macmillan, 1953. 247 pp.

This story of the Rebellion of 1837 has neither the period charm of Emily Weaver's *The Only Girl* nor the excitement of John Hayes' *Rebels Ride at Night*, which have the same background.

COOK, LYN. *The Secret of Willow Castle.* Illustrations by Kelly Clark. Toronto, Macmillan, 1966. 235 pp.

The everyday life of a well-to-do little girl in Napanee, Ont., is enlivened by festivities and two friendships, one with her older cousin, John Alex Macdonald. Lacking a strong plot line, and crowded with bits of social history and with the business and politics of the time, this is little more than a rather tedious period piece. However, it is a welcome change from more conventional historical fiction dealing with Indians, explorers, and settlers.

CRAIG, JOHN E. *The Long Return.* Illustrated by Robert Doremus. New York, Bobbs-Merrill, 1959. 255 pp.

A straightforward account of the capture of a white boy and his journey back to his own people after several years with the Ojibways. The rather hackneyed theme is treated with simplicity and insight.

CUTT, W. TOWRIE. *Carry My Bones Northwest.* Toronto, Collins, 1973. 144 pp.

The story moves from the Canadian prairie in 1794 to the Orkney Islands and back to Canada with the Selkirk settlers. As in Cutt's first book, *On the Trail of Long Tom*, the hero is a half-breed torn by his double heritage. In spite of the heavy use of dialect, the Scottish scenes have a greater impact than the Canadian ones, perhaps because the first are fictional and the second are more or less straight history.

CUTT, W. TOWRIE. *On the Trail of Long Tom.* Toronto, Collins, 1970. 189 pp.

Western Canada in the days of the Riel Rebellion. A boy is caught in conflicting loyalties between his Indian and Scottish backgrounds as he becomes involved in the struggle. A skilful blending of historical events and personal narrative makes this better-than-average historical fiction.

DOWNIE, MARY ALICE and JOHN DOWNIE. *Honor Bound.* Illustrated by Joan Huffman. Toronto, Oxford, 1971. 192 pp.

The background of this novel is conventional enough—the trials of a hard-pressed Loyalist family who eventually reach a farm near Kingston, Ont. However, the children become involved in a mystery and an adventure that are not completely dependent upon the larger historical background. Thus it is genuine historical fiction rather than fictionalized history; it also has humour and a refreshing childlike quality. These are rare attributes in Canadian historical fiction.

EATON, SARA. *Moccasin and Cross*. Illustrated by Merle Smith. Toronto, Copp Clark, 1959. 181 pp.
An account of the establishment and destruction of the Jesuit missions to the Hurons—St Joseph, Ste Marie, and St Ignace—with a minimal story line. The tone of the book is completely that of the seventeenth century when no man, whether soldier, statesman, or priest, had any doubts about the righteousness of his position in regard to the Indians.

FAULKNOR, CLIFF. *The Smoke Horse*. Illustrated by W. F. Phillips. Toronto/ Montreal, McClelland and Stewart, 1968. 187 pp.
The third book in the author's trilogy of the Piegan Indians. The incidents are much the same as in *The White Calf* and *The White Peril* and so may simply reflect the repetitive life of a people whose main concern had to be the search for food and the 'undoing' of the neighbouring tribes. But the lack of development in incident, insight, or style is disappointing.

FAULKNOR, CLIFF. *The White Calf*. Illustrated by Gerald Tailfeathers. Toronto. Little, Brown, 1965. 180 pp.
The adventures of a twelve-year-old Piegan Blackfoot boy, Eagle Child, provide the rather loose thread that holds together this interesting picture of Indian life in the 1850s. Humour and suspense make this an above-average story of Indian wars and life on the prairie, and it is uncluttered by the 'white man' versus 'red man' theme.

FAULKNOR, CLIFF. *The White Peril*. Illustrated by Gerald Tailfeathers. Boston/ Toronto, Little, Brown, 1966. 166 pp.
In this sequel to Faulknor's *The White Calf*, the 'white peril' is the increasing numbers of white men, with their repeating rifles, who are crossing the prairie. But the life of the Indians is not yet completely disturbed. Eagle Child, now older, and his companions hunt the buffalo, fight with other Indian bands, and try to acquire guns. The episodic plot is strengthened by the simplicity of the style, the naturalness of the conversation, and the piquant commentary on the human condition, Indian and white.

FREEMAN, MADELINE A. *A Horse for Running Buffalo*. Illustrated by Alan Daniel. Toronto, Van Nostrand Reinhold, 1972. 88 pp.
This story was obviously told to describe the customs of the Blackfoot Nation and is reinforced by thirteen pages of notes. Yet in its simplicity it conveys a feeling of the prairies and of what it must have been like to be young and Indian in those early days. The illustrations, some on coloured paper, have considerable dignity and power.

FRITH, AUSTIN F. *The Lost Stagecoach: A Story of Gold-Rush Days on the Cariboo Trail.* Illustrated by Leo Rampen. Toronto, Gage, 1962. 168 pp. ('Frontier Books'.)

Two modern children learn, in piecemeal fashion, about the early days in the Cariboo when they meet a former stagecoach driver and help him fix up an old BX stagecoach for a parade. This is a mundane question-and-answer story, with a few contrived and unbelievable incidents thrown in for excitement.

GOODSPEED, DONALD J. and HERBERT F. WOOD. *The Night Riders* by John Redmayne (pseud.). Illustrated by John Lawrence. Toronto, Macmillan, 1967. 150 pp.

Another Peter Maclean book, a sequel to *Substitute General.* The writing and historical background are again competent but interest lags because of the stock characters and the uninvolving narrative, which lacks suspense.

GOODSPEED, DONALD J. and HERBERT F. WOOD. *Redcoat Spy* by John Redmayne (pseud.). Illustrated by John Lawrence. Toronto, Macmillan, 1964. 163 pp.

A young British officer and a younger Spanish countess spy for Napoleon during the Peninsular War in 1812. The characterization is deeper and the the style more polished than in the usual run of Canadian historical novels with Canadian themes.

GOODSPEED, DONALD J. and HERBERT F. WOOD. *Substitute General: A Peter Maclean Story* by John Redmayne (pseud.). Illustrated by John Lawrence. Toronto, Macmillan, 1965. 158 pp.

For a brief time young Peter Maclean is part of the tangled web of intrigue surrounding Napoleon as he seeks to gain control of the government of France. The fast-paced plot completely meshes with the historical background, and the characters, both historical and fictional, are most convincing.

GREENE, MARION. *Canal Boy.* Illustrated by Vernon Mould. Toronto, Macmillan, 1959. 152 pp.

The theft of Colonel By's pistols begins the action in this fast-paced and believable story of a boy's efforts to clear his name in the rough society of Ottawa and Montreal in 1828.

HAIG-BROWN, RODERICK L. *The Whale People.* Illustrated by Mary Weiler. London, Collins, 1962. 184 pp.

The West Coast Indian tribes have provided inspiration for some of the finest Canadian children's books. In *The Whale People* the daily round of life is balanced by the magnificent whaling scenes. These evoke astonishment at puny man with his primitive weapons pitting himself against the monarch of the sea.

HARRINGTON, LYN. *The Luck of the La Vérendryes*. Toronto, Thomas Nelson & Sons, 1967. 157 pp.
The author tries hard to give shape and meaning to the events that surrounded the La Vérendryes and their involvement in them as soldiers, explorers, and fur-traders. But the book is little more than a confusing welter of excursions. The fictional element is provided by invented conversations, which add immeasurably to the dullness of the book.

HARRIS, CHRISTIE. *Cariboo Trail*. Toronto, Longman, 1957. 188 pp.
The Hawthorne family journey with a hundred gold-seekers from Fort Garry to the Cariboo in 1862. This is an unusual Canadian book because a girl is the central character and it attempts a portrayal of family life. The trek itself is memorable; the people who make it are not.

HARRIS, CHRISTIE. *Forbidden Frontier*. Drawings by E. Carey Kenney. New York, Atheneum, 1968. 210 pp.
Both Indian life and the fur trade are threatened by the discovery of gold in the Cariboo and the arrival of settlers. The major conflict is worked out in terms of a more personal one, between two immigrants to the area and the daughter and son of two Scottish factors who married Indian women. Harris's always-accurate background is marred by a loose plot and a style that is sometimes prosaic and sometimes pretentious.

HARRIS, CHRISTIE. *Raven's Cry*. Illustrations by Bill Reid. Toronto/Montreal, McClelland and Stewart, 1966. 193 pp.
This is a cry of protest against the treatment of the Haida by fur-hungry traders and missionaries and indifferent government officials. With magnificent tragic material provided by her research, Harris dissipated the impact of the reality with mundane fictionalization. She also neglected to consider the seeds of weakness in Haida life (all nations have weaknesses). Thus, although *Raven's Cry* is a *cri de coeur* on their behalf, it is a failure in a literary and historical sense.

HARRIS, CHRISTIE. *West with the White Chiefs*. Illustrated by Walter Ferro. Toronto, McClelland and Stewart, 1965. 214 pp.
This account of Viscount Milton and Dr Cheadle and their hazardous crossing of the Rockies in 1863 is based on Dr Cheadle's journal. It is better-than-average historical fiction because of the surprising and interesting events upon which it is based.

HAYES, JOHN F. *Buckskin Colonist*. Illustrated by Fred J. Finley. Toronto, Copp Clark, 1947. 251 pp.
A white boy and an Indian boy help to foil the Métis and their employers, the Nor'Westers, who are determined to destroy Lord Selkirk's colony. A lively story, but it is filled with too many similar adventures that strain credulity.

HAYES, JOHN F. *Bugles in the Hills*. Illustrated by Fred J. Finley. Toronto, Copp Clark, 1955. 312 pp.

A teen-age boy travels with the last of the Red River cart trains in 1873 and later joins the newly formed Mounted Police as a bugler. The bringing of law and order to the prairies was one of the most dramatic and significant movements in Canadian history. The author's premise that 'Fiction, in most cases, appears pallid and lifeless when set alongside plain, unvarnished fact' is demonstrated in a novel in which the actual historical details are the most interesting parts of the book.

HAYES, JOHN F. *The Dangerous Cove.* Illustrated by Fred J. Finley. Toronto, Copp Clark, 1957. 265 pp.
In 1676 the settlers on the coast of Newfoundland are attacked by the Fishing Admirals who have the sanction of the Crown to expel the fishermen from their homes and so usurp the season's catch. Two teen-age boys have a large share in helping to thwart the attack and save their own village. A fast-moving story with crisp and natural dialogue.

HAYES, JOHN F. *Flaming Prairie.* Illustrated by Fred J. Finley. Toronto, Copp Clark, 1965. 313 pp.
Young Jeff Carson is in the forefront of the North West Rebellion of 1885. While the details are historically accurate, the young reader might well be forgiven if he finishes with the impression that without the aid of the fictional but omni-present Jeff, events might well have turned out differently.

HAYES, JOHN F. *A Land Divided.* Illustrated by Fred J. Finley. Toronto, Copp Clark, 1951. 285 pp.
A colourless tale of the expulsion of the Acadians.

HAYES, JOHN F. *On Loyalist Trails.* Illustrated by J. Merle Smith. Toronto, Copp Clark, 1971. 234 pp.
The adventures and sufferings of the Loyalist families who escaped to Canada after the American War of Independence have a built-in drama. Here they are combined with a personal vendetta against the younger son in the Hunter family, who finally finds peace again with his young bride on land close to Frederick Town. The events are exciting enough to carry the prosaic writing.

HAYES, JOHN F. *Quest in the Cariboo.* Illustrated by Fred J. Finley. Toronto, Copp Clark, 1960. 240 pp.
The rough and turbulent days of the Cariboo Gold Rush are pictured as two teen-age boys, one white and one Chinese, set out on a journey of rescue. The plot of the story is highly original, the action straightforward, and the whole is more unified than the author's other novels, which rely more heavily on actual historical events. The writing, however, is often flawed and even amateurish.

HAYES, JOHN F. *Rebels Ride at Night.* Illustrated by Fred J. Finley. Toronto, Copp Clark, 1953. 286 pp.

The final events of the Rebellion of 1837 are recorded accurately, but the plot depends on too many contrivances, as when a member of the 'in group' reveals his sympathies to a teen-age boy. The story also lacks impact, mainly because the young protagonist supports Mackenzie through reasons of expediency rather than belief.

HAYES, JOHN F. *The Steel Ribbon.* Illustrated by Fred J. Finley. Toronto, Copp Clark, 1967. 211 pp.
The struggle to complete the CPR is highlighted in the events at Jackfish Camp on northern Lake Superior. Two smart boys in their mid-teens encounter, and finally outwit, saboteurs responsible for serious explosions in the CPR work camp. The relevant historical and geographical data are conscientiously recorded, but through weak characterization and weaker style, the story fails to excite and convince.

HAYES, JOHN F. *Treason at York.* Illustrated by Fred J. Finley. Toronto, Copp Clark, 1949. 314 pp.
Most of the major events of 1812–14 are mentioned in this story. The writer tries to indicate both the complexity and the futility of the War of 1812, but the theme weakens under the distractions of fights, spying, captures, etc. As is usual in Hayes' books, great attention is paid to historical detail.

HILL, KAY. *And Tomorrow the Stars: The Story of John Cabot.* Illustrations by Laszlo Kubinyi. New York, Dodd, Mead & Co., 1968. 363 pp.
A fictional account of John Cabot's life with eleven pages of 'Historical Notes' on which some of the invention was based. A dull, lengthy, ponderous piece of work far removed from the author's lively writing in her Indian tales, such as *Glooscap and His Magic.*

HOUSTON, JAMES. *Eagle Mask: A West Coast Indian Tale.* Illustrated by the author. Toronto, Longman, 1966. 64 pp.
A slight, episodic tale of West Coast Indian life just as the white men were making their appearance. In very few pages, and with authentic illustrations, the author manages to reveal and yet synthesize a whole way of life for younger children.

HOUSTON, JAMES. *Ghost Paddle: A Northwest Coast Indian Tale.* Illustrated by the author. Toronto, Longman, 1972. 64 pp.
When the Raven Clan tries to make peace with the Gwenhoots (they regret the loss of oolichan oil), young Prince Hooits has a chance to show his bravery. This is a more dramatic and tightly knit story than Houston's *Eagle Mask,* for the same age group.

KING, DONALD R. *Sukanabi.* Toronto, Longman, 1955. 237 pp.
For three years a teen-age boy lives a Robinson Crusoe life in the foothills of the Rockies in what is now southern Alberta. This episode gives the story its greatest merit; the rest of the book adheres to the conventional

fur-trading, life-with-the-Indians type of historical fiction. The sequel, *Spitzee Anota* (Toronto, Longman, 1957, 252 pp.), is little more than a rehash of *Sukanabi*.

KNOX, OLIVE E. *Black Falcon*. Illustrated by Clarence Tillenius. New York, Bouregy and Curl, 1955. 192 pp.

John Tanner was kidnapped by the Shawnees in 1789. This true story has many interesting and little-known facts of Indian life, particularly family life, but it is swamped with detail at the cost of a strong, selective, dramatic presentation.

KNOX, OLIVE E. *By Paddle and Saddle*. Toronto, Macmillan, 1943. 270 pp.

In accompanying Sir George Simpson on his trip around the world in 1841, a sixteen-year-old Scottish boy has every adventure that Canada at that time could possibly offer. While it is packed with information that has been lifted from sound sources, the loosely strung story line vitiates interest.

KNOX, OLIVE E. *The Young Surveyor*. Toronto, Ryerson, 1956. 164 pp.

A bookish boy accompanies Edward Warrel Jarvis on his CPR survey route of 1874–5 in British Columbia. The writer copes well with the details of the expedition, but not with the fictional plot and characters.

LEITCH, ADELAIDE. *The Great Canoe*. Illustrated by Clare Bice. Toronto, Macmillan, 1962. 115 pp. ('Buckskin Books'.)

A little Huron boy attaches himself to Champlain in 1615 when Champlain and the Hurons were defeated by the Iroquois. The major historical event is a fact of history, narrated by Champlain, but the author's strong implication that the part of her story that relates to the boy is also true shows no respect for history, for fiction, or for children.

LEITCH, ADELAIDE. *Lukey Paul from Labrador*. Illustrated by Joe Rosenthal. Toronto, Macmillan, 1964. 116 pp. ('Buckskin Books'.)

Although this story of a ten-year-old boy in Labrador tells of fishing, trading, Eskimos and Eskimo carving, an iceberg, a whale, and Dr Wilfred Grenfell, Labrador itself is unportrayed. A 'reader-like' action book.

MACDONALD, ZILLAH and COLIN MACDONALD. *Prisoner in Louisbourg*. Toronto, Macmillan, 1966. 231 pp. (First published in 1944.)

The events in the story lead to the capture of Louisbourg in 1745 by the New Englanders. However, the plot turns into a 'Gothic tale', with secret passages, disguises, escapes, hurried journeys, and mysterious strangers. While these adventures provide some relief from the usual Canadian penchant for an overdose of history, the plot is one of appalling confusion, with a bevy of minor characters that bear little relationship to the whole.

MCFARLANE, LESLIE. *The Last of the Great Picnics*. Illustrated by Lewis Parker. Toronto, McClelland and Stewart, 1965. 99 pp.

Young David had never realized that a statesman could be a living person until he met Sir John A. Macdonald at one of the famous Ontario political picnics. A refreshing and charming vignette of Canadian history.

MCLAUGHLIN, LORRIE. *The Trouble with Jamie.* Illustrated by Lewis Parker. Toronto, Macmillan, 1966. 98 pp. ('Buckskin Books'.)
Young Jamie, who can 'sweet talk' his way out of anything, accidentally stows away on the brigantine *Rover* sailing out of Liverpool, N.S., on June 4, 1800. In his duties as cabin boy Jamie does a man's work and learns to hold his tongue—unfortunately, since his 'sweet talk' was the liveliest part of the book! A period piece for younger children characterized by the usual 'Buckskin' mildness of incident and style.

MCLAUGHLIN, LORRIE. *West to the Cariboo.* Illustrated by Joe Rosenthal. Toronto, Macmillan, 1962. 122 pp. ('Buckskin Books'.)
Two brothers, eighteen and twelve years of age, make the long trek from Minnesota to the Cariboo to find their father. The theme of the story is too heavy to be encompassed in a limited vocabulary and in 122 small pages of large type.

MCNAMEE, JAMES. *My Uncle Joe.* Illustrated by Lewis Parker. Toronto, Macmillan, 1962, 63 pp.
'I will always remember Mr Riel. As long as I live I'll remember. . . . And he never once pretended I wasn't there, he made me forget I was the smallest kid, he shook my hand.' In this oblique look at the North West Rebellion, the author reveals a deep sense of history as well as a knowledge of the cruelty and kindness and humour that make up life itself.

PACKARD, PEARL. *The Reluctant Pioneer.* Montreal, Palm Publishers, 1968. 231 pp.
Mrs Jane McIntyre, the wife of a Hudson's Bay factor, was a truly feminine woman of her time—spirited, fun-loving, fond of pretty clothes and the happy, gentle way of life she had known in England as the daughter of a clergyman. In 1849 she made the hazardous trip, with her infant daughter, to her husband's post, 900 miles from Lachine, in Northern Ontario, where they lived for six years. The authentic facts are based on the experiences of the author's grandmother. Fortunately some of them are exciting enough to compel interest. For older readers.

PFEIFER, LILLIAN. *The Wolfers.* Illustrated by David Craig. Toronto, Burns and MacEachern, 1967. 167 pp.
The son of a Montana trader follows a group of 'wolfers' or whisky traders into what is now south-western Alberta to avenge the murder of his father and mother. The period of the 1870s was a turbulent one—mostly because of the illegal sale of whisky to the Indians—and culminated in the arrival of the North West Mounted Police in 1874. The richly detailed, accurate background is a strong foil for the plot and characters.

RADDALL, THOMAS H. *Son of the Hawk.* Illustrated by Stanley Turner. Toronto, Doubleday, 1950. 247 pp.

An unfamiliar episode in Canadian history was the brief attempt in Cumberland County, N.S., to bring about an uprising against the British, while the Nova Scotia Yankees in general tried to remain neutral. Although the story lacks the virtue of simplicity, being crowded with events and people, it has considerable atmosphere and excitement and brings the past alive in vivid style and characterization.

REANEY, JAMES. *The Boy with an R in His Hand*. Illustrated by Leo Rampen. Toronto, Macmillan, 1965. 102 pp.
A young boy is involved in the destruction of Mackenzie's printing office in 1826. In plot, this story is a heavily moral tale of Good against Evil, but it manages to catch some of the spirit of York at the time of the Family Compact.

REDMAYNE, JOHN. See GOODSPEED, DONALD J. and HERBERT F. WOOD.

REEKIE, ISABEL M. *Journey to Red River*. Illustrated by Anne Fines. Toronto/ Montreal, Holt, Rinehart and Winston, 1973. 199 pp.
The Mackay family is forced to leave their Highland home and join Selkirk's group travelling to the Red River Settlement, where they endure terrible hardships during their first year. As usual Reekie has done her homework—the book is well researched—but the dialogue is unbelieveably dull and awkwardly expressed.

REEKIE, ISABEL M. *Red, Horse of the West*. Illustrated by Alan Daniel. Holt, Rinehart and Winston, 1972. 96 pp.
In Brandon, Man., in 1885, the uneasy inhabitants hear the news of the Riel Rebellion. A young boy also learns to trust the Indians when his horse is stolen. A dull little period piece for younger children.

REEKIE, ISABEL M. *Red Paddles*. Illustrated by Dennis Hutchins. Vancouver, Mitchell Press, 1968. 99 pp.
A dugout canoe, with red paddles that were presented to young David by an Indian chief, helps to save lives when the community around Burrard Inlet is swept by fire in 1886. This is local history lightly set in a fictional mould.

SHARP, EDITH L. *Nkwala*. Illustrated by William Winter. Boston, Little, Brown, 1958. 125 pp.
This fine book has two levels. It is an Indian adventure story, with an appealing young hero of the Spokan tribe in what is now British Columbia. It also has the 'inner eye' that shows a happy picture of a people who loved their young and gave examples to them of quiet good deeds, good taste, good judgement, and bravery—then stood away and let them come to maturity on their own.

SWAYZE, BEULAH G. *Father Gabriel's Cloak*. Illustrated by Douglas Sneyd. Toronto, Macmillan, 1962. 122 pp. ('Buckskin Books'.)
A little white girl is carried off by the Indians and discovered six years later

by La Salle, Tonty, and Father Gabriel. The author tries to pack too much information into a story that is intended for younger readers.

SWAYZE, FRED. *The Fighting Le Moynes*. Toronto, Ryerson, 1957. 201 pp.
The famous Le Moyne brothers helped to save Canada for France, to extend her empire to the Mississippi, and to make the fur trade prosperous for the king. This is an overly detailed mixture of history, biography, and fiction.

SWAYZE, FRED. *Fire Over Huronia*. Illustrations by Fred Oakley. Toronto/ Montreal, McClelland and Stewart, 1968. 144 pp.
According to the *Jesuit Relations*, Jean Amiot was a boy who served with the Huron Missions; he was given to the Jesuit missionaries to be trained as an interpreter with the Indians. The well-known Huronia drama is seen through his eyes in a story that never rises much beyond bald fact. Indian attitudes and customs are given a more adequate treatment here than in Sara Eaton's *Moccasin and Cross* (1959), but the style is equally devoid of grace.

SWAYZE, FRED. *Iroquois War Trail*. Toronto, Ryerson, 1965. 146 pp.
The lack of a central character and a central plot in this story results in a series of disjointed adventures. The author has a good knowledge of the geography and history of early Canada (the year is 1683), but his insistence on larding the story with facts impedes an already sluggish plot.

SWAYZE, FRED. *Tonty of the Iron Hand*. Toronto, Ryerson, 1957. 194 pp.
A detailed account of the explorations of La Salle and Tonty, his lieutenant. Concern for historical accuracy over-shadows the imaginative inventiveness that is necessary for good fiction. In merely trying to make history palatable, the author fails to achieve the aims of history or of fiction.

TAIT, HERBERT. *Redwulf the Outlander*. Toronto/Vancouver, Clarke, Irwin, 1972. 187 pp.
The Viking and Saxon world of the ninth century. A Viking boy, forced to leave his home, finds shelter in the East Wessex dales, to be finally caught up in King Alfred's victory over the Danes. Though it goes on a bit too long and lacks the masterly touch of the Viking novels of Henry Treece, this is a rich and carefully constructed novel.

THOMPSON, FRANCES C. *Danger in the Coves*. Illustrated by Lloyd Scott. Toronto, Macmillan, 1963. 122 pp. ('Buckskin Books'.)
The daily life of a family in Quebec (the father is Scottish and the mother French Canadian) in the year 1845. Excitement is caused when the two boys are kidnapped briefly by a press gang.

THOMPSON, FRANCES C. *Escape from Grand Pré*. Illustrated by David Craig. Toronto, Macmillan, 1966. 118 pp. ('Buckskin Books'.)
Young André escapes to live with the Indians during the expulsion of the Acadians, but returns finally with his grandfather to work for the English

who have taken over their farms. A mild and shallow treatment of one
of the most dramatic moments in Canadian history.

WEAVER, EMILY P. *The Only Girl: A Tale of 1837.* Toronto, Macmillan, 1925.
289 pp.
As a description of everyday pioneer life in Ontario, this is a charming
period piece. That it takes place in the exciting year of 1837 is almost
incidental.

WEEKES, MARY L. *The Silver Pelt.* Illustrated by W.B. White. London, Blackie
1960. 174 pp.
A fifteen-year-old boy, less than six months out from Scotland, manages
to survive for a few days in the Mackenzie District when he is separated
from his half-breed companion. He also successfully and humorously
barters with an Indian chief for a valuable silver-fox fur. This glimpse of
fur-trading in 1862 is a slightly better-than-average story because of its
unity of action.

WOOD, KERRY. *The Boy and the Buffalo.* Illustrated by Audrey Teather
Toronto, Macmillan, 1963. 120 pp. ('Buckskin Books'.)
A six-year-old Indian boy is lost on the prairies and is adopted by two
buffalo cows. Kipling treated the story of Mowgli the jungle boy as fantasy
but Wood expects us to believe that a small boy could survive an Alberta
winter.

WOOD, KERRY. *Samson's Long Ride.* Toronto, Collins, 1968. 77 pp.
A ten-year-old boy of the Stoney Indian tribe runs away from a mission
school in October and travels 400 miles to find his father's band before
winter sets in. It is not easy to write for younger children—to have drama
without sounding like a TV cartoon program—but here is proof that it can
be done.

YOUNG, DELBERT A. *Last Voyage of the Unicorn.* Illustrated by Mary Cserepy
Toronto/Vancouver, Clarke, Irwin, 1969. 182 pp.
This account of the ill-fated Munck expedition of 1619 to search for the
Northwest Passage is related by a fifteen-year-old boy, one of the three
to survive the harrowing journey. The narrative, based on Captain Munck's
Relation, is true adventure lightly touched with fiction, but it makes a
compelling story because of the innate drama of men endeavouring to
survive.

YOUNG, DELBERT A. *Mutiny on Hudson Bay: A Story about the Last Voyage
of Henry Hudson.* Illustrated by Doug Sneyd. Toronto, Gage, 1963. 200
pp. ('Frontier Books'.)
A cabin boy on Hudson's ship, the *Discovery,* tells the story of the last
ill-fated voyage. Fiction and history are well blended here, particularly in
the first part of the book, and the slight use of conventional seventeenth
century speech helps to draw the reader into the past.

5 | the realistic animal story

In the late nineteenth and early twentieth centuries, when most writers of fiction were slavishly following the accepted English literary tradition, the realistic animal story appeared in Canada as a genuine native product and spread outward to influence the animal story around the world. It was the creation of two Canadians, Ernest Thompson Seton and Charles G.D. Roberts, and it was their works that gave it both its definition and its highest form.

The realistic animal story can best be described as animal biography in fictional form. Although it can vary greatly in the amount of fiction purposefully used, it is founded upon scientific observation and a profound knowledge of animals. Using his knowledge, and with affection and respect, the writer brings his animal hero alive in its own world and in complete harmony with its own nature. The realistic animal story is not concerned with talking-animal fantasies and fables or with satires based on animals, such as George Orwell's *Animal Farm*: these genres do not really contain works about animals but about human actions and aspirations. Neither should it be confused with the kind of story in which a child's adventure is the main subject, and an animal, usually a horse or a dog, plays an auxiliary role: the horse is stolen or the pet dog is blamed for killing sheep. The realistic animal story under discussion here has its closest link with the writings of naturalists like Raymond L. Ditmars, Gerald Durrell, and Jean Henri Fabre.

It is obvious that the naturalist would not indulge in anthropomorphism—the endowment of animals with human traits. It is not so clear that the writers of even the best animal stories should not or do not do so. Some transference of human intelligence and emotion to the animal character can, in good hands, heighten the emotional impact of a story and strengthen the rapport between writer and reader. Animal lovers, both children and adults, often ascribe super-animal qualities to their pets and it should be no surprise that some of this feeling has worked its way into animal literature. But it takes a sure sense of the limits of credibility to keep the realistic animal story from being maudlin or, worse, so confused as to be neither animal story nor outright fantasy. Seton and Roberts trod this line and in the main successfully, as will be noted later in this chapter.

That the realistic animal story should first have appeared and developed in Canada is not entirely the result of chance. When Seton and Roberts wrote, knowledge of animals, especially wild animals, was still a necessity for Indians, who depended upon them for food, for those who hunted for profit, and for those concerned with conservation; and of course protection and interest have always made some knowledge essential. In a sparsely populated country the forces of nature still played a major role, as indeed they do today in many parts of Canada. Probably in no other part of the world were the cities so close to the forests. In Canadian art, in Canadian novels, in Canadian poetry there was still an intense concentration on descriptions of nature. Seton and Roberts maintained this emphasis, but added to it a new dimension—a genuine insight into the nature of the animals that roam our woods and forests.

The novelty and scope of their achievement may best be seen in relation to the general pattern of the animal story that had been established earlier. It is easy to imagine that the first animal stories ever told must have been highly realistic; a primitive hunter relates his escape or his kill to an admiring group of friends—colouring his account a bit, perhaps, but telling the truth nonetheless. Later, the primeval relationship between man and animal became encased in mythology and legend, and the denizens of forest and field, sky and water, were used mainly to point a moral for the benefit of mankind. From this outlook came the medieval bestiaries (very shaky nature lore indeed) and fables—those of Aesop and Lafontaine and the anonymous *Reynard the Fox*. Writers for children in eighteenth- and nineteenth-century England produced highly moralistic animal stories, on the assumption that faults and virtues would be made clearer to children if they were attributed to animals. For example, in a charming book by Dorothy Kilner, *The Rational Brutes; or, Talking Animals* (1799), an ass is made to remark: 'Well, I think it would be the happiest thing for this nation that ever yet was thought of, if some plan could be contrived to destroy every boy upon this island.' The theme, of course, is cruelty to animals. The moralistic animal story and 'talking animals' (though not the kind used in fantasies) reached a culmination in 1877 with Anna Sewell's *Black Beauty*. Written in the heavily sentimental style of the Victorian era, this book became the first of the tear-jerking 'hanky' animal stories. In 1894 the Canadian writer, Marshall Saunders, duplicated Sewell's effects and phenomenal success with *Beautiful Joe*. In short, whatever the variety of purposes and techniques, the animal stories before Seton and Roberts had one trait in common: animals were employed and not described.

For the moralizing and sentimentality of their predecessors, Seton and Roberts substituted a rigorous naturalism. They were interested in their animal subjects as animals, not as devices. They assumed that their animal heroes were as intrinsically worthy of interest as any human being might be and they created, in effect, 'animal biographies'. Like the biographer, then, they undertook an analysis of character that was based on the influence of environment, youthful training, and education, with a selection of facts and events to make the portrait emerge clearly. Their animals are not mere automatons, led by blind instinct; they are creatures that possess the faculty of reason—but not human reason. The plots are chiefly life-and-death struggles in the wilderness. Most of the animals fall to the laws of nature, and usually if man is pitted against them, man is the victor. As Seton put it, 'The fact that these stories are true is the reason why all are tragic. The life of a wild animal always has a tragic end.' (*Wild Animals I Have*

Known.) Roberts, with his greater poetic skill, put it thus, 'And death stalks joy forever among the kindred of the wild.' (*The Kindred of the Wild.*)

Both Seton and Roberts frequently used composite animal characters. That is, although the incidents related happened to an animal, they would not all have happened to the same animal or in the sequence presented. Both writers wisely used the short-story form and the novella. Lengthy animal stories, especially those about wild animals, can easily become repetitious, and a preponderance of gory detail can surfeit the reader and break the dramatic impact.

The first collection of stories by Seton appeared in 1898 (*Wild Animals I Have Known*) and by Roberts in 1902 (*The Kindred of the Wild*). The two men had much in common. They were born in the same year, 1860; each respected the other's work; each succeeded at his chosen occupation and regarded his animal stories as something of a sideline. Seton was a naturalist and a hunter; his scientific work, *Lives of Game Animals*, is still useful. Roberts came to be considered the dean of Canadian letters because of his poetry and his novels. It is somewhat ironic that the enduring fame of both men now rests on their animal stories, which have largely been kept alive by the young: *The Biography of a Grizzly*, *Lobo*, *Silverspot*, *Arnaux*, *Raggylug* (Seton) and *Kings in Exile*, *Red Fox*, *The Haunters of the Silences* (Roberts).

One of Seton's collections of stories is called *Animal Heroes*. Each of his stories, however, has an animal hero, either an appealing one like Raggylug the rabbit, whose story ends while he is still alive and thumping, or one that is simply 'wild' like Wahb (*The Biography of a Grizzly*), the ferocious, truculent bear whose character remained sour all his life because he grew up without love.

Many of Seton's best attributes as a writer can be seen in *The Biography of a Grizzly*: his clear, straightforward, still-modern style, his humour, and especially his ability to create an intimate picture of animal life. That Seton gave in to sentimentality and archness is shown in *The Biography of a Grizzly*; but in general these qualities do not destroy the overall clarity of his vision of wild-animal life. The sentimental touch is sometimes quaint—an attempt on Seton's part to link animals to human behaviour without anthropomorphism.

They [the bear cubs] were well acquainted with the common little brown ants that harbour under the logs in the uplands, but now they came for the first time on one of the hills of the great, fat, luscious Wood-ant, and they all crowded around to lick up those that ran out. But they soon found that they were licking up more cactus-prickles and sand than ants, till their Mother said in Grizzly, 'Let me show you how.'

She knocked off the top of the hill, then laid her great paw flat on it for a few moments, and as the angry ants swarmed on to it she licked them up with one lick, and got a good rich mouthful to crunch, without a grain of sand or a cactus-stinger in it. The cubs soon learned. Each put up both his little brown paws, so that there was a ring of paws around the ant-hill, and there they sat, like children playing 'Hands', and each licked first the right and then the left paw, or one cuffed his brother's ears for licking a paw that was not his own, till the ant-hill was cleared out and they were ready for a change.—The Biography of a Grizzly.

Neither in Seton nor in Roberts does an animal actually talk, but they communicate in such a way that a kind of conversation is frequently suggested. Seton explained his theory about this in *Raggylug*:

Truly rabbits have no speech as we understand it, but they have a way of conveying ideas by a system of sounds, signs, scents, whisker-touches, movements and example that answers the purpose of speech: and it must be remembered that though in telling this story I frequently translate from rabbit into English, I repeat nothing that they did not say.

He also repeats nothing that an animal could not do. For example, his greatest story, *Lobo, The King of Currumpaw*, is based on personal observation. Seton actually trailed the great wolf in New Mexico. He tells us there is almost no deviation from the truth and that the great wolf's death happened precisely as related. Lobo is finally captured because of his love for his mate,

Blanca. Forgetting his usual, almost super-animal cunning, he trails her body to the ranch, is captured, and, although offered food and water, steadfastly refuses it and dies (who can say otherwise?) of a broken heart.

Though the incidents of Lobo's life did actually happen, the emotions with which they are invested are anything but naturalistic. The death of a wolf is made to evoke from the reader feelings of pity and terror that are akin to the moving quality of *Wuthering Heights*. There is no doubt that Seton here strove deliberately for the effects of tragedy and in so doing came very close to justifying the charge of anthropomorphism that was frequently laid against him. But he delicately questions rather than states— and so the skeptics have as much evidence as the believers.

Seton often came just as close to the borderline in his comic effects. In a humorous episode in the otherwise moving and tragic story of Wahb, in *The Biography of a Grizzly*, a smaller bear craftily conducts planned manoeuvres against Wahb. He climbs on logs and stones to rub his head upon a tree and thus show his height as greater than that of eight-foot Wahb.

It is difficult, and probably pointless, to try to decide which of his stories Seton particularly intended for children, for of all types of writing the realistic animal story makes perhaps the least distinction in the age of its readers. Who could say—certainly their authors gave no clue to the answer—whether *The Call of the Wild* (Jack London), *Tarka the Otter* (Henry Williamson), or *Rascal* (Sterling North) were meant for children or adults? The one instance in which we can be certain of Seton's intended audience suggests that he would have done better not to try to pinpoint his target. In straining for what he thought would appeal to children in *Bannertail* (1922), Seton produced his poorest story. Although it is an accurate picture of squirrel life, he indulges excessively in cuteness, even to the extent of personifying nature as 'Mother Carey'. *Bannertail* is his closest approach to the pathetic fallacy. In writing down for children to the extent of distorting animal nature, Seton almost emerges in *Bannertail* as the forerunner of those concoctors of animal travesties, Thornton Burgess and Walt Disney.

Seton was a professional naturalist and his stories were based on the scientific observations of an adult. The stories of Charles G.D. Roberts derived from recollections of his boyhood in the forests of New Brunswick. This association gives Roberts' work a romantic cast, in contrast with Seton's more matter-of-fact approach to the wilderness. Here, in two sentences, Roberts sets the stage and mood of 'The Boy and Hushwing' in *The Kindred of the Wild*:

A hollow, booming, ominous cry, a great voice of shadowy doom rang out suddenly and startled the dark edges of the forest. It sounded across the glimmering pastures, vibrating the brown-velvet dusk, and made the lame old woman in the cabin on the other side of the clearing shiver with vague fears.

Roberts can write with equal excitement of the largest animal (and his favourite), the bear, in a group of stories brought together in 1947, *Thirteen Bears*, and of the tiny ant in 'The Prisoners of the Pitcher Plant' (*The Haunters of the Silences*). Roberts often became intoxicated with words. Phrases such as 'the intense sapphire of the zenith thrilled and melted' (*The Haunters of the Silences*) and 'his baby face of tenderest cream and pink . . . the hair . . . like a fleece all over his head, enmeshing the sunlight in its silken tangle' (*Jim, the Story of a Backwoods Police Dog*) suggest nineteenth-century floridity. But in books such as *Red Fox*, *Thirteen Bears*, and *The Feet of the Furtive*, the description adds beauty to the stories and gives them individuality and distinction.

There is infinite variety in Roberts' nature themes. Fate or pre-ordained doom, mother love, the tragedy of growing old in the wilderness, the balance of nature and the chain of events resulting from killing, by animal or man, are only a few examples. Roberts ranged much further than Seton in the kinds of animals he treated, writing about tropical creatures as well as the inhabitants of Canadian forests.

Roberts' animal stories have been criticized more harshly than those of Seton. His book-length story, *Red Fox*, for example, is not as scientifically presented as are most of the works of Seton. In his attempts to bring drama to his stories and to emphasize the personality and cunning of his hero, he often strains credulity. That animals are instinctively on guard against man-made traps is a fact of hunting. But when Roberts has Red Fox and his mate deliberately leave the trap uncovered 'so that no other of the forest dwellers might be betrayed by it', and then go off to find out what other treasons man had plotted against the wild folk, he leaves reality for fantasy. However, as Frank Underhill once pointed out, 'biography only becomes interesting and alive when the biographer is partisan', and perhaps this is Roberts' way of being partisan to *his* hero. The story of Red Fox is spellbinding. He is shown as the strongest and most intelligent of the litter and is the only one to survive, even outwitting his human captors twice by playing 'dead'. At the end of the story he has triumphed over the hunters and the hounds and finds a home in a new wilderness. This ending represented to Roberts the triumph of the wild animal and a glorification of its freedom and strength.

Not all of Roberts' animals are endowed with the intelligence of Red Fox. Sometimes a beast's limitations are humorous: a young muskrat belonging to a litter of nine is killed by a duck. 'The attention of the little mother was just then occupied, and never having learned to count up to nine, she, apparently, never realized her loss.' ('The Calling of the Lop-Horned Bull' in *The Secret Trails*.)

Many of the stories of Seton and Roberts would be wearisome if they had been dragged out to a full-length book, and the reader would be far more conscious of, and probably repelled by, the wholesale slaughter animals inflict on one another and man inflicts on animals. As it is, they preserve suspense which, together with the genuine emotions they arouse for their animal heroes, has kept them very much alive.

In the 1930s another naturalist, born in England a generation after Seton and Roberts, won international fame as a portrayer and champion of wild life. He was George Stansfeld Belaney, who preferred to be known by his adopted name, Grey Owl. After spending some years as a trapper and hunter in Ontario, he became repelled by the cruelty and senseless killing and turned to conservation instead. His dream was of a time when all animals in the wilderness would have sanctuaries set aside for them. While trying to establish his own beaver sanctuary, he began to write stories in order to support his family. They were first pub-

lished in England and it was in that country that his books had
their greatest success. His one children's book, *The Adventures
of Sajo and Her Beaver People*, was published in 1935, the year
after his autobiography, *Pilgrims of the Wild*, appeared. *Sajo* falls
into the category of the realistic animal story, since it deals with
a year in the lives of two beaver kittens, Chilawee and Chikanee.
In the preface Grey Owl maintains that all events, 'although they
might not have occurred in the chronological order as presented',
were recorded either from first-hand experience or from 'first-
hand narrations'. The story tells how the two beaver kittens were
rescued by an Indian, who took them home as a birthday present
for his daughter Sajo. Both Sajo and her brother Shapian become
attached to the helpless, lovable little animals, and Sajo in particularly lavishes upon them the love she herself has lacked since
the death of her mother. Much of the first part of the book is
concerned with the play and learning habits of the kittens and
particularly with the emergence of their different temperaments.
Chikanee is the quieter, more helpless one and has a special love
for Sajo; Chilawee 'had a rather jolly way about him, and was
more of a roisterer, one of the "all for fun and fun for all" kind
of lads to whom life is just one big joke.' As there was no doubt
about their affection for, and their dependence upon, the children,
so there was no doubt about their love for one another. They had
never been separated for a minute of their young lives.

Hard times come and the father is forced to sell one of the
kittens to pay part of his debt at a company store and then to go
off on a trip to make up the rest. With true Indian stoicism Sajo
and Shapian stand by as the company trader picks the more
delicate and gentle Chikanee to be sold to a city zoo. Sajo begins
to pine, Chilawee mopes, and in a dream Sajo understands that
she must go to the city to rescue Chikanee. Sajo and Shapian go
off together, and on the way Shapian saves his sister's life in a
forest fire—a vivid and realistic bit of writing. The children eventually come in contact with white people who help and speed them
on their mission. Towards the end of the book this becomes a
'hanky' story, but it is saved by Sajo's dignity and because the
animals are pathetic even without the attempt to humanize them.
Chilawee is put down in the cage with Chikanee: 'Then, the

truth slowly dawning in the little twilight minds, they crept to one another, eyes almost starting out of their heads, ears wide open, listening, sniffing. . . .' The story ends with the return of the two beavers to their home pond—a realistic note—and with Grey Owl's views on conservation triumphant. As an animal story for children, *The Adventures of Sajo and Her Beaver People* is significant because it is the only one written in Canada that preserves realism and still shows a highly emotional link between children and animals.

The real heir of Seton in the writing of the realistic animal story is Roderick L. Haig-Brown, one of Canada's foremost writers in many fields. *Silver: The Life of an Atlantic Salmon* was published in 1931 and *Ki-Yu: A Story of Panthers* in 1934. *Silver* describes the life cycle of a salmon from the time he is spawned until he is finally caught in his own stream by the 'Good Fisherman' in true sportsmanlike fashion. Completely authentic in its details of salmon life, it is lightened by an intimate, at times almost lyrical style. Haig-Brown addresses his readers as if he were telling the story in person and is quite explicit when he is 'making things up', such as what Silver might have said or thought. Fishing skills, sportsmanship, and conservation are skilfully woven into a story. It takes a craftsman to make something as narrowly special as salmon interesting to the general reader, but Haig-Brown manages to do it.

Ki-Yu: A Story of Panthers is Seton and Roberts brought to complete realism. Ki-Yu is by no means an attractive character. (Even the most predatory animals of the earlier writers are appealing.) The wilderness is presented in all its starkness and there is little to show 'the kindred of the wild'. Ki-Yu is perhaps more a documentary of wild-animal life than a sympathetic animal biography. Haig-Brown simply prefers to let the facts speak for themselves. The drama of the story appears in the deliberate stalking of Ki-Yu by a professional panther hunter; when his dogs are killed by the panther, the sympathy is with the dogs and the man rather than with the hunted animal. Although man plays no more important a role here than in Seton, we are made to feel much more the depredations of wild animals upon domestic animal life.

Haig-Brown, like Roberts and Seton, also shows the inevitable-ness of death in the wilderness. In the end, when Ki-Yu is old and wounded and caught between two enemies, man and wolves, it is his own wild kind that tear him apart.

Ki-Yu is over-long and sometimes wearying, particularly in the description of the constant killing and feeding of the wild animals. Even so, all the details in the story are so realistically presented that they have a considerable holding power. Haig-Brown convinces by realism, not by invention. When Ki-Yu's mother, Nassa, is training her cubs—a surprisingly long, slow job—she wants to leave them at times, and the cubs seem to know when not to follow her. Haig-Brown is careful not to indulge in imagination at this point. 'She dropped them now, at the foot of the lake. What she did, how she persuaded them to stay behind instead of following her as they had followed her all the morning, it is difficult to say.' He ascribes feelings to animals, but in this form:

> *Ki-Yu, in killing and feeding and sleeping, in roaming by himself and with females, was beginning to find his life. His joys were utterly sub-conscious joys, utterly joys of the senses. As he turned down from the heather-laden breezes of the Plateau, the damp, earthy scent of the woods was pleasant to him—though he did not know it and would never have turned back from the Plateau to find the scent.*

Basically Haig-Brown does not care to engage our sympathies for Ki-Yu; he is concerned to present life in the wilderness—in this case Vancouver Island—and in carrying the realistic animal story to its logical conclusion he has perhaps gained in accuracy and restraint, but at the expense of dramatic emotion.

From Haig-Brown to the most popular recent exponent of the Canadian animal story is a long jump and one that ends in a form that is really *sui generis*.

No definition quite encompasses or fits animals like Mutt, the Prince Albert (?) retriever, the hero of Farley Mowat's *The Dog Who Wouldn't Be* (1957), written for adults and adopted by children, or Wol and Weeps, the equally surprising owls of Mowat's *Owls in the Family* (1961), written for children and adopted by adults. Both books brought joy and exuberance and a sense of fun and mischief into Canadian children's literature.

Mutt, the dog who wouldn't be, was a dog all right, but he was also sensitive to his appearance and to comments made about him. He early learned to avoid trouble with more combative dogs by balancing on the top of back fences; then he graduated to tree and ladder climbing. He was a traveller, sailing on the Saskatchewan River with Farley's father and on land in the Mowat car, suitably dressed in dark glasses. He became the most noted, but not always the most loved, dog in Saskatoon, maybe because of, maybe in spite of, the competition offered him by Farley's madcap father. Though a super-canine, Mutt was not immortal, and in old age he did not evade the destructiveness of the hit-and-run driver. Death on a back road in eastern Ontario ends his story—the ending does not come as a surprise: it is inevitable. The fast and furious sense of fun has been gradually disappearing and the reality of the ending casts an aura of credibility, even over the bizarre incidents that have gone before.

All the Mowat animals are presented as eccentric individualists, memorable for their refusal to accept the limitations of an animal's life. The truth or untruth of any particular incident is immaterial; disbelief is suspended and the reader does not doubt either the genuineness or the exaggerations of the Mowat way of life. If animals do take on the characteristics of the family with whom they live, then Mutt is completely credible.

Owls in the Family is an extension of one of the episodes in *The Dog Who Wouldn't Be*. No more readily classifiable than its predecessor, it purports to be a factual account of a family and its peculiar pets. The element of realism does exist—the owls are owls and the boys are boys—and there is a sharp sense of prairie sky and sun and cottonwoods. The details are wholly convincing, from the statement 'You can't walk quietly on the poplar bluff because of all the dead sticks underfoot' to the delineation of the contrasted characters of Wol and Weeps—Wol the extrovert and Weeps the introvert. But it is also a fast-moving adventure story about a search for the baby owls, the boys' animal circus, an encounter with the toughest kids in town. Most of all, it is an autobiography, recalling and conveying with humour, sometimes farcical and sometimes wry, a sympathetic but unsentimental feeling for animals and the values the author holds important: generosity, justice, and compassion. And it always rings true, for the boy who recounts the tale is honest and sensitive, and as colloquial as only a boy can be.

Mowat is a natural writer for children. He writes from his own experience, both childhood and adult. With his direct, simple, and lively style he can reveal aspects of life that are necessary in good children's literature if it is to have any enduring value. Qualities such as cruelty, irony, satire—gentled of course—give life and depth to children's literature and they are present in all Mowat's animal stories. They are implied in the style and confronted squarely in the realistic details.

Although Mowat's *Never Cry Wolf* (1963) was, again, not written deliberately for children, there is much in it of wolf life that has the same appeal for children as the books of Seton and Roberts. It is different from them in that it is related more explicitly to everyday Canadian life than are the stories of the two earlier writers. The chief interest of the book is in Mowat's daily observations of one particular family of wolves in the North. He had been asked by government officials to assess the habits of wolves in general and their supposedly ruinous effects upon the caribou. He becomes fascinated with their family life and finds himself adapting to their schedule—even to the point of learning to 'wolf-nap' so that he can observe them more closely. There is room for satire of government departments, officialese, and red tape, and Mowat makes the most of his opportunities, but the strength of the book is in the truly Canadian picture of wild-animal life. We are struck by the fact that most of his major points had been made by Seton and Roberts. If the government department concerned had read and understood these two great masters, however, Mowat might not have had his trip and the literature of the Canadian animal story would have been the poorer.

Alongside Mowat's highly personal narratives, others seem bland. But the impersonal animal story may have its own virtues, and chief among them is the sense of universality. Just such a story is Fred Bodsworth's *Last of the Curlews*. It received acclaim first when it was published in *Maclean's* and later in 1954 when it appeared in book form.

The Eskimo curlew, on its long migrations from the Arctic to the grasslands of South America, always returns to the Arctic to mate. Through the years and the depredations of the hunters the breed has become almost extinct. Bodsworth tells of one curlew who returned to the north several times and always found himself alone. At last a mate comes and loneliness disappears. On a flight north the female is killed, leaving the male to fly on alone; we know that he will now be alone until he dies.

Although the author could not have observed all the details, the reader is not conscious of fiction among the facts. All is so well blended that there is never a jarring or obtrusive note.

Behind them now the Arctic's aurora borealis was flashing vividly above the Labrador sky-line, but when they came to earth again, with flight feathers frayed and their breast muscles numbed by fatigue, it would be in dank jungle river-bottom of the Guianas or Venezuela. Yet there was no fear or hesitation now with the takeoff, no recognition of the drama of the moment. There was only a vague relief to be off. For it was a blessing of their rudimentary brains that they couldn't see themselves in the stark perspective of reality—minute specks of earthbound flesh challenging an eternity of sea and sky.

Last of the Curlews is a story that haunts the reader with its feeling of loneliness and sadness; it is also a poignant protest against the wanton destruction of wild life. In beauty of writing and in its perception of nature and universal values, it matches in many ways the writings of the great naturalist W.H. Hudson. A single sentence may sum up Bodsworth's spare and restrained approach to animal portrayal: 'It was a blessing of their rudimentary brains that they couldn't see themselves in the stark perspective of reality.' For Bodsworth, honesty of depiction is the paramount virtue and only such dramatic values as are wholly justified by the actual circumstances of the natural environment may be attached to his subject.

This faithfulness to reality, of course, is hardly the road to popularity. The great mass of readers will prefer a more romantic colouring. *Last of the Curlews*, highly esteemed but rather little known, thus forms an interesting contrast with *The Incredible*

Journey, the outstanding 'success' among Canadian children's books of our time.

The Incredible Journey (1960), written by Sheila Burnford, an Englishwoman long resident in Canada, was made into a motion picture almost immediately after publication and for good reason. The book represents almost all the virtues and failings characteristic of popular films: a simple plot, a strong emphasis on characterization, a large measure of sentimentality, and a compelling vividness, pace, and charm.

The plot itself is well worn, paralleling at many points Eric Knight's *Lassie Come Home*. Two dogs and a cat, beloved household pets, have been left with a friend while their owners are in Europe. The younger dog, a Labrador retriever, determines to make his way back home and leads his companions on a 250-mile trek through the Northern Ontario wilderness to do so. En route they face every hazard, including starvation, wild animals, cold, weariness, and near-drowning. And still, of course, they succeed.

The journey is imaginary, but the animals are modelled after the author's own pets and are given all the human attributes that pet-lovers are apt to ascribe to their charges. Thus the Labrador is represented as following not instinct, but consistent, logical thought. 'Only one thing was clear and certain—that at all costs he was going home, home to his own beloved master. Home lay to the west, his instinct told him; but he could not leave the other two—so somehow he must take them with him, all the way.' Indeed, when the dog sees a 'temporary master' leaving, so firmly does he know that this is a time for departure that he presents his paw to the master in a gesture of farewell.

So, too, the cat exhibits such motivations as selflessness (it attacks a bear cub and even a bear on behalf of the bulldog) and generosity (continually hunting food to give to the older dog). And there is not a moment's altercation among the three animals; they treat each other with complete sweetness throughout a long and difficult journey when their own survival was hourly at stake.

All this Burnford relates so graphically and even poetically that it very nearly convinces. But not quite. The journey remains incredible and, despite its undoubted emotional impact, the book is not entirely honest in the sense that the stories of Seton, Roberts,

Haig-Brown, and Bodsworth are basically honest in their treatment of animals. *The Incredible Journey* will be read and remembered, but not as a true exemplar of the realistic animal story. It should be considered rather as the heir of *Black Beauty* and *Beautiful Joe*, in which there is a deliberate attempt to use animals as the vehicles for human emotions.

That there can be emotion in the animal story without arrant emotionalism is triumphantly seen in books by two new and very different writers—*The Black Wolf of River Bend* (1971) by Helene Widell and *The Winter of the Fisher* (1971) by Cameron Langford.

The Black Wolf of River Bend begins, as do most animal biographies, with the birth and survival of the best and luckiest of the litter and his normal adventures as a creature of the wild. But the scene shifts dramatically when a forest fire drives Blackie from the Cariboo Mountains into new territory, Robson Valley. Here he gradually adopts an immigrant ranch family, driving in game, playing tag, calf-sitting, guarding the youngest child, but never allowing himself to be petted or even touched. Human cruelty brings the idyll to an end when Blackie is shot by a pair of drunken hunters in front of a busload of school children. Helene Widell can generate the kind of moral outrage displayed by Farley Mowat in *A Whale for the Killing*, but she also cushions the shock with the attitude of the sensitive and sensible parents. In this story the natural caution and instincts of a wild animal are not betrayed; it is logically surmised that the wolf, having once escaped from a steel trap, could never take the one step necessary for escape from the valley—the crossing of the steel railway tracks. The story is told very simply—there are no frills, no flourishes—much as it might be told to children around a campfire with the song of wolves echoing from a distance.

Cameron Langford's *The Winter of the Fisher* is at once a full-length animal biography and a fully crafted novel. It begs immediate comparison with Roberts' *Red Fox* (1905), not only because of its length—it is 222 pages of close type without illustration—but because of the sustaining of interest within that length. But in literary power and in the delight it arouses it is closer to two classics by the English naturalist Henry Williamson:

Tarka the Otter (1928) and *Salar the Salmon* (1935). Langford's narrative, which is without dialogue, has neither Seton's sometimes coy and often didactic manner of addressing the reader directly, nor Roberts' almost intrusive chatter among his human characters.

In the gray dark of a hunter's moon, the mother fisher led her brood along the eastern shore of the lake. Occasionally, she glanced behind to see if they were keeping their proper stations. They had come far in the eight weeks since their first wild and hilarious hunting foray. Now they slipped in disciplined quiet through the classroom of the night. Yet, for all their stealth, the hushed night sounds died at the moment of their passing, to whisper forth again when they had gone. They moved as in a soft cocoon of tiny silences.

The protagonists are never named; they are identified only as 'fisher', 'trapper', and 'Ojibway'. The landscape is never made explicit; it is the vast wilderness of Northern Ontario, which becomes apparent only through internal evidence. The slight delineation of character needed for the dramatic action is handled so skilfully that both men and animal are raised to archetypal proportions—the humans becoming symbols of their kind and the fisher the symbol of all wild animals. In the same way the setting is never specifically identified; rather there is 'the cabin on the shore', 'the head of the lake', 'the den beneath the old spruce', which each of us knows or can imagine. By establishing an aesthetic distance between the reader and the background of his story, Langford requires that we reach into our own memories to participate in the creation of a landscape and setting that are much more familiar and intimate than word-pictures would make possible.

Much of the conflict, and the climax, comes from the contrasting characters and attitudes of the two humans in the story: the old Ojibway who hunts only for sustenance and who befriends and protects the fisher, and the white commercial trapper who is at first annoyed with the fisher for robbing his traps and who then pursues him with a relentless, almost mindless fury. The author analyses the struggle in reasoned terms and keeps it always within the bounds of possibility:

The trapper had his human brain, experience and skill in his trade. Against these, the fisher pitted his natural intelligence and wiliness, both highly developed qualities in his kind, plus his exceptional agility and incredibly delicate senses. In truth, it was the trapper who held the edge. But the fisher had luck, and a silent ally in the Old Ojibway.

Like Red Fox, the fisher escapes in the end, scarred, wiser, and still independent.

Considering the limited characteristics of animals, it is not surprising that there is a certain sameness, and even repetition of particular incidents, in most animal biographies. Roberts' Red Fox reacts to the horrors of the trapline much as Langford's Fisher. Seton's wolves behave as Mowat's do. All the outstanding writers of the realistic animal story have been conservationists and protectionists; they have treated animals with respect and honesty in their natural habitats. Their themes are timeless and therefore timely—and similar. They either state or imply that we must respect and ultimately love nature for what it is, and that we must see it for what it is in order to understand man's place in the scheme of things. Following the example of Seton and Roberts, they have wished to spare the reader emotionalism and sentimentalism (indeed, they encourage neither); and they have all chosen the same method—the placing of an aesthetic distance between their readers and their animal characters. We know their animals but we do not identify ourselves completely with them.

All of this is to say that realistic animal stories, taken as a group, present a rather static composite picture. Canadian writers seem to eschew the kind of mystical rapport between man and animal that can be found in the writings of the French writer René Guillot in such books as *The Elephants of Sargabal* and *Fodae and the Leopard-Men*. Nor, with the exception of Grey Owl's *Sajo and Her Beaver People*, and Roberts' short story 'The Boy and Hushwing', do they capitalize upon children's affection for animals. Sterling North, the American writer, used this theme in *Rascal* (a lonely boy's love for his pet racoon) and it became an international best-seller. These particular books are still part of the realistic animal stream because the habits of these tamed creatures of the wild are so well delineated. Most books about children and their pets—horses, dogs, etc.—are usually a branch of the adventure novel; the child's involvement and emotions are more pronounced than the study of the animal. But even with these slightly differing approaches, it is difficult to see how there can be any dramatic changes or developments in the genre.

Nevertheless, Canadians, working within a stable viewpoint, are all the more to be appreciated for their individual styles: the lyricism of Roberts and Bodsworth, the directness of Seton, the documentary approach of Haig-Brown, the taut control of Cameron Langford. Indeed, the writing in this field is far generally superior to that of most Canadian writing for children. This may be because the books are not specifically directed at children and so there is less 'writing down'. Or it may be that the practitioners in this genre genuinely respect and understand their subjects, while many writers dealing with children do not.

A great many other books about animals have been written and published in Canada. Most of them, however, are not concerned to tell about animals in a narrative or literary form but constitute a branch of popular science. The number of animal stories proper is surprisingly small and it may be that the sheer productivity of Seton (ten books) and Roberts (fifteen books) in this vein has inhibited successors. After all, between them Seton and Roberts have left hardly a species of animal or bird unportrayed.

Yet we need not fear for the decline of the animal story in Canada. If the quantity has been low, the quality has been consistently high. The best of the Canadian publications in this genre have attained a world-wide audience unmatched by any other type of Canadian children's book. With Haig-Brown, Mowat, and Bodsworth still active, and with such newer writers as Widell and Langford, the tradition of achievement will surely be maintained. After all, the animals of Canada are still there for the seeing and the telling and their appeal is perennial and universal.

BELANEY, GEORGE STANSFELD. *The Adventures of Sajo and Her Beaver People* by Grey Owl (pseud.). Toronto, Macmillan, 1935. 256 pp.

This is a love story—the love of two Indian children for their pet beavers, Chikanee and Chilawee, and the love of the beavers for each other. Sajo and her two friends are among the few characters in Canadian children's books that linger fondly in the memory.

BODSWORTH, FRED. *Last of the Curlews.* Illustrated by T.M. Shortt. Toronto, Dodd, Mead, 1955. 128 pp.

In its migrations from the Arctic breeding grounds to the pampas of South America, the Eskimo curlew has fallen prey to the depredations of hunters. The last of the curlews finds a mate, then loses her to the guns and flies off, an infinitesimal speck in the vast sky. This story is full of pathos, but it does not indulge in pathetic fallacy.

BRAITHWAITE, MAX. *Voices of the Wild.* Illustrated by Karl S. Pogany. Toronto, McClelland and Stewart, 1962. 122 pp.

An omniscient uncle discourses on various animals and birds for the edification of his young niece and nephew. Brief incidents of adventure involving the children are interspersed with the nature lessons. The book is partly redeemed by the realistic drawings of Karl S. Pogany.

BURNFORD, SHEILA. *The Incredible Journey: A Tale of Three Animals.* Illustrated by Carl Burger. Boston, Little, Brown, 1960. 145 pp.

Two dogs and a cat find their way home through 250 miles of northern Ontario wilderness. This popular story combines the realistic and the sentimental approach.

GREY OWL. See BELANEY, GEORGE STANSFELD.

DUNFIELD, CLIFFORD. *Rusty and Susie.* Illustrated by Ray Taylor. Toronto, Musson, 1965. 180 pp.

A beaver family is transported to a conservation area in northern Saskatchewan as part of a fur rehabilitation and native re-establishment program. While this is an informative book, the shifting of the narrative from humans to animals and the overt anthropomorphism give it many discordant moments. It is in no way as realistic or as moving as Grey Owl's *Sajo and Her Beaver People.*

HAIG-BROWN, RODERICK L. *Ki-Yu: A Story of Panthers.* Illustrated by Theyre Lee-Elliott. Boston, Houghton, Mifflin, 1934. 214 pp. (Also published under the title *Panther.* London, Collins, 1934. 191 pp.)

In describing the life cycle of a Vancouver Island panther, Haig-Brown emphasizes the truths of wild animal life to an even greater degree than Roberts and Seton.

HAIG-BROWN, RODERICK L. *Silver: The Life of an Atlantic Salmon.* Illustrated by Bernard Venables. London, Black, 1931. 96 pp.

A light and joyful book that tells as much about the skill and sportsmanship of fishing as it does about the life cycle of the Atlantic salmon.

LANGFORD, CAMERON. *The Winter of the Fisher*. Toronto, Macmillan, 1971. 222 pp.
With the help of an old Ojibway, the one-year-old fisher eludes both the impersonal dangers of the wilderness and the calculated pursuit of the white trapper. A distinguished full-length animal biography.

MOWAT, FARLEY M. *The Dog Who Wouldn't Be*. Illustrated by Paul Galdone. Toronto, Little, Brown, 1957. 238 pp.
The outrageous adventures of Mutt are somehow made completely believable, so much so that his death brings genuine sadness. Mowat's capacity for true humour that is never divorced from reality and kindliness is shown here at its best.

MOWAT, FARLEY M. *Never Cry Wolf*. Toronto, McClelland and Stewart, 1963. 247 pp.
Mowat writes bitterly about government and sympathetically about wolves. His personal observation of a wolf family and his trenchant style have added a new dimension to the Canadian realistic animal story.

MOWAT, FARLEY M. *Owls in the Family*. Illustrated by Robert Frankenberg. Boston, Little, Brown, 1961. 107 pp.
The recollection of a boyhood in Saskatoon that has fun and liveliness rather than nostalgia. Wol and Weeps, the two owls, have built up a wide and admiring audience. This is possibly our most deservedly popular Canadian children's book.

PEARSON, CAROL. *Brown Paws and Green Thumbs*. Illustrated by Lewis Parker. Toronto, Clarke, Irwin, 1961. 215 pp.
The author reminisces about animals she has known as a 'housemother'. Too many animals are dealt with too quickly and superficially to give the book any validity.

ROBERTS, CHARLES G.D. *Jim: The Story of a Backwoods Police Dog* [and other stories]. New York, Macmillan, 1919. 216 pp.
When Roberts turned from wild animals to domestic ones he was far less successful in his portrayals. Here the police dog Jim forms a link between the stories of life in a small town in New Brunswick.

ROBERTS, CHARLES G.D. *The Kindred of the Wild: A Book of Animal Life*. Illustrated by Charles Livingston Bull. Boston, Page, 1902. 374 pp.
While based on the truth and reality of wild-animal life, these stories are touched with a poetic imagination that makes them literature as well as natural history. This is Roberts' first collection of animal stories. Other collections are: *The Feet of the Furtive* (London, Ward Lock, 1912, 277 pp.); *The Haunters of the Silences* (Boston, Page, 1907, 316 pp.); *Kings in Exile* (London, Ward Lock, 1909, 306 pp.); *The Watchers of the Trails* (Boston, Page, 1904, 361 pp.). *King of Beasts* (Toronto, Ryerson, 1967, 237 pp.) is the most recent edition of some of Roberts' tales for young people.

ROBERTS, CHARLES G.D. *Red Fox: The Story of His Adventurous Career in the Ringwaak Wilds and of His Final Triumph Over the Enemies of His Kind.* Illustrated by Charles Livingston Bull. Boston, Page, 1905. 340 pp.

Roberts' only full-length animal biography makes us see the qualities that men and animals have in common. A moving, exciting, and fast-paced story.

ROBERTS, CHARLES G.D. *Thirteen Bears.* Chosen and edited by Ethel Hume Bennett. Illustrated by John A. Hall. Toronto, Ryerson, 1947. 254 pp.

The bears vary in kind and temperament but they all provide exciting reading.

SAUNDERS, MARGARET MARSHALL. *Beautiful Joe: An Autobiography.* Philadelphia, American Baptist Pub. Soc., 1894. 304 pp.

This Canadian imitation of Anna Sewell's *Black Beauty* is as far beyond objective literary evaluation by most readers as is its prototype. It is about a dog, and its appeal lies in a combination of ease of reading and high emotionalism. It is of some significance that Saunders' other stories have dropped into oblivion. In *The Wandering Dog* (1916), for example, the author showed herself to be nothing but a very poor writer.

SETON, ERNEST THOMPSON. *Animal Heroes.* Illustrated by the author. New York, Grosset & Dunlap, 1905. 362 pp.

Eight spirited stories that show sympathy and admiration for the courage of wild animals.

SETON, ERNEST THOMPSON. *Bannertail: The Story of a Gray Squirrel.* Illustrated by the author. New York, Scribner, 1922. 265 pp.

This is Seton in a softer mood. As a charming, rather sentimental look at an animal, it differs from Seton's typical realistic—and so more honest and dignified—approach.

SETON, ERNEST THOMPSON. *Wild Animals I Have Known; Being the Personal Histories of Lobo, Silverspot, Raggylug, Bingo, The Springfield Fox, The Pacing Mustang, Wully and Redruff.* Illustrated by the author. New York, Scribner, 1898. 359 pp.

These stories, upon which Seton's fame has rested, are as contemporary as the day they were written. The collection is foremost of its kind and is deservedly a Canadian classic. Other collections are *Lives of the Hunted* (1901) and *Wild Animals at Home* (1913). Many of Seton's animal stories have been published separately.

WIDELL, HELENE. *The Black Wolf of River Bend.* New York, Farrar, Straus & Giroux, 1971. 156 pp.

'Blackie' was born in the Cariboo Mountains. Driven from his home by a disastrous forest fire, he escapes to a remote valley where he eventually 'adopts' an immigrant family. A realistic animal story for younger children that has the pace, tautness, and the impact of fiction as well as the humour and tragedy of real life.

6 | realistic fiction

The miscellany is the classifier's traditional recourse for dealing with phenomena too few or too diverse to warrant groupings of their own. This chapter encompasses those realistic works of fiction that do not lend themselves to more rigorous classification—books that are not historical narrative, fantasy, or legend. It includes sub-categories as varied as the adventure yarn, the semi-naturalistic account of family life, the mystery story, and horse and dog stories.

Most dictionaries define realism, as related to art and literature, in terms of fidelity to truth and accuracy of representation. Leaving aside philosophical considerations of truth, the reader of fiction asks: 'Does it seem true? Am I convinced both intellectually and emotionally?' If the answer is an unequivocal yes, he might well have read a work of art. However, surface truth—visual accuracy—is more commonly achieved in fiction than inner truth. What the stories discussed below ask of the reader is simply belief —belief without effort or imagination. There is no 'willing suspension of disbelief', no payment of 'a little extra' to enter the world created by the author. Without attempting to achieve depth or an 'inner consistency of reality', the authors of these stories strive for outward consistency. They may not grip the imagination, but they do try to achieve a measure of conviction and many of them succeed.

These books also have in common technique and setting. Most of the books lean heavily on the well-tested appeal of 'Change the name and the story is about you!' And so the protagonist is of the same age and sex as the intended reader. In fact these books often have no characters outside the predetermined age group; if grown-ups do appear, they exist mainly for purposes of plot advancement. As for their setting, the stories are aimed for the most part at the Canadian market. Written by people who are themselves residents of Canada, they are almost invariably set in Canada and make much of their locale. At their worst, such books utilize locale as only one more ploy in saleable familiarity: a Toronto background promises more interest for Canadian readers than does Nashville or Manchester. At their best, they make the setting an integral part of the action and the results contribute to a distinctively Canadian literature for children.

TALES OF OUTDOOR LIFE AND ADVENTURE

The theme of conflict against the wilderness, though it is one of universal appeal, is very Canadian. Inherently dramatic and evoking one of the most distinctive and recognizable features of the Canadian scene, familiar yet out of the ordinary, it requires only reasonable craftsmanship and knowledge to make a competent book. Probably no branch of Canadian children's literature has produced so uniformly high a level of attainment as the tale of outdoor adventure. With the exception of certain books treasured for reasons of nostalgia and sentimentality (*Anne of Green Gables, Beautiful Joe*), not many Canadian children's books have lasted for more than one generation. Significantly, most of the survivors have been based on Canadian outdoor life. The struggle with nature calls for courage, endurance, effort, skill, loyalty, and tolerance. These are timeless virtues and the qualities to which children of every generation can respond.

The literary and cultural themes that Margaret Atwood has identified as 'survival' can be seen in such books in their most direct and forceful form. In the Canada they represent, the land is overwhelmingly larger than its people; only occasionally does a scene of cosiness or domesticity intrude on the all-pervasive presence of nature in the raw and nature in the grand. The plots are almost inevitably played out with casts of animals, Indians, fur-traders, trappers, fishermen, or others battling the environment. And because the environment is seen in purely physical terms, conflicts are overcome by 'manly' virtues. The protagonists are, with the merest handful of exceptions, young males who overcome their natural 'enemies' by dint of their courage, endurance, self-reliance, and woodsman skills.

Where our adult literature equates 'survival' with alienation, coldness, and hostility, our children's books equate it with challenge—and an almost joyous one at that. A favourite plot is how a young man comes to feel at home in the wilderness. Even in our earliest books there is a celebration of nature rather than antagonism towards it—a responsiveness, a zest, an exuberance. Perhaps Ballantyne set the tone in 1856 in *The Young Fur Traders* when he wrote: 'All nature was joyous and brilliant, and bright and beautiful. Morning was still very young—about an hour old.' Often the Canadian wilderness is presented, as in Ballantyne, as a friendly playground, or at least as something that can be handled.

The combination of dramatic setting and narrative skill that makes for a compelling tale is best exemplified in the books of Roderick Haig-Brown and Farley Mowat. These writers stand far above their Canadian contemporaries and rank high internationally.

Both Haig-Brown and Mowat have come to the writing of outdoor books almost inevitably. Confirmed naturalists who have given years of their lives to exploring the Canadian wilderness, active and dogged campaigners for conservation, they have a feeling for the Canadian land and a knowledge of it that are genuine and deep. More important, they are thoroughly professional writers who have learned how to shape their feelings rather than just express them; they know that even in children's stories a character remains vivid long after the most ingenious contrivances of plot have been forgotten.

Haig-Brown's *Starbuck Valley Winter* (1943) and *Saltwater Summer* (1948) were obviously inspired by tremendous feeling for particular places—British Columbia's range lands and the ocean that washes its coastline. However, there is more than feeling in these books. Haig-Brown has looked at what he describes and so feels with his hero not only a 'sudden pride' in his surroundings but also a 'sense of ownership through knowledge'.

He invests his readers with this sense of ownership and can thus impart to them, without ever veering into pedagogy, many unfamiliar activities, like trolling, seining, skinning a buck, making a water-wheel, canoeing up a river, setting traps. He has a Homeric appreciation of the well-done task, the well-made artifact, and an observant eye that is never sentimental. He more than sees: he understands and feels as well. 'He looked at everything, trying to use it and make it his own'—this describes Haig-Brown as well as his hero. Such an intimacy between the hero and what he makes or creates enables Haig-Brown to escape the common pitfall of obtrusive information and explanation. (Such an error of style, however, can have unintentional charm. The reader will recall Father Robinson, in the very act of escaping from the wreck, pausing to explain to his children the principle of the lever—'as well as I could in a hurry'.) Haig-Brown is always sure-footed in traversing detail. *Starbuck Valley Winter* and *Saltwater Summer* are *real* stories as *Swiss Family Robinson* and *Kidnapped* are real.

Haig-Brown's honesty of description is reflected in his plots, which have drama but no impossible deeds. In *Starbuck Valley Winter*, Don's initial decision to save his friend's life is grandly heroic, but the actual journey he undertakes turns out to be almost devoid of sensational incident. The plots of both books are extremely simple but have implicit moral dimensions. In *Starbuck Valley Winter*, Don Morgan and his friend spend a winter trapping in the woods; in *Saltwater Summer* they spend the summer in commercial fishing. Both are basically chancy enterprises and it is the natural hazards, the inherent violence of outdoor life, rather than artificial 'adventures' that give the tales their impact. The mistakes made, while adding to the suspense, are those that would plausibly be made by anyone of youth and inexperience.

Don Morgan's personality is as believable as his experiences. Haig-Brown presents him as a rather complex person, by no means as straightforwardly 'nice' as his great friend Tubby Miller. He is more moody, more ambitious, and impulsive enough to break the law on one occasion. His path to heroism is a process of development, not a melodramatic change of heart. Perhaps even more remarkably, Haig-Brown knows how to handle adults. In most Canadian children's books the world of youth is quite divorced from the world of adults. The latter are shadowy figures who are almost nameless: simply the Father, the Mother, the Boss, etc. Almost never do we find grown-ups as vivid and as memorable as Alan Breck or Long John Silver. Haig-Brown's adults do not catch the imagination as do Stevenson's great creations, but at least they exist. They have mixed motives, complexity, reality. We understand how they have come to live in isolation on range or coast and what their environment has done to them.

Farley Mowat's stories are somewhat more conventionally adventurous and less thoroughly realistic than Haig-Brown's. *Lost in the Barrens* (1956) recounts the experiences of a white boy, Jamie, and an Indian boy, Awasin, who become separated from the Indian band. They encounter every test the North can impose upon them. They suffer near-starvation and snow blindness. They fight to the death with a Barren Lands grizzly and with almost unbearable suspense they miss by a hair's breadth the Indian band they were supposed to join for the return. Somehow they survive it all and grow up in the process.

Mowat's strength lies in the sense of pace and breathless suspense he gives to his tale. The boys almost reel from crisis to crisis. But Mowat is far too good a writer, and he knows the North too well, to strain credibility in the interest of narrative. Beneath the overlay of adventure there is always the solid substance of the North itself and the kind of character development it imposes on those who live there. Awasin, the son of a Cree chieftain, explains to Jamie, the city boy, that one must conform to the North rather than fight it, and so the interest of the story is fundamentally based on the way that adaptation is made rather than on the events that precipitate it.

Mowat's steady hand on the world of reality can be seen even more clearly in his modern pirate story, *The Black Joke* (1962). Here are the hard economic facts of life in the Newfoundland outports in the 1930s. The power of the traders, the father's need to find a profitable cargo so as to retain his ship, form a springboard for the incidents. *The Black Joke* is also a first-class tale of the sea in the grand, a-little-larger-than-life tradition: seafaring boys navigating in stormy waters, brave seamen and scheming merchants, rum-runners and castaways, a fine schooner shipwrecked and seized but brought home safely to port. Mowat's beautifully outrageous imagination is shown particularly in the gusto with which he delineates character. His villains are properly evil. There is even a touch of grandeur about Captain Smith: 'Back to the ship,' he bellowed, 'or I'll drill the rotten lot of you'—an imprecation in the best tradition of pirates' curses. Yet all this is set against a background of precise detail, whether Mowat is describing a Newfoundland outport or catching a salmon or sailing a ship through the fog. The humour in the story is not particularly subtle, though perhaps it is well calculated for its audience. The two young heroes, Peter and Kye, who are capable of doing a man's job in sailing the *Black Joke*, indulge in pranks dear to their age—squirting bilgewater at the unpleasant trader, Mr Barnes, and frying salt pork when he is seasick. The style, as in *Lost in the Barrens*, is simple, exact, and detailed, in the tradition of the plain English of Defoe and Swift.

As Black Joke *cleared the end of Long Island and encountered the Atlantic again, she began to rise to a head sea. The sky was a sombre grey and the wind was still freshening. The ship's course lay southeast around the tip of Hermitage peninsula and then across the bay to the town of Fortune, where all vessels outward bound for St. Pierre were required to clear through customs.*

Such plain words are often the prelude to momentous events. 'It was a magnificent night,' says Mowat quietly, and then launches into the crescendo of the story in which the boys cause an explosion on the *Black Joke* and rout the villains. These pages are probably the most exciting in Canadian children's literature. *The Black Joke* is a latter-day *Treasure Island*, a story whose gusto and toughness are generally lacking in Canadian books for children.

In such works as *Starbuck Valley Winter* and *The Black Joke*, Haig-Brown and Mowat owe most of their success to their respect for their readers. When that fails, craftsmanship falters, as is evident in Mowat's *The Curse of the Viking Grave* (1966), a sequel to *Lost in the Barrens*. A tedious re-working of material is a fault in many sequels, but here the careless writing, lack of attention to detail, and a dull plot (there is not even a good old-fashioned curse) presumably led Mowat himself to describe it as a 'pot-boiler'.

Of the many possible variations on the theme of conflict against the wilderness, Eskimo life has proved especially fruitful. Perhaps it is because the struggle of human beings with nature is here revealed at its starkest. Or it may be because Eskimo life is so far removed from ordinary experience as almost to guarantee that only authors who really know their subject will dare to write about it. And who should know it better than an Eskimo? The first piece of Eskimo fiction to be published in English is *Harpoon of the Hunter* (1970) by Markoosie, who writes of the adventures of a sixteen-year-old boy in the not-so-distant past as if he had lived them himself.

The word 'survive' occurs frequently in the story:

Maybe they would be lucky and get a polar bear. But Kamik knew that hunting bear is not easy. He knew that many times hunters come back empty handed after many sunrises of chase, sweat, and exhausting work. Bear hunting is the hardest thing in the north. The bear, if cornered, can kill many good dogs or men, if he gets the chance. But that is life. To survive in this wild land, man and beast kill for food. This is the land where the strong survive. The weak do not survive.

But even the strong are defeated here, thus making *Harpoon of the Hunter* one of the most sombre as well as moving experiences in Canadian children's books. The artless style, almost devoid of adjectives and adverbs, matches the landscape, which is empty of all but threats to life, except for the people who live and love and help one another. The form of this novelette is sophisticated and dramatic. It moves in brief episodes, from the hunters who go in search of a rabid bear, to events in the base camp, to the people who go for help, to the wounded bear itself. Together these episodes make a perfect whole.

Film-like episodes are also a feature of *The Story of Comock the Eskimo* (1968), perhaps more naturally so, since the story was related by Robert Flaherty, who made the famous film *Nanook of the North*. It is, however, Comock's story, based on actuality and written down by Flaherty years later. As in *Harpoon of the*

Hunter, the events have a starkness and reality that rise to an almost unbearable pitch. Two Eskimo families make a hazardous journey to an island rich in game; only one family survives to return to the mainland ten years later. The style is succinct but has a touch of poetry:

> *My wife said, 'It is well, Comock, we have something.'*
>
> *'Yes,' I said, 'but no spears, no harpoons—we cannot kill bear —we cannot kill seal.'*
>
> *'There are the dogs,' my wife said, 'and there are the harnesses of the dogs that are gone. We can eat them,' my wife said.*
>
> *'No,' said my eldest son, 'we cannot eat the harnesses. The harnesses they are gone. They were tied to the lost sleds.'*
>
> *'Well, anyway, there are the dogs,' my wife said.*
>
> *'Ae,' I said, 'there are the dogs.'*
>
> *'Ae,' said everyone.*

An Eskimo desert island may support game, though not the amenities of a Coral Island or of Robinson Crusoe's island. *The Story of Comock the Eskimo* was not intended particularly for children, but its integrity, subject matter, style, and a multitude of small drawings may make it the prerogative of children rather than adults.

Eskimos have had outstanding interpreters in several writers with a wide experience of the Arctic and a respect and affection for the Eskimo way of life: Douglas Wilkinson, James Houston, and Vilhjalmur Stefansson. Wilkinson was a film-maker in the North who spent over a year as the 'adopted son' of an Eskimo family on Baffin Island. James Houston, as well as being a traveller in and a painter of the North, helped to bring the now-famous Eskimo carvings to the attention of art lovers of the world. Stefansson was the famed explorer who first showed how to live in the Arctic and not just traverse it.

Wilkinson's *Sons of the Arctic* (1965) is perhaps an important book rather than a great one. Its setting is wholly in the Arctic, which is not contrasted in any way with the sophisticated world 'outside'. Yet the results of the Eskimo's ever-increasing contact with the white man's technology are implicit in the story. Wilkinson's book points up the fact that all too many conventional

'Eskimo stories' perpetuate an outdated picture: nomads huddled in igloos or hunting polar bears with spears. In *Sons of the Arctic*, the boys had .22 rifles and long for 30:30s. The family own a motor boat, boil water in a tin kettle on a primus stove, and drink tea from mugs. Even so, there is no attempt at any refinement of a still-harsh and primitive existence, though the Eskimos' delight in their simple life is made plain. There is an occasional touch of unheard-of luxury in our Kleenex society, as when the boys wipe their greasy hands on the fine white feathers of a ptarmigan.

Like *Lost in the Barrens*, this is basically a survival story. Three young Eskimo boys disobey instructions and take a different route home because they want to kill a caribou. They are caught in a sudden Arctic blizzard and struggle with the elements for five days. However, the reader does not fear for them—even in a difficult situation they know exactly what to do—until they are attacked by a bear that has been looming in the background throughout the story.

As memorable for the reader as the swift adventure is an overall tone that sounds for the Eskimos themselves and that lingers when the details of the adventure have faded. There is the happy delight of a simple joke or in family teasing; there is the affectionate relationship between old and young. At the end of the story, when the bear has been killed and all has turned out happily:

> *Kyak looked at his three boys and a surge of pride rose in his breast. 'What more could a man want?', he asked himself. 'Meat and fat, skins for boots and clothing, and three fine sons to help me as I grow older.'*

The impact of new technology upon the Eskimo is seen even more clearly in Margery Hinds' *Makpa: The Story of an Eskimo-Canadian Boy* (1971), but although this is now an important aspect of Eskimo life, and more books on the subject would be welcome, *Makpa* simply fails in its storytelling quality.

James Houston has not only been the most prolific spokesman for the Eskimo in children's literature, but the most artistic writer. In *Tikta'Liktak* (1965), *The White Archer* (1967), *Akavak* (1968), and *Wolf Run* (1971) he has distilled the essence of the heroic in Eskimo life, as in a broader sense the stories of King Arthur,

Roland, and Beowulf bring to a culmination the essence of the civilizations they represent. Legend is by definition 'some wonderful event handed down for generations among a people and popularly believed to have historical basis, although not verifiable: distinguished from myth'. Certainly all the events that James Houston records in his stories *could* have happened, and he has clothed them in the dignified language that befits a legend. But in the timeless world that he describes, his heroes are as modern as those in Roderick Haig-Brown's *Starbuck Valley Winter* or David Walker's *Pirate Rock* or Jean Mackenzie's *River of Stars*. As Houston's Eskimo characters complete their quest, they have changed, become aware of themselves and their environment, and so achieve a new inner power.

Tikta'Liktak is closest to legend. The story of the young man (less than twenty years of age) who escaped from his floating prison to equal danger and hardship on a barren Arctic island, and who then, by courageous and ingenious means, made his way back to the mainland, had become famous in the Arctic when James Houston first heard it. (Tikta'Liktak's method of saving himself appears in *The Story of Comock the Eskimo*, also based on fact; the reality of both stories is therefore reinforced.) The boy's long period of loneliness and isolation in *Tikta'Liktak* and his knowledge that there will be no rescue search on his behalf make his story more powerful than that previous classic of the North, Wilfred Grenfell's *Adrift on an Ice-Pan* (1909).

Stories of Eskimo life have little internal variety. The basic needs of food and shelter are at the root of all those we have for children, whether written in another era, such as Stefansson's *Kak the Copper Eskimo* (1924), or Doug Wilkinson's *Sons of the Arctic* (1965). The harsh realities of the northern landscape and climate cannot be denied. The traditional antipathy between Eskimo and Indian, which forms a minor theme in Mowat's *Lost in the Barrens* and in legendary material, is the major one in Houston's *The White Archer*. Survival, however, is still the underlying ingredient. The plot is a simple one—although, as is usual with James Houston, it is designed more for the insight it gives into the Eskimo people and their ways than for narrative interest. An Eskimo family is forced by its laws to offer hospitality to three strangers (also Eskimo) who had just returned from Indian territory—the Land of Little Sticks—where they had desperately hunted game and robbed an Indian camp. The Indians, following their trail, retaliate by mass murder of the Eskimo family who sheltered the strangers. Twelve-year-old Kungo escapes and his young sister is carried off by the Indians. Kungo trains himself for revenge under the guidance of an old, wise, nearly blind archer. Four years later Kungo, now 'the white archer', sets out on his odyssey of hate, his all-white clothes perhaps signifying the North as much as the purity of spirit that is to come to him in the final moments of his revenge. At any rate the story is charged with a mysticism not usual in Eskimo stories. The motif—man's finding himself—is of course basic to all literature.

Akavak and *Wolf Run* are simpler stories but are all the more welcome as books of quality and integrity for younger children.

Stefansson's book, *Kak the Copper Eskimo*, was published in 1924. Stefansson provided the facts and incidents and Violet Irwin made them into a story. It has only a tenuous plot: it is really no more than a series of incidents. Kak often acts as a Tom Sawyer of the North, getting into scrapes, having accidents and getting out of them with considerable credit, and seeking the opportunity to boast about his exploits as tough youngsters around the world love to do.

The most significant difference between Wilkinson, Houston, and Stefansson lies in their style. Wilkinson's is direct, simple, crisp, and modern; Houston almost underwrites to catch the starkness of the Arctic and the stoicism of the young hero; Stefansson, or perhaps Violet Irwin, used the more colloquial and jocular approach that was considered suitable for children in the late nineteenth and early twentieth centuries.

Had Kak been an English or American schoolboy he would doubtless have mumbled, 'All right, Dad', and gone on eating his breakfast without giving any visible sign of this thrill. But an Eskimo never learns to disguise his feelings, so Kak grinned all over his round face and cried: 'Bully! Bully! Me for it! Do you hear, Noashak? I'm to drive the team.'

Strangely enough, and tiresome though its telling may sometimes be, *Kak* is much the most effective book in the portrayal of character. Wilkinson's heroes are only representatives of their type, while Kak is a person with charm, zest, and insouciance. The reader remembers Kak himself, but the boys in *Sons of the Arctic* and even *Tikta'Liktak* are memorable only for their adventures. *Kak the Copper Eskimo* has vitality and verve that have given it a deservedly long life.

Whether written by Eskimo or non-Eskimo, all these stories speak of an eternal struggle with their environment of a people who seemingly will never change. In *Ningiyuk's Igloo World* (1972) Anne Rokeby-Thomas brings the Eskimo world closer to the present with pictures of the trading post, the trek to meet the yearly arrival of the big ship, and above all the erosion of traditional Eskimo beliefs in the face of Christianity.

> *Christmas lasted for many days. The people went back time and time again to the mission. 'Jesus is one of us,' they said, remembering the Christmas story. And they felt a great desire to learn more about Him.*
>
> *But, as in previous visits to the mission, some of the old folk refused to hear the message. 'How can you learn if you refuse to listen?' Ningiyuk begged her grandmother.*
>
> *'Leave me as I am. I'm too old to change.' Itow would shake her head sadly.*

Ningiyuk is a little Eskimo girl, lovable, playful, sometimes protesting over 'women's work'. She enjoys the old tales of her grandmother but accepts her father's and mother's new religion. She learns that she is an adopted child (the Eskimos have a natural, informal style of adoption) and is given a choice of staying with her foster family or joining her real father who has succumbed to the white man's style of living.

With its little-girl character and its intimate view of Eskimo family life, *Ningiyuk's Igloo World* introduces into children's literature about Eskimos a bit of relief from the survival theme. A simple little story, it is all the more revealing for being naive: it was published by a Bible Institute in the United States, but it cannot be dismissed as a piece of religious propaganda. The author spent several years among the Ekaluktuk group near St George's

Mission on Victoria island and from this experience she is able to describe their way of life through the daily activities of a small Eskimo girl who could be any child with a problem similar to hers. The few verses or songs in the book are fundamentalist rather than poetically Eskimo and there is the assumption that Christianity is 'right' for the Eskimo. Yet surely the writer indicates through the character of the grandmother, Itow, that Christianity can be only a veneer on the Eskimo's traditional beliefs. (The great debate on this issue is presented in the very fine adult novel, *The White Eskimo*, by Harold Horwood.)

Two early books—Norman Duncan's *Billy Topsail* (1906) and Ernest Thompson Seton's *Two Little Savages* (1903)—still have something to say to present-day readers. As the son of a deep-sea fisherman in the early 1900s in Newfoundland, Billy Topsail knows no other life than that dictated by the harsh realities of his livelihood. By current standards of social and economic egalitarianism, the book may at times grate, for it conveys an implicit sense of caste; 'people know their place' in life and seek no other. At the end of the rather episodic story, Billy is 'on the books'— accepted as a man by his crew mates, while the son of the owner of the fishing vessel learns that the men who sail his father's ships are everyday heroes. Life for fishermen has changed in the last sixty years, but not in the essential qualities by which men face and wrest a living from the sea. In this major aspect, *Billy Topsail* is part of the continuing tradition of great sea stories.

Seton's *Two Little Savages: Being the Adventures of Two Boys Who Lived as Indians and What They Learned* is in many ways the apotheosis of Canadian children's literature. His two boy heroes, Sam and Yan (Seton himself), are archetypal Canadian boys as they play at being Indians. But the play is serious, as all children's play is serious, although not solemn. As with Seton's animal stories, this book was written out of the author's childhood experiences when he first went to the forests and streams of Ontario to satisfy his 'torment of thirst' for knowledge about woodcraft, birds, animals, and the disappearing customs of the Indians. Seton was a dedicated naturalist and *Two Little Savages*, with its detailed illustrations and marginal sketches, can serve almost as a handbook to the woods. The book's setting is the bushland country around Lindsay, Ont., at the turn of the century. Its theme is man's necessarily close relationship with nature and wild life; its message is survival. Seton was an idealist who loved to learn things and to impart knowledge to others; the didactic approach was integral to his writings—whether subtle (as in his animal stories) or outright (as in *Two Little Savages*). Yet Yan and Sam, particularly Yan, are two of the most appealing boy heroes in Canadian fiction. They are filled with curiosity, prank-ish, high-spirited, and yet, when the occasion arises, they are serious woodsmen.

It may seem odd to group together two authors as disparate as Seton and the modern writer David Walker. Yet the juxtaposition is revealing, for it illustrates the almost infinite malleability of the conflict-within-nature theme. For Seton it serves as the narrative thread for the exposition of woodlore; for Walker it provides the fillip of exciting incident in a story that centres on character rather than on episode or setting.

Walker's *Dragon Hill* (1963) is set vaguely somewhere on the Atlantic coast—perhaps New England or the Bay of Fundy, it does not really matter. Nor does its old-hat theme matter—the crusty, terrifying curmudgeon tamed by children—for this is far from being a stock story. Its author is observant and uncommonly per-ceptive, almost introspective in his search for the truth about his fictional creations. He has not betrayed the grown-up world in order to entertain the half-grown, and the half-grown will enjoy the book all the more for its honest, wry, and sometimes terrify-ing glimpse of the adult world. Instead of the usual shadowy and laughable adults, there is Pugsy the gardener—kind, sane, and perfectly ready to put the boy William in his sometimes small, mean place. So too William's parents are not pieces of cardboard perfection. They have life and vitality of their own; they change and are changed by each other.

Although the motif is familiar, the working out of the plot is highly original. During a hot summer on the Atlantic seaboard, William first dislikes and then forms a bond with his Scottish cousin, Mary, who has come to spend the summer. The children get to know a hermit-like former sea captain, E. McDurgan. Their first reactions are hostile, but half fearing, half fascinated, they go to visit him when ordered; they are particularly taken with a model ship that the captain has taken sixteen years to carve. As the summer draws to an end, the heat increases and tension rises. William's father, who is trying to finish a book, becomes cross and withdrawn; the family finances flounder, with no money to buy a battery for the car or to provide the father with a glass of domestic sherry to help the creative process. The dénouement comes in the form of a hurricane. E. McDurgan rushes to warn the children at their home. The house breaks adrift, and as the father types furiously up in the attic to the music of Bach, all unconscious of what is going on, the captain sails the house like a ship and orders everyone around as if they were his ship's crew. 'Murder and the lash,' he shrieks, and 'Curs-ed wummen!' Finally even the hurricane cannot prevail against him. Is the ending conventional? The reader has to decide.

The settings—coast, woods, trout stream—are freshly conveyed and so is the trimness of the ship's model and her owner's skill in making it. The brief, emphatic, impressionistic style is jagged and jerky, almost deliberately awkward. Occasionally William's comments are sharply reminiscent of Holden Caulfield's: 'He was a very funny man saying crazy things' or: 'He's just about the most famous writer who can't write any more.' Nevertheless, *Dragon Hill* is an always honest and usually successful attempt to employ for children modern techniques of prose writing.

The old man spoke of fall, but he was weeks and weeks too early. Now the days were nearly ninety and the nights were hot. Now it was fierce summer, and the islands shimmered double— real islands and a mirage of them in the heat. Now the blueberries were ripe. Blaeberries she called them until he told her to snap out of it, the whole world wasn't Scotland. Now the woods grew dryer day by day, and a haze of smoke was added to a haze of heat. But forest fires had not come here. Now in the woods you felt the tinder-dryness in your nose. One match—and pouff!— that feeling, even wanting, wicked, no.

The story, slight as it is, is rooted in the moral problems of the real world, not the storybook one—problems of friendship, prejudice, hatred, and sacrifice. It is not quite a great children's book, but it has qualities of truthfulness that lift it out of the class of stock children's stories that were written to sell.

In an even faster-paced novel of intrigue, *Pirate Rock* (1969), David Walker's sure eye for detail, insight into character, and skill in handling conversation never falter. The Bay of Fundy is no vague setting; the two young heroes are at home in it and their knowledge becomes ours (as did that of the boys in De Mille's *B.O.W.C.* a hundred years before). The plot is out of John Buchan, but it has all the rich and convincing touches that have made John Buchan's suspense novels re-readable. The established residents resent the arrival of Frank Becker, obviously wealthy and *nouveau riche* at that, who indulges in fast speed-boats, gourmet picnics, and who fences in the animals (for their protection, he says). The two boys who work for him one summer are the direct cause of his undoing and his death. But they also feel they have betrayed him. Their father, a biologist, acquires the dream of his life—an aquarium—as the result of events. The boys show no interest in it and their mother tries to reason with them:

> *Their father went to the door, turned to speak, but thought better of whatever he had been going to say, and left the room. Soon the Volkswagen drove away.*
>
> *Keith and Nelson stacked the breakfast dishes. 'Boys!' she said before they could escape. 'It would please him so much if you went along.'*
>
> *'I know,' Keith said.*
>
> *'Yeah, I know, Mum,' said Nelson.*
>
> *'But you're not going, is that it?'*
>
> *The boys said nothing.*
>
> *'There are fences and fences,' she said.*
>
> *'How do you mean, Mum?'*
>
> *'There was the one we all hated, and that came down. But you've built another, haven't you?'*
>
> *'We just don't want to go there,' Nelson said. After the first days they had never talked about it to one another, not to Dad and Mum, not to anyone. Shut it off, you could forget about it.*
>
> *'Young people never know how much we depend on you, that's why Dad is so edgy and bothered—because you won't have any part of the things he has slaved for. Do you realise that?'*

Keith nodded, but Nelson said it straight out, 'Dad didn't kill Frank Becker.'

'And Dad didn't do what we did to Mrs. Becker.'

'You're so comforting for someone young,' she had said one day.

For most writers this concluding conversation would be the 'lesson' of the book. For David Walker the lesson grows out of the characters of the boys, which have already been built into the story, and is natural, inevitable, and satisfying.

Stories of outdoor life are not generally written by women. *The Forest Is My Kingdom* (1952) by Janet Carruthers can in no way be described as a feminine look at the wilderness, though the book has a tender quality that is not generally associated with the rough and tough life of the out-of-doors. In dealing with the aspirations of an Indian half-breed boy to become an artist, the author sees more in the northern Ontario wilderness than a challenge to existence and livelihood.

Over in the village there were other children, but Bari had never been drawn to them. They didn't like the things he liked nor did they join him in his wanderings through the deeper bush.

His mother told him stories of far places and peoples, but forest life satisfied him. In his heart he dreamed dreams about trees, flowers and fur-folks, and with a burnt stick tried to make pictures of them on scraps of paper. When his mother bought him pencil and scribbler his joy was complete.

The link between art and outdoor life has always been strong in Canada (the life and work of Paul Kane, Tom Thomson, and A.Y. Jackson, among other painters, have revealed this to us), but only in this book has it been reflected in a way that a child can understand.

The Forest Is My Kingdom is not a tale of high adventure but an episodic account of a boy's development, under adverse circumstances, from childhood to young manhood. Bari's everyday life with a trapper is described, along with his days at an Indian school, his first job at a lumber camp, his relations with the not-always-understanding adults who make up his orphaned world. The writing is casual, unforced, at times colloquial, portraying with some skill the life of a people who do not seek the refinements of civilization. Though the ending assumes that talent is always recognized—that Bari will become a famous painter and his friend Oney a famous singer—and there is no indication that the road to success can be a hard one, optimism has its place in life, and where else should it be found if not in a children's book?

The strong emotional link between our writers and the landscape is nowhere better demonstrated than by a book that does not even have Canada as a background: *The Bushbabies* (1965) by William Stevenson, set in Kenya. Unlike most Canadian outdoor fiction, this story deals not only with the landscape, which is described unforgettably, but with a very modern human problem: race relations. It is as unmoralistic and successful in its treatment of this subject as Mowat's *Lost in the Barrens*. There are three bushbabies. Kamau (the tiny African lemur) is the reason for the week-long trek through the jungles of Kenya; Tembo is the African headman who follows when he is in the white man's world and leads when in his native jungle; Jackie is the thirteen-year-old daughter of a game warden, the owner of Kamau and the instigator of the journey. Mistakenly thinking that Kamau, her beloved pet, is threatened, Jackie leaves the ship that is to carry her back to England, sees it sail without her, finds her father's headman, Tembo, and persuades him to conduct her 100 miles up country to return Kamau to the place where he was first captured. On the way she hopes to train him to hunt for himself. Event piles upon event, and danger upon danger. Jackie is listed as a white girl kidnapped by an African and eventually the order comes: 'Shoot to kill.' Jackie and Tembo meet the perils of jungle animal life; they are shot at by a pygmy, mistakenly 'rescued', wind their way through a forest fire, and finally survive the beginning of the famous Hundred Days of storm and flood. Too much? Well, it is all grippingly believable.

The landscape itself is part of the story, not only determining the action but often actively participating in it. Although we feel the immense sweep of East Africa, Mr Stevenson's small and intimate details of life and lore gradually lend to an unknown country complete familiarity. This is undeniably one of the finest novels for the young written by a Canadian.

The more immediate sociological and racial implications of the meeting of European and indigenous cultures in modern times have provided the theme for a few books about modern Indians: *No Word for Good-Bye* (1969) and *Zach* (1972) by John Craig, *River of Stars* (1971) by Jean MacKenzie, *A Nice Fire and Some Moonpennies* (1972) by Dorris Heffron, and *Never Step on an Indian's Shadow* (1973) by Diana Walker.

In all these stories the cultural difference becomes a 'problem' and is the *raison d'être* of the novel—that is, the problem provides the only plot mechanism. In describing John Craig's *No Word for Good-Bye*, one would not say 'this is the story of a friendship between two boys', but between a white boy and an *Indian* boy. Such books also veer away from a completely outdoor setting to a semi-urban or urban one. *No Word for Good-Bye* is set in a summer resort in Manitoba within commuting distance from the city. *Zach* is a peripatetic highway novel with glimpses of small-town life in the midwestern United States and of Winnipeg and Thunder Bay in Canada. *River of Stars* reveals the life of a fishing community (Rivers Inlet) on the coast of British Columbia. *A Nice Fire and Some Moonpennies* moves in locale from Kingston to Yorkville Street in Toronto and *Never Step on an Indian's Shadow* is set in Moosonee, Ont.

John Craig's *No Word for Good-Bye* is the most generally satisfying novel of the group, with straightforward, competent writing and a conclusion that is based on the inner inevitability of events. In the face of prejudice and accusations against a nearby Ojibway band, Ken's father and some of the local adults support the Indians. They try, but fail, to establish the Indians' rights to the land on which they have settled. When Ken returns at Thanksgiving to spend a planned weekend with his Indian friend Paul, the band has disappeared and Paul has been left no message. An earlier conversation between the two boys gives the explanation.

'By the way,' Ken asked, 'how do you say good-bye in Ojibway?'

'We don't say it,' Paul answered. He thought for a moment.

'We say B'jou when we meet somebody, and the same thing when we leave them. But in Ojibway there is no word for good-bye.'

Zach is a far more contrived novel and the machinery shows—i even creaks. Although written in 1972, it uses the slang and th 'going down the road' formula of the youth cult of the 1960s, both of which seem a hundred years old. Zach is an Indian youth o sixteen who suddenly learns that he is not an Ojibway but ar Agawa and the last of his tribe. (Agawa is apparently fictitiou and should perhaps be taken as a symbol.) He sets out to try t find his people and on his journey meets a black youth who had been tricked by his sports promoters and a young girl who ha thrown off the bonds of her middle-class family. With othe travellers they finally decide to try communal living. As artificia as the story is, John Craig has an eye for place and his descrip tions of the seedy parts of small towns and of some eccentri characters in them give the book its only memorable moments.

Jean MacKenzie's *River of Stars* tells of an Indian boy's struggle against the racial antipathy of some of the fishermen who sai out of a small British Columbia fishing community and of his attempt to instil in his father some pride in his heritage In many ways the unpolished style suits the rough setting an characters, but the writing is totally undistinguished. Yet it carries the story with an honesty and unpretentiousness that is com pletely lacking in Diana Walker's *Never Step on an Indian's Shadow*. A young Montreal girl, visiting her sister in Moosonee is bored with her summer and makes friends with an Indian youth Teresa is a selfish young teenager, always concerned about he own reactions. She feels satisfied only when she acquires a white boy friend at the end of the story. Her contacts in the Indian vil lage are treated subjectively, on her terms. When Teresa gives ar old Indian a pie she has baked, the Indians express their thanks by organizing a dance.

At first she was stiff and self-conscious, afraid that they would laugh at her, but soon the closely swaying bodies, the weird chant- ing and stamping of feet began to hypnotize her. She felt an exhilarating freedom sweep over her, a feeling of belonging to a tremendously ancient culture. At last she could abandon hersel,

entirely to the music. The shacks of Indian Village disappeared.
She was no longer Teresa Denys of Montreal. Now she, too, was
a child of the wind, a daughter of the white whales, and she was
dancing with her brothers. We are all one, she kept thinking. We
are all the same now.

The author seems to know nothing of the fantastical elements
involved in such a ritual but uses the incident merely as a superficial, romantic, and (considering Teresa's character) quite unconvincing injection of brotherhood.

There is no sociology at all in Dorris Heffron's *A Nice Fire and*
Some Moonpennies, which is refreshing, considering the subject.
The story is told by a sixteen-year-old Iroquois girl who lives with
her highly artistic mother in a 'pad' in Kingston. The language is
that of a highly intelligent girl but it is steeped in the teenage
patois of the 1960s. It is sad that the writer, beginning with an
unusual and potentially rich background, should move Maizie on
to the drug scene in Yorkville (Toronto), for here the setting
becomes a stereotype of all the articles and news items written
about the place at that time. The Yorkville drug scene might have
been described truly and powerfully in retrospect, but there is
little here to understand or savour.

These few novels of modern Indian life and problems represent
almost the only Canadian examples of the new 'realism' that has
infiltrated children's books, particularly those from the United
States, since the beginning of the 1960s. In a sociological sense
these books were undoubtedly the outcome of a fast-changing
society and its great and all-pervasive voice—television. By reason
of their harsh interpretation of reality they have tended to push
children out of their childhood into an ever-more youthful adoles-
cence, but with the knowledge and weight of adult problems upon
them. These books seemed to revolutionize children's literature,
but it was not a true revolution and it can be seen now as unfortunate. The American writers of the new realism in fact adopted
the old-fashioned and narrow view of nineteenth-century realism:
'the deliberate refusal to select subjects from the beautiful and
harmonious, but instead and even more deliberately to select un-
savoury and distasteful topics' (*Encyclopaedia Britannica*). In this

pursuit the average American work of fiction for children lost its shape as a novel. The story-cum-adventure became the fictional equivalent of the 'young person's guide to problems'—psychological, physical, and sociological—and had as little artistry or depth in its style as a TV script. Not surprisingly, the majority of them became formula books with token characters. As a colleague of mine has said: 'Take two representatives of oppressed minority groups, assorted sleazy settings and happenings, lashings of social protest, abundant enthusiasm and minimal skill—feed this into a writing machine and out pops another pot-boiler.'*

Almost none of these quite dramatic shifts in subject, taste, and style showed up in Canada during the same period. Canadian children's books, whether deliberately or because of the innate conservatism of their writers, did not join the mainstream of current writing. While American (and to a lesser extent, British and Australian) children, as seen through the books written for them, were coping with ineffectual parents, no parents, one parent, being unhappy, growing up, tuning in, dropping out, or brushing up against drugs, alcohol, homosexuality and racism, Canadian children were still visiting a lighthouse, crossing the barrens, discovering a cache of Indian relics, catching a bank robber, or getting a pony for Christmas. Two books published in the 1970s, however, indicated that Canadian writers might not let the wave of American realism expend itself without attempting this kind of fiction themselves. *Just Gin* (1973) by Wallis Kendal describes in rather sub-standard language a year in the school life of a teen-aged girl who is parentless, and in *Fly Away, Paul* (1974) Peter Davies (a newcomer to Canada) includes explicit scenes of cruelty and sexuality in his story about a boy's home in Montreal.

Most of the American problem books seem to demand an urban setting, and it may be Canadian writers' lack of interest in such a setting that has prevented the development of a similar type of novel in this country. With regard to fiction for children generally, this is an unfortunate blind spot, considering that about eighty per cent of our population lives in cities and that children

*Roy Stokes in a speech to the Canadian Association of Children's Librarians, Winnipeg, Man., June 25, 1974.

ike to identify themselves with fictional characters who share their own experiences. This sense of identification has been a strong element in the attraction of children to the American realistic novel, but in Canada the exploitation of city life has been largely left to the superficialities of the career story and a few mystery stories.

STORIES OF CHILD AND FAMILY LIFE

After the strong outdoor settings of most of the boys' adventure stories of Seton, Haig-Brown, Mowat, and Walker, some recent minor but often more charming books have what might be described as a semi-urban setting. One such, *Kristli's Trees* (1948), was published over twenty years ago but has recently been republished in paperback. It is set in the Mennonite community just outside Kitchener. As a long-time librarian in Kitchener, Mabel Dunham understood and appreciated the Mennonites' determination to make and keep their own patterns of living, and her book reflects that knowledge and love. A very simple tale for younger readers, it tells of the rather quiet everyday doings of Kristli, a little Mennonite boy; the climax of the story is a struggle with his conscience. The book has the honesty, serenity, and deliberate simplicity that we associate with Mennonite life.

Luella Creighton in *The Hitching Post* (1969) has added a touch of romance to goodness, and in so doing has almost re-created Frances Hodgson Burnett's *A Little Princess*. In the village of Crabtree lives a poor little girl whose only possession is a hitching post that she believes is a magic horse that will bring her mother back to her. But the magic really comes from an elderly gentleman who provides her with marvellous meals, served by his man-servant in an old shoemaker's shop. One day a car is driven to her door and a tall man gets out:

'I'm looking,' said the tall old man, 'for a young lady called Cecilia Crabtree. My name is McGinty and I'm a dealer in magic.' He looked up at the sky as if he expected, perhaps, that Cecilia Crabtree might drop from a passing cloud.

Cecilia edged over to the hitching post horse and touched his iron curls.

'I am Cecilia Crabtree.'
'You are? How extremely fortunate.'
He leaned into the car and picked out a big box. He dropped it
at Cecilia's feet. 'Parcel for you,' he said briefly, leapt into his car,
and was gone.

This is the kind of story that went out of style with the late Victorian age, but in the midst of the ugly realism of most modern American children's books, the quality of innocence and artlessness in a child character and the atmosphere of a small village untouched by modern problems are most refreshing. It is also an exciting little tale.

The quintessence of the authentic fictional treatment of family life, at least where Canadian children's books are concerned, is represented by Judith St John's *Where the Saints Have Trod* (1974). For its warm and honest portrayal of the everyday life of a close-knit family in a small community, one has to seek comparison with two charming books about Eskimos, Stefansson's *Kak the Copper Eskimo* and Rokeby-Thomas's *Ningiyuk's Igloo World.* St John, however, deals with life in the family of a Methodist parson in southern Ontario some fifty years ago. It is not a novel in the strict sense, since it is a collection of episodes, but it conveys a small happy world of children's pastimes and mild small-town incidents with great warmth, believability, and quiet humour. The Methodist affiliation of this family was of course central to all its activities, but religious observances and the serene life that surrounded them are unaffectedly presented. The book portrays a way of life that will be recognized nostalgically by many adults. Whether children will respond to it with interest is a question, for its depiction of a joyful childhood unmarked by jarring episodes is far removed from the world of today's TV watchers. However, in its artless handling of simple concerns and enjoyments that to some degree are part of almost any childhood —having scarlet fever, moving, a makeshift wedding—it is a book that anyone can savour.

Cliff Faulknor's *The In-Betweener* (1967) is closer to the theme of many a modern American realistic novel—the alienation of a young teenager from his father. But here Canadian restraint is imposed, along with common sense: the hard-working father is often no more than justly impatient with his son's lapses into carelessness and dilatoriness (farm life is hard), but he also recognizes his son's need for a dog, which comes to be a bit of a trial. The story is shaped by a strong setting (West Vancouver, probably in the first quarter of the twentieth century) and by an adventure—Chad runs into and eludes a gang of bank robbers and is able to clear his uncle's name. As in Faulknor's Indian stories of the past, the conversation is both natural and enlightening.

'Why do people drive into the bush and drink this stuff?' Jinx wondered, wrinkling his nose in distaste. 'Sure doesn't smell very good to me.' One of the bottles had a patch of mildew in the bottom.

Chad shrugged indifferently. 'I dunno. My dad says once you start drinking, it sort of takes ahold of you and you can't quit. He'd be plenty mad if he heard about me carting these things up to Riverside.'

'Can't see him objecting to your making a bit of money. Pop says your dad still has the first nickel he ever got, and the hand that gave it to him.'

'Never you mind what your pop says,' Chad told him belligerently, 'or I just might bop you with one of these here beer bottles. Now grab onto this sack and boost it up on my shoulder. Do I have to do all the work around here?'

MYSTERY—ADVENTURE STORIES

The transition now shifts abruptly to lesser authors and to works that, in a country with more first-class books, would perhaps not warrant description. To consider them at all raises the question: does it matter that they are not very good? In what way are they not as good as the best?

Does it matter? A great part of many people's reading is for pastime. No one pretends that the average Canadian adventure or mystery story is great literature. Many of these books are read to be enjoyed and forgotten, and so it can easily be maintained that there is no point in considering them further. Yet even among 'entertainments' (to use Graham Greene's famous classification), there are marked gradations in value and success. Since no author deliberately intends to produce a poor book, we cannot help trying to account for the failures.

In many of the middling and forgettable stories for children there is a sort of dishonesty. It is generally a sin of omission. The adult world is left out and along with it the complexities, sorrows, and humdrum difficulties of everyday life. When adults appear (generally parents), they are simply foils for the child protagonists, who effortlessly manipulate and triumph over their simple-minded and good-natured seniors. The device is borrowed from the comic strips and unfortunately it makes many books as empty and as unreal as comic strips.

Another glaring omission in many different stories has to do with the descriptive matter. Crusoe's possessions, the size of the Lilliputians, the design of the *Nautilus* are remembered by many of us because their authors envisaged them in detail. The second-rate writer is content with vague descriptions that cannot convey more than hazy impressions.

To compensate for deficiencies, the mediocre writer will rely on 'effects': frequently on an unnaturally fast pace and endless turns of plot; sometimes on a billboard-like display of background. Or he may use a plethora of unbelievable incidents in an attempt to obscure the lack of inner inevitability in the development of the story.

Most of the characteristic defects of the unsuccessful 'entertainment' can be found in the 'Secret Circle Mysteries', which contain such titles as *The Mystery of Monster Lake* (1962), *The Mystery of the Muffled Man* (1962), *The Mystery of the Missing Emerald* (1963), *The Clue of the Dead Duck* (1962). It is an open publishing secret that a title containing the word 'mystery' or its synonym has a good chance of selling well. That mystery stories have an immediate and genuine appeal for children is beyond dispute, and that a reading of a few silly stock ones won't do any harm even if it won't do any good is also unarguable. Some children enjoy them as pastime reading, much as children of a previous generation whiled away hours on the stories of English boarding schools. However, the exploitation of the word 'mystery' in children's books is a little more serious than in those for adults.

An adult pursuing books like *The Mystery of the Black Orchid* and *The Case of the Missing Secretary* has his tastes settled and probably wouldn't enjoy the outstanding mysteries, such as Josephine Tey's *The Daughter of Time* or Dorothy Sayers' *Gaudy Night*, anyway. Many outstanding children's books are also good mysteries in the broad sense—Stevenson's *Treasure Island*, Masefield's *Jim Davis*, Leon Garfield's *Smith*, and David Walker's *Pirate Rock*. The trouble with books, and particularly a series of books, that emphasize the word 'mystery' and then turn out to be not so mysterious after all is that they tend to limit a child's idea of what a really good mystery can be.

The 'Secret Circle' books are not wholly bad; a few have a certain narrative power and a good sense of pace. Most of them have been written by professional writers—Robert Thomas Allen, Lawrence Earl, Max Braithwaite, among others—some of whom have achieved commendable standards in other fields of literature. However, they suffer more from dishonesty than do most of the poor and middling books written for adults. The advertising claim that 'each story [is] set in a different part of Canada' lends them a potential interest that the treatment never realizes. The characters are so busy scrambling from one incident to the next that the reader has no opportunity to form an impression of the surroundings. The authors lack either the feeling, the power of expression, or the space to create atmosphere. Since the number of pages in each book varies only from 156 to 160, we must presume that the author has been required to write to a set length. This hardly allows him any individuality of approach. Indeed, it is possible to chart these books by patterns: villains break into the hero's house —six books; central cast of two boys and one girl—six books; central character kidnapped or held prisoner—seven books; and so on.

Unfortunately some of the 'Secret Circle' books attempt to 'teach', and this neutralizes whatever merit they may have as mysteries. Thus *The Mystery of the Disappearing Dogs* by Arthur Hammond, while using some of the techniques of Kästner's *Emil and the Detectives* quite effectively, also uses an adventure as a diatribe against animal vivisection and in so doing gives a completely unfavourable and unfair picture of medical research. In

The Secret Tunnel Treasure, also by Arthur Hammond, the children are given to laboured sociological disquisitions that presumably represent French-Catholic and English-Protestant viewpoints. In *The Valley of the Vanishing Birds*, Max Braithwaite endeavours to interpret white-Indian relationships. All these problems are handled ineptly, they have no real connection with the main stream of the story, and they jar whatever storytelling quality there is. To compare the 'Secret Circle' books with one another (they could never stand up to competition outside the series), *The Clue of the Dead Duck* by Scott Young is outstanding. More characterization is attempted here than in the other books and the children have some genuine emotions and believable problems. Yet basically it reads like a caricature of a novel for adults.

In tune with the Canadian penchant for outdoor life, most Canadian mysteries for children take place in large settings: the coastal waters of British Columbia, the woods of Northern Ontario, the Athabaska tar sands. As these environments are developed, they demand special skills, knowledge, and physical strength from those who would move capably through them. It is quite understandable, then, for the protagonists of such stories to be men and young men whose abilities in sailing, flying, and woodcraft play a key part in the plots. In Edmund Cosgrove's *Windigo Wings* (1967) and *The Terror of the Tar Sands* (1968) two veterans of the Korean War operate a small bush airline. In Ted Ashlee's *Voyage into Danger* (1971) and *Night of the Sasquatch* (1973) the crew of the *Gabriola*, which plies the waters of the British Columbia coast, are rough and tough, have hearts of gold, and often bow to the wisdom of the sixteen-year-old cabin boy.

There is no reason why children should read only about children and, in fact, they do not. In the mystery-story field, for example, they range from Conan Doyle to Alfred Hitchcock. But books such as those by Cosgrove and Ashlee do not have the insight into child-life of a good children's mystery (such as Philippa Pearce's *Minnow on the Say*) or the full-bodied characteristics of an adult mystery. They remain 'junior plots', copying the poorer intrigue and spy aspects of adult stories and relying, as Cosgrove does, on such stock descriptive phrases as 'the big Indian' or 'the slender French-Canadian' to indicate character.

That the outdoor mystery can be successful is seen in Lucy Berton Woodward's *Kidnapped in the Yukon* (1968). Woodward not only has a firm hand on the Yukon wilderness but an even surer touch with her boy hero who, although summoning resourcefulness and courage for his ordeal in the wilderness, is prey to boyish fears and misery. Instead of the large-scale international conspiracies of Ashlee and Cosgrove, there is simply a poor old prospector who, suddenly maddened by years of being unable to find gold, makes up for his failure by robbing a bank. In his flight he accidentally kidnaps a young boy who is sleeping in a canoe (against his father's orders) and there are days of flight through the wilderness with the boy as a prisoner. This is a childlike story that enlists the reader's sympathy by means of protagonists who are not clever and able-bodied men.

The use of children, however, is no guarantee of success. In Carl Barton's *Robber's Roost* (1972) three children (of assorted ages) set out to solve the mystery of some articles that have disappeared from their island summer cottages. The ingredients seem just right: the children are self-reliant, but subject to adult care; the details and hazards of sailing are realistic; various clues are followed up. But the story fails chiefly from dullness. The final revelation is accidental rather than the result of detective work, and the style, and so all that goes with it, is completely lacking in conviction. Girls do play a major role in this book, but not with any sparkle. It is a nine-year-old boy who is the major hero at the end and who also indicates his disdain of females at two points in the story. The book might well call down the wrath of the Women's Liberation Movement except that it is hardly worth being taken seriously.

Pace—or a reader's compulsion to keep turning a page to find out what happens next—is important in a novel, especially a mystery novel. Clark Wallace's *Montreal Adventure* (1967) sustains interest to the end not only through its tightly knit plot but through the plausibility of the children's actions within it. Listening to their home-made radio, they stumble upon a 'gang' engaged in an international art theft and with the final help of the police they 'foil the villains'. This is the traditional form of the mystery story for children: the youthful characters are both childlike and competent and they never over-step either characteristic; the adults are first skeptical, then helpful and rescuing, and the Montreal place-names and buildings are not belaboured. Some expertise in style would have made *Montreal Adventure* a first-rate story. Richard Wright's *Andrew Tolliver* (1965), which is almost a 'tour de force' as a mystery story for younger children, is a spoof on the mystery story. Harmony is celebrating its one hundredth anniversary with a fair, a circus, decorations, speeches, and the mayor dressed up as Sir John A. Macdonald. When a bank robber also appears as Sir John the amusement begins. It is original, exciting, and presents a vivid picture of small-town life.

Yet the dominant impression left by all Canadian mystery-adventures is that anything is good enough for a child reader. If children themselves do not have the experience to resent the condescension, then the responsible adult should be resentful on their behalf. After all, there are more than enough examples of first-rate mystery-adventure or detective stories for children to prove that popularity and excellence are quite compatible in even this least pretentious of genres. Erich Kästner's *Emil and the Detectives* (Germany), Cecil Day-Lewis's *The Otterbury Incident* (England), and Paul Berna's *The Horse Without a Head* (France) are only a few examples that contain fast-paced action, exciting detective work, and believable events and children.

The mystery story, like so much other Canadian writing for children, has strength in its settings but fails through poor writing and a propensity to teach or inculcate good values. Cosgrove and Ashlee introduce characters belonging to ethnic groups other than Anglo-Saxon and do it quite naturally; but then they leave them looking somewhat ridiculous. A band of Indians decide to flee their land because of their superstitious fear of the Indian evil spirit, the Windigo *(The Terror of the Tar Sands)*. A Chinese family is effusively grateful to the point of caricature *(Voyage into Danger)*. There is also in these books an effort to make sure that improper behaviour is at least recognized as such.

Children, wishing to escape their home to continue their investigations, say, 'Well, I'll tell mother a lie, but she will understand when all is known' (a paraphrase from two novels, Joan Seager's *The Vengeance of Wol* and Clarke Wallace's *Montreal Adventure*). In the outstanding children's mystery-adventures—Walter Macken's *The Island of the Great Yellow Ox* or T.H. White's *The Master*, for example—children are plummeted into adventures when their parents are not around. This, of course, relieves them of such moralistic decisions and offers readers what they want in a mystery—larger-than-life situations that can be coped with through courage, ingenuity, and the outwitting of adults. And, of course, the divorce from the child's everyday world gives the good mystery an especially chilling and spine-tingling quality. The antiseptic quality of Canadian mystery stories for children makes one long for the irrationality and the fantasy of *Doc Savage* and *Dr. Fu Manchu*.

HORSE AND DOG STORIES

The literature of the domesticated (or semi-domesticated) pet is far too wide-ranging for any rigid classification. It can encompass a straightforward story like Eric Knight's *Lassie-Come-Home*, in which the dog's instinctive journey home provides the drama, or a novel such as William Armstrong's *Sounder*, in which the ravaged and mutilated dog symbolizes the suffering of oppressed humanity; or Norman Duncan's *Billy Topsail* (1906) which, though mainly a sea story, has a memorable account of Billy's life being saved by his Newfoundland dog. In a great many horse and dog stories the plots almost always concern their young owners, who change and develop because of their love for and their responsibilities to their charges. They are therefore more accurately described as stories of child and family life. But the pet is the 'deus ex machina' for the events and a natural focal point for the young reader's sympathy and interest.

Morley Callaghan's *Luke Baldwin's Vow* (1948; reprinted in 1973) is now even more old-fashioned than *Billy Topsail* and far more didactic. Callaghan used the boy-dog theme to present a conflict between materialism and idealism. On the death of his father, Luke goes to live with his uncle in Collingwood, Ont., a setting that does give the story an attractive quality. He has been brought up in the humanistic tradition of his doctor-father, but is suddenly faced with the utilitarianism of his uncle; whatever is not useful must go, including the old, sick dog on whom Luke, in his loneliness, has lavished all his affection. The boy's love and courage and the pragmatism of another adult eventually save the dog. Like many other didactic writers, Callaghan trips himself with his ending. Does humanism really win?

Putting his head down on the dog's neck, he [Luke] vowed to himself fervently that he would always have some money on hand, no matter what became of him, so that he would be able to protect all that was truly valuable from the practical people in the world.

With this message, *Luke Baldwin's Vow* is memorable only for its reciprocal love between boy and dog.

The two children in David Walker's *Big Ben* (1969) are not so emotionally involved with their St Bernard, although they love Ben and are equally protected by him and protective of him. The major difference between *Big Ben* and *Luke Baldwin's Vow* lies in David Walker's more optimistic view of life. He always provides his child protagonists with interesting and decent parents. When Ben is unjustly accused by a crude and eccentric neighbour of killing his sheep, it is the mother who takes to the barricades in the dog's defence. *Big Ben* is a simply told book for younger children, but even here David Walker shows his firm, sane grasp on reality.

In Charles Perkins' *Molly*—the story of a boy and another St Bernard dog—the life of the town is a strong part of the story:

Our town was on the edge of the great northern forest that stretches across Canada from the Prairies to the Arctic tundra. When I was a boy it was almost as untouched and unknown as in the days of the early explorers, and men came into town out of the north woods where they had lived for months and perhaps years in isolation, hunting and trapping or prospecting for gold in the mountain streams.

The town, which seems to have a timeless quality, is the kind of place where boys can be boys, break a leg on a dare, get acquainted with a timber wolf, and be friendly with the Mounted Police. But it is not always an understanding place. Even though Molly has saved a child's life, the townspeople protest when, after the loss of her puppies, she becomes over-protective of her young master. After several incidents when she threatens people who she thinks are harming the boy, she has to be given away. And, with her going, the boy's childhood seems to end.

Irony gives the story depth, as it also does in Adelaide Leitch's *The Blue Roan* (1971). Roddy does not quite know why he chose the little blue roan over the horse that had been recommended to him, but he quickly finds in the roan and in its skill at competition some compensation for his unhappiness at school and for his father's lack of attention to him. In many modern books for children, such a boy would turn to drugs or crime, etc. Here the boy's problem is worked out in terms of his relationship with the horse. When it throws him, the resulting broken leg is less painful than the shock to his ego. At the end he has to come to an understanding of his horse and to help his little sister. 'Old-hat' though it is, this theme of child-animal relations has been used in a well-crafted and believable story.

OUTDOOR LIFE AND ADVENTURE

BICE, CLARE. *Across Canada: Stories of Canadian Children.* Illustrated by the author. Toronto, Macmillan, 1949. 122 pp.
An attempt to instruct children about Canada in fictional form.

BICE, CLARE. *A Dog for Davie's Hill.* Illustrated by the author. Toronto, Macmillan, 1956. 120 pp.
This story of the training of a sheep dog on a Highland farm has considerable atmosphere and a few exciting moments. All in all it holds the interest more firmly than Bice's stories with a Canadian setting.

BICE, CLARE. *Jory's Cove: A Story of Nova Scotia.* Illustrated by the author. New York, Macmillan, 1941. 104 pp.
A story of boats and the sea for young children. Although the plot lacks continuity, the atmosphere and background of a small fishing village give life to the various episodes.

CARRUTHERS, JANET. *The Forest Is My Kingdom.* Illustrated by P.A. Jobson London, Oxford, 1952. 231 pp.

The background is conventionally Canadian: life in the northern Ontario woods, animal lore, the passing of the seasons. Bari, a half-breed boy wants to draw and has the compulsion of genius to capture his 'forest kingdom' on whatever scraps of paper he can find, beg, buy or steal. Looked after by a lonely trapper and attending an Indian school, he faces doubt and bewilderment in himself as well as (at times) the misunderstanding of the adults who make up his orphaned world. The dialogue is natural and the events are gently paced, but the ending almost verges on the sentimental. However, while the whole is something of a forest 'idyll', the treatment shows a sensitivity to nature and people that is rare in this type of outdoor story and as a result the book is firmly grounded in reality.

CHILDERHOSE, ROBERT J. *Fighter Pilot.* Illustrated by William Wheeler. Toronto, McClelland and Stewart, 1965. 158 pp.

A self-taught Canadian pilot of seventeen eventually joins the RAF and fights in the Battle of Britain. The author's ability to describe action cannot hide the mediocre dialogue and characterization. The penchant that Canadian writers have for larding fiction with dragged-in fact has some advantage here because, as a war story, the facts do give some depth to the hero's personal crisis.

CLEMSON, DONOVAN. *Lost Mine.* Illustrated by David Craig. Toronto, Macmillan, 1967. 176 pp.

Sixteen-year-old Paul accompanies his uncle on a prospecting trip into the interior mountains of British Columbia. The story is rich in prospecting lore and dull in adventure.

COMOCK. *The Story of Comock the Eskimo.* As told to Robert Flaherty. Edited by Edmund Carpenter. New York, Simon & Schuster, 1968. 90 pp.

Faced with starvation, two Eskimo families risk a journey to an island rich in game. Ten years later one family makes the equally hazardous journey back to the mainland. Their true adventures, written down years later by Robert Flaherty, are recounted in the voice of the father, Comock, and presented in sharp, film-like episodes. This powerful story was not particularly intended for children, but its simple style, a multitude of small drawings from the collection of the Royal Ontario Museum, and its picture-storybook format should be an enticement to them.

CRISP, WILLIAM G. *Ook-Pik: the Story of an Eskimo Boy.* Illustrated by Jean Crisp. Toronto, Dent, 1952. 151 pp.

The details of Eskimo life, both old and new, are presented through the adventures of a twelve-year-old Eskimo boy. Simply written for younger children.

DEWDNEY, SELWYN H. *The Map That Grew.* Illustrated by the author. Toronto, Oxford, 1960. 32 pp.

The intention of this book is avowedly informational, although it is cast in fictional form. It is quite effective, however, in making mapping and surveying a fascinating topic for younger readers.

DUNCAN, NORMAN. *The Adventures of Billy Topsail.* New York, Revell, 1906. 331 pp.
This has provided good reading for many years. Although somewhat old-fashioned in style and outlook, it still holds its place by reason of its integrity as it tells of the men who fought for a living in the fishing grounds of Newfoundland in the early twentieth century. This was the first in a popular series of Billy Topsail books.

FEATHER, JEAN HAYES. *Sawtooth Harbour Boy.* Illustrated by Lisa Calvert. Toronto, Nelson, 1973. 128 pp.
The harshness of existence and the joys of family life in an outpost in Newfoundland in the 1920s are revealed through the exploits of Billy at school, at play, and at work. This is a gentle narrative, almost a memoir (it is based on the author's own family experiences), and so never rises to the dramatic tension of Farley Mowat's *The Black Joke* (Newfoundland in the 1930s) or of the classic tales of Newfoundland, *Billy Topsail* and *Captains Courageous.*

FORD, FRED. *Atush Inlet.* Drawings by Anne Fines. Toronto, Nelson, 1972. 148 pp.
Two boys learn the skills of water and wilderness from experienced and friendly adults along the northern British Columbia coast. The author has the knowledge to write a useful 'how-to-do-it' book but little idea of the craftsmanship necessary for fiction.

HAIG-BROWN, RODERICK L. *Mounted Police Patrol.* London, Collins, 1954. 191 pp.
The everyday work of a Mountie in a district of Alberta is presented without fanfare, but the overtly moral tone makes this a far less compelling book than the author's *Starbuck Valley Winter* and *Saltwater Summer.*

HAIG-BROWN, RODERICK L. *Starbuck Valley Winter.* New York, Morrow, 1943. 310 pp.
Seventeen-year-old Don Morgan spends a winter trapping in the wilds of British Columbia. An outstanding tale of the outdoors and a perceptive look at a boy reaching out to be a man.

HAIG-BROWN, RODERICK L. *Saltwater Summer.* New York, Morrow, 1948. 256 pp.
In this sequel to *Starbuck Valley Winter,* Don Morgan and his friend Tubby engage in the hazards of commercial fishing. The excitement and drama created by the sea do not over-shadow the drama of people's lives.

HAMBLETON, JACK. *Abitibi Adventure.* Decorations by Thoreau MacDonald. Toronto, Longman, 1950. 173 pp.

The standard attained by Canada's most prolific writer for boys is less than average. While the author's knowledge of such topics as bush flying, forest fires, conservation, and the forestry industry is extensive, the writing is invariably coy, puerile, or at its best a mere recounting of facts. His chief hero, Bill Hanson, has some incredibly responsible jobs for a person who is often described as a 'youngster' or a 'boy' or a 'youth'. His dog, of course, is almost human. The author's books provide a good example of how outdoor action tales can be made popular with little or no writing ability. Other titles are: *Forest Ranger* (1948), *Cub Reporter* (1951), *Charter Pilot* (1952), and *Wings Over Labrador* (1957).

HINDS, MARGERY. *Makpa: The Story of an Eskimo-Canadian Boy.* Illustrated by Doug Sneyd. Toronto, McGraw-Hill Ryerson, 1971. 142 pp.
The story covers one year in the life of Makpa, an eleven-year-old Eskimo boy living in a remote community of Baffin Island. The hardship of life in a barren land and the changes brought by modern technology are realistically examined as Makpa, accompanying his father on a trip by dogsled to gather food, manages to kill a polar bear, which he decides to sell for a snowmobile. The story lacks excitement and a sense of adventure and mystery.

HOUSTON, ALMA G. *Nuki.* Illustrated by James Houston. Philadelphia, Lippincott, 1953. 151 pp.
Nuki, an eleven-year-old Eskimo boy of Baffin Island, does not have 'adventures' but takes part in the hunting when his father is lost, with the resulting daily drama that is forced upon those who hunt daily for their food. The style of writing has a simplicity and a restraint that the North seems to impose on those who write about it.

HOUSTON, JAMES. *Akavak: An Eskimo Journey.* Illustrated by the author. Toronto, Longman, 1968. 80 pp.
Akavak's grandfather wants to see his brother before he dies and the young boy supports him on a long and difficult journey, only to see him die as it is accomplished. The wisdom and strength of the old man are a reassurance to the boy in the face of terrifying hardships. The narrative has a simple, pure line; this, combined with effective pictures, offers a powerful revelation of Eskimo life for younger children.

HOUSTON, JAMES. *Tikta'Liktak: An Eskimo Legend.* Illustrated by the author. Toronto, Longman, 1965. 63 pp.
The young Eskimo who survived on a floating ice-pan, existed on a barren island, and made a startling escape to the mainland has now become a legend in the Arctic. Like all great legends and hero stories, this one is stronger than the immediate actions described and distils the essence of the heroic in Eskimo life. A memorable book.

HOUSTON, JAMES. *The White Archer: An Eskimo Legend.* Illustrated by the author. Toronto, Longman, 1967. 95 pp.

A young Eskimo trains himself for an act of revenge, but his bitter feeling is finally conquered by the wisdom and kindness of an old couple who befriend him. In all his writing Houston continues to show a people who overcome their problems of living in a frozen land by an inner warmth and love.

HOUSTON, JAMES. *Wolf-Run: A Caribou Eskimo Tale.* Illustrated by the author. Toronto, Longman, 1971. 64 pp.
This simple story of a search for food has a slightly mystical quality: two wolves after caribou seem to help young Punik, bringing him closer to the teachings of his grandparents. James Houston has a remarkable ability for making the strange, hard world of the Eskimo believable to the city dweller.

HYDE, LAURENCE. *Under the Pirate Flag.* Illustrated by Victor Mays. Boston, Houghton Mifflin, 1965. 196 pp.
A Canadian contribution to the pirate story in the tradition of *Treasure Island.* That it begins and ends in Nova Scotia in the late 1700s is incidental to the fact that it has an engaging hero, a whole parcel of convincing cutthroats, and a fast-paced plot.

MCEVOY, BERNARD (ed.). *Stories from Across Canada.* Toronto/Montreal, McClelland and Stewart, 1966. 109 pp.
A miscellany of thirteen short stories and chapters from novels. The writing is good but the choices represent merely the traditional wood-and-forest aspect of Canadian children's literature. The format is very dull.

MacKENZIE, JEAN. *Storm Island.* Illustrated by Gordon Rayner. Toronto, Macmillan, 1968. 115 pp.
In many ways this is the typical Canadian outdoor-adventure story: it has an authentic setting (here a lighthouse off the northern coast of British Columbia), a city boy who has to adjust to isolated living, a dog (and its attendant problems), a secret cave, and a storm. But it fails because of a lack of characterization and a nondescript style.

MARKOOSIE. *Harpoon of the Hunter.* Illustrations by Germaine Arnaktauyok. Montreal/London, McGill-Queen's, 1970. 81 pp.
Kamik, a sixteen-year-old Eskimo, is the lone survivor on a hunt to kill a rabid bear. As conventional as the plot may sound, this is an outstanding novelette, the first to be written by an Eskimo. The simple style, virtually lacking in adjectives and adverbs, not only reveals a rich pattern of Eskimo life (all too often hidden) but heightens the intense emotional impact of the final events.

MOWAT, FARLEY M. *The Black Joke.* Illustrated by Douglas Johnson. Toronto, McClelland and Stewart, 1962. 177 pp.
A modern pirate story set in and around Newfoundland in the 1930s. This adventure has the zest and liveliness characteristic of all Farley Mowat's writing. A very good book.

MOWAT, FARLEY M. *The Curse of the Viking Grave*. Illustrated by Charle
Geer. Boston/Toronto, Little, Brown, 1966. 243 pp.
This sequel to Mowat's *Lost in the Barrens* suffers the fate of many sequel
and for the usual reasons—careless writing and a tedious re-working of the
same material. Yet at his worst Mowat is better than many of our writer
at their supposed best.

MOWAT, FARLEY M. *Lost in the Barrens*. Illustrated by Charles Geer. Toronto
Little, Brown, 1956. 244 pp.
A white boy and an Indian boy face the North alone and survive. Mowa
interprets the North so that the very landscape participates in the story
One of the few Canadian children's books that have achieved an inter-
national reputation.

RINGWOOD, GWEN PHARIS. *Younger Brother*. Decorations by E. Harper Johnson. Toronto, Longman, 1959. 213 pp.
Although the setting is an Alberta farm close to a Blood reservation and
the plot has plenty of excitement, this is chiefly the story of a boy, living
on the recollections of his brother killed in the war, endeavouring to 'find
himself'. The unusual combination of introspection and action is not
entirely successful; the solutions are a little too 'pat' and foreseeable to
sustain interest.

ROKEBY-THOMAS, ANN E. *Ningiyuk's Igloo World*. Pictures by James N.
Howard. Chicago, Moody Press, 1972. 94 pp.
The author spent several years among the Ekaluktuk group near St George's
Mission on Victoria Island. From this experience she is able to describe
their way of life through the daily activities of a small Eskimo girl who,
facing a problem, could be any child in the world. The missionary influence in the book is strong, but it is integral to the story — at least as
the author sees it.

ST PIERRE, PAUL. *Boss of the Namko Drive: A Story From the Cariboo Country*. Toronto, Ryerson, 1965. 115 pp.
When rancher Frenchie Bernard is injured, his fifteen-year-old son must
take charge of a 200-mile cattle drive. This is a story that offers more than
'an authentic Canadian setting' and more than the physical action of a
traditional western adventure when, at the climax, each character exhibits
a surprising aspect of his personality. The reader ends the book believing
that such people could exist, that such events actually happen.

SETON, ERNEST THOMPSON. *Two Little Savages; Being the Adventures of Two
Boys Who Lived as Indians and What They Learned*. Illustrated by the
author. New York, Doubleday, 1959. (First published in 1903.)
In a narrow sense this is an account of Seton's own boyhood in Ontario.
In a wider sense it speaks to all boys who have loved and learned from
nature.

STEFANSSON, VILHJALMUR and VIOLET IRWIN. *Kak the Copper Eskimo*. Toronto, Macmillan, 1924. 253 pp.

With a fund of knowledge, Stefansson presents the life of a happy, light-hearted Eskimo boy—an interpretation of Eskimo character that has validity for a race that has been described as 'the smiling people'.

STEVENSON, WILLIAM. *The Bushbabies*. Illustrated by Victor Ambrus. Boston, Houghton Mifflin, 1965. 278 pp.

The bushbabies—a tiny African lemur, a thirteen-year-old white girl, and an African headman—journey 100 miles into the jungle of East Africa. A compelling and sensitive story of friendship and adventure. *The Bushbabies* is a 'real' children's book and an outstanding contribution to children's literature.

WALKER, DAVID HARRY. *Dragon Hill*. Illustrated by Robert Hodgson. London, Collins, 1963. 157 pp.

A violent storm and an even more violent sea captain bring to a dramatic climax a most unusual summer for a boy and a girl. This book is well written and the adults are characterized in some depth—an unusual accomplishment in Canadian children's fiction.

WALKER, DAVID HARRY. *Pirate Rock*. London/Toronto, Collins, 1969. 190 pp.

This Buchan-type adventure on the Bay of Fundy shows David Walker's always sure touch as a novelist. It has a magnificently described setting, believable adults, and three children who, while coping admirably with strange events, are moved and saddened by what they have to do.

WILKINSON, DOUG. *Sons of the Arctic*. Illustrated by Prudence Seward. Toronto, Clarke, Irwin, 1965. 179 pp.

This is an Eskimo story with the traditional survival plot, but it contains interesting details of modern Eskimo life as well as considerable excitement. There is authority in the writing and authenticity in the detail.

STORIES OF SOCIOLOGICAL INTEREST

CRAIG, JOHN. *No Word for Good-Bye*. Illustrated by Harry Alto. Toronto, Peter Martin, 1969. 194 pp.

A young teenager loses his Indian friend after efforts to save the land of an Ojibway band in Manitoba fail; the whole band, including his friend, silently disappears—there is no word for good-bye in Ojibway. By virtue of its realistic detail and convincing plot, this is a more satisfactory piece of writing than other stories that emphasize social consciousness.

CRAIG, JOHN. *Zach*. New York, Coward, McCann & Geoghegan, 1972. 254 pp.

An Indian youth, a black youth, and a white girl—all fleeing from their past and not sure where to go—join forces 'on the road'. This, however, is chiefly the story of Zach and his attempt to find his (symbolic?) people, the Agawas. The sometimes enlightening glimpses of the towns the young people pass through and of the eccentrics they meet are marred by the conversational jargon of the 1960s, which is drearily repetitive and stale, as is their final idea to try communal living.

DAVIES, PETER. *Fly Away, Paul.* New York, Crown Publishers, 1974. 213 pp.
Paul has his fourteenth birthday in a Boy's Home in Montreal—an institution that reflects the tyranny, cruelty, and repressed sexuality associated with prison life. The author has no ability to distil these experiences. He recounts them, incident by incident, so monotonously and unskilfully that the book could be begun in the middle.

HEFFRON, DORRIS. *A Nice Fire and Some Moonpennies.* Toronto, Macmillan, 1971. 160 pp.
Maizie is an ebullient, intelligent, well-read Iroquois girl who decides to leave her home in Kingston for a day's try at the marijuana scene on Toronto's Yorkville Street. The book's potential for charm, modernity, and originality is lost in a stereotyped presentation of the pad-and-drug scene that existed on Yorkville in the 1960s.

MACKENZIE, JEAN. *River of Stars.* Illustrations by Tom McNeely. Toronto, McClelland and Stewart, 1971. 160 pp.
An Indian boy faces the hostility of some white men and the inertia and despair of his father as he tries to engage in commercial fishing. The rough (but not coarse) language is appropriate to the rough life of the fishing community, and the story moves at a good pace.

WALKER, DIANA. *Never Step on an Indian's Shadow.* New York, Abelard-Schuman, 1973. 189 pp.
A young girl from Montreal spending a summer in Moosonee, Ont., is attracted to an Indian boy and takes up the Indian cause. As with so many novels-with-a-purpose, this is superficial and unconvincing. The girl's motives spring more from her unhappiness with herself and her situation than from altruism.

CHILD AND FAMILY LIFE

COOK, LYN. *The Bells on Finland Street.* Illustrated by Stanley Wyatt. Toronto, Macmillan, 1950. 197 pp.
Elin, a little Finnish girl in Sudbury, Ont., is inspired by her grandfather to love her new country but also to be sustained by the old tradition. This could have local interest for northern Ontarians, but otherwise it is too contrived to merit serious attention.

COOK, LYN. *Jady and the General.* Illustrated by Murray Smith. Toronto, Macmillan, 1955. 242 pp.
The hazards of life on a peach farm in the Niagara Peninsula, 4-H Clubs, a boy and his horse, his parents and his friends, are all part of a loosely knit plot replete with moral.

COOK, LYN. *The Little Magic Fiddler.* Illustrated by Stanley Wyatt. Toronto, Macmillan, 1951. 252 pp.
The city of Winnipeg, Ukrainian customs, and the fictionalized childhood of the Winnipeg violinist, Donna Grescoe, make this book more valuable for its unusual content than for its writing.

COOK, LYN. *Pegeen and the Pilgrim.* Illustrated by Pat and Bill Wheeler. Toronto, Macmillan, 1957. 248 pp.
The setting is Ontario's Stratford and the beginning of the Shakespeare Festival. Twelve-year-old Pegeen is seen as her mother's helper in a boarding-house, at school, as she daydreams about being an actress, and as the friend of a Shakespeare expert who is working for the Festival as a carpenter. Crowded with slight incidents, this book fails both as a story and as a dramatic picture of the Festival itself.

COOK, LYN. *The Road to Kip's Cove.* Illustrated by William Wheeler. Toronto, Macmillan, 1961. 222 pp.
A rather spoiled boy is forced to change his holiday plans but has a good time after all and learns about the countryside, history, and Indians. Some characters move around on the printed page, but this is not a real story.

COOK, LYN. *Samantha's Secret Room.* Illustrated by Bill McKibbin. Toronto, Macmillan, 1963. 210 pp.
With a Penetanguishene, Ont., farm as the setting, the author writes of twelve-year-old tomboyish Samantha and her family and friends. As is usual in Cook's books, there is no plot as such but rather a string of incidents that record the happenings in a modern family.

CREIGHTON, LUELLA. *The Hitching Post: A Story Dealing in Magic.* Illustrated by Tom McNeely. Toronto/Montreal, McClelland and Stewart, 1969. 94 pp.
A little girl, through her goodness and with the help of wishing, acquires a fortune and finds her mother. This romance for younger children has the sentimental but compelling attraction of a novel by Frances Hodgson Burnett.

DAVELUY, PAULE. *Summer in Ville-Marie.* Translated from the French by Monroe Stearns. New York, Holt, Rinehart and Winston, 1962. 142 pp.
Summer is the time for romance, but Rosanne finds in it as much misery as joy. This story of a girl's first teen-age infatuation offers a clear-eyed view of life that does not omit the realities of friendship, tenderness, and humour. A welcome translation from French-Canadian writing.

DUNHAM, BERTHA MABEL. *Kristli's Trees.* Illustrated by Selwyn Dewdney. Toronto, McClelland and Stewart, 1947. 198 pp. (Reissued in 1974 in 'Canadian Favourites'.)
An intimate picture of Mennonite family life in Ontario of the 1940s, relating the everyday adventures of a seven-year-old boy who lives beside the Conestoga River. A beguiling book.

FAULKNOR, CLIFF. *The In-Betweener*. Illustrated by Leonard Shortall. Boston/ Toronto, Little, Brown, 1967. 166 pp.

There is an unusual set of ingredients in this boys' adventure tale: the growing-up problems of an adolescent, a believable mystery, and a West Vancouver setting in the recent past. The author has a touch of Mark Twain's skill in reporting the conversation of boys.

KENDAL, WALLIS. *Just Gin*. Illustrated by Ib Ohlsson. Toronto, Macmillan, 1973. 159 pp.

Gin, a junior-high-school girl, tells of her daily experiences in school and with her friends—and enemies. Told in what is supposed to be 'up-to-date' language, the story lacks plot, background, and characterization, as well as style.

LITTLE, JEAN. *Home from Far*. Illustrated by Jerry Lazare. Toronto, Little, Brown, 1965. 145 pp.

Two foster children are taken into a home, one of whom is the same age and has the same name as the boy in the family who has recently been killed. A 'problem' story that is a little more contrived than the author's earlier book, *Mine for Keeps*.

LITTLE, JEAN. *Mine for Keeps*. Illustrated by Lewis Parker. Toronto, Little, Brown, 1962. 186 pp.

The trials and successes of a child crippled by cerebral palsy as she learns to adjust to normal school and family life after five years at a special school. A conventional attempt at 'bibliotherapy'.

MCKIM, AUDREY. *Lexy for Short*. Illustrated by Charles Geer. New York, Abingdon Press, 1961. 159 pp.

In moving from Ontario to Edmonton Lexy meets mild problems of adjustment and growing up. This story is similar in content to hundreds of American books but is here told in a Canadian context. Unfortunately the difference is only geographical. The setting is in no way distinctive.

MCKIM, AUDREY. *That Summer With Lexy!* Illustrated by Charles Geer. New York, Abingdon Press, 1964. 144 pp.

A loose sequel to *Lexy O'Connor* in which Lexy and her friend have a string of summer adventures. Light, pleasant, and forgettable.

ST JOHN, JUDITH. *Where the Saints Have Trod*. Illustrated by Robin Jacques. London, Oxford, 1974. 118 pp.

A warm, authentic re-creation of a childhood in a Methodist minister's family in southern Ontario fifty years ago, drawn from the author's recollections. It is a well-written, charming book in which the various episodes—which seem tame and uneventful today but had great importance for the children of an earlier generation—are filled with childhood joys and concerns and described with gentle humour. The drawings by a well-known English illustrator are decorative but provide no visual complement to the charm and the Canadian flavour of the book.

MYSTERY-ADVENTURE STORIES

ASHLEE, TED. *Night of the Sasquatch*. Toronto/ Montreal, Holt, Rinehart and Winston, 1973. 182 pp.
The setting for this badly written novel is Vancouver and the coastal waters of British Columbia. There is a huge cast of characters, including Sasquatches and Boy Scouts, a plot that involves villainy, both legal and illegal methods to save the ecology, and fights galore. If only it were *good* melodrama. A sequel to *Voyage into Danger*.

ASHLEE, TED. *Voyage into Danger*. Toronto/Montreal. Holt, Rinehart and Winston, 1971. 134 pp.
Ashlee has a great knowledge of seamanship and West Coast commercial shipping, but this seafaring mystery gets bogged down in a welter of events and artificially created characters.

BARTON, CARL. *Robber's Roost*. Toronto/Montreal, Holt, Rinehart and Winston, 1972. 142 pp.
Articles have been disappearing from summer cottages on an island off the coast of British Columbia. The setting and the children's knowledge of boats are rather attractive, but the plot, characterization, and style are weak indeed.

BELL, ELEANOR. *The Black Totem*. Toronto, Ryerson, 1960. 180 pp.
The shoreline of British Columbia, north of Vancouver, provides a dramatic setting for the events surrounding four young people who become involved with a bank robber. A better-than-average plot with below-average writing.

BICE, CLARE. *The Great Island: A Story of Mystery in Newfoundland*. Illustrated by the author. Toronto. Macmillan, 1954. 103 pp.
Bice can create atmosphere because he knows his setting so well, but he manages to make a search for treasure humdrum.

BICE, CLARE. *Hurricane Treasure*. Illustrated by the author. Toronto, Macmillan, 1965. 190 pp.
Nova Scotia's famous 'Oak Island' (thinly disguised as 'Gull Island'), and the incidental descriptions of life in a modern Atlantic fishing village, give this story its only authenticity. The plot is dull and contrived and the characters completely forgettable.

BOYLE, JOYCE. *The Stone Cottage Mystery*. Toronto, Macmillan, 1958. 151 pp.
A mystery story for girls that involves the finding of documents to clear a family name. An inconsequential plot is given some weight by the method of historical research used by the young heroine.

COLLINS, ROBERT. *Rory's Wildcat*. Illustrated by Douglas Johnson. Toronto. McClelland and Stewart, 1965. 160 pp.
This mystery-adventure based on oil prospecting in the Northwest Ter-

ritories is marred by an instructional purpose. The young hero's friendship with the French-Canadian cook and two Indian children is treated almost as a social problem.

COOK, RONALD J. *Algonquin Adventure*. Toronto, Ryerson, 1958. 138 pp.
Two boys are sadistically left to die by fur thieves whom they have discovered. They escape and are pursued through the northern-Ontario woods. A plot that is slight and improbable is further marred as the boys pause to explain to one another some techniques of survival in the wilderness.

COSGROVE, EDMUND. *Windigo Wings*. Illustrated by the author. Toronto, Burns and MacEachern, 1967. 140 pp.
'Windigo Wings' is a bush airline run by two veterans of the Korean War. With two younger companions they become involved in espionage centred on uranium discoveries at Elliott Lake, Ont. Informative as it is about airplanes, this is a stereotyped spy-intelligence plot with stereotyped characters. *The Terror of the Tar Sands* (1968) has the same characters and a similar plot.

FALKNER, FREDERICK. *The Aqualung Twins and the 'Iron Crab'*. Illustrated by Frank Grey. Toronto, Dent, 1959. 188 pp.
Both the setting (the Caribbean) and the events (a new type of atomic underwater vessel) are reminiscent of a James Bond story, but unfortunately the author lacks Ian Fleming's bravura.

MCKIM, AUDREY. *Thorny's Hideaway*. Illustrated by Don Lambo. Toronto, Nelson, 1961. 147 pp.
The adventures of some children on a ranch in Alberta. They include helping a runaway boy, a rodeo, and a mystery that turns out not to be so mysterious. The story is jammed with events and not much else.

MCLAUGHLIN, LORRIE. *The Cinnamon Hill Mystery*. Illustrated by Leonard Shorthall. New York, Crowell, 1967. 234 pp.
A twelve-year-old boy is the 'deus ex machina' who solves the problem of a family will and generally straightens things out for everybody. A summer-holiday family mystery that is both dull and implausible.

PEREZ, NORAH A. *Strange Summer in Stratford*. Illustrated by Robert Ihrig. Toronto, Little, Brown, 1968. 176 pp.
Mystery at the Stratford Festival with lessons on Shakespeare from an insufferably knowledgeable family. If the book had been widely read, the Stratford Festival might have had a serious decline in business.

RILEY, LOUISE. *The Mystery Horse*. Illustrated by John Merle Smith. New York, Messner, 1950. 200 pp.
Ranch life in Alberta is lightly described in this mediocre 'mystery adventure' story as a group of children thwart two horse thieves.

SEAGER, JOAN. *Mystery at Lynx Lodge*. Illustrated by Douglas Johnson. Toronto, McGraw-Hill, 1965. 114 pp.

The incidents and characters in this short book are so artificial as to be ludicrous. It is too bad the author didn't write it as a parody of a children's detective novel.

SEAGER, JOAN. *The Vengeance of Wol*. Toronto, McGraw-Hill, 1966. 124 pp.

Jeff and his biologist uncle are in serious danger from an escaped mental patient. The story, which moves from one sensational incident to another, has no redeeming features.

'Secret Circle Mysteries, The'. Toronto, Little, Brown. General Editor: Arthur Hammond.

1. Gammon, David. *The Mystery of Monster Lake*. Illustrated by Frank Davies. 1962. 156 pp.
2. Earl, Lawrence. *The Riddle of the Haunted River*. Illustrated by Douglas Sneyd. 1962. 160 pp.
3. Collins, Robert. *The Legend of the Devil's Lode*. Illustrated by Douglas Sneyd. 1962. 156 pp.
4. Hammond, Arthur. *The Secret Tunnel Treasure*. Illustrated by Douglas Johnson. 1962. 158 pp.
5. Braithwaite, Max. *The Mystery of the Muffled Man*. Illustrated by J. Rosenthal. 1962. 160 pp.
6. Young, Scott. *The Clue of the Dead Duck*. Illustrated by Douglas Johnson. 1962. 159 pp.
7. Allen, Robert Thomas. *The Mystery of the Missing Emerald*. Illustrated by Gordon Collins. 1963. 160 pp.
8. Braithwaite, Max. *The Valley of the Vanishing Birds*. Illustrated by Wendy Hagwood. 1963. 160 pp.
9. Hammond, Arthur. *The Mystery of the Disappearing Dogs*. Illustrated by Lewis Parker. 1963. 160 pp.
10. Gammon, David. *The Secret of Spaniards Rock*. Illustrated by William Wheeler. 1963. 158 pp.

These are caricatures of adult mystery stories with superficially described Canadian settings.

WALLACE, CLARKE. *Montreal Adventure*. Toronto, Burns and MacEachern, 1967. 123 pp.

Montreal, three children, radio expertise, and an art theft provide exciting ingredients for this mystery. It is well plotted and full of suspense, which makes it all the more regrettable that the style is so mundane.

WARREN, ARNOLD. *The Stolen Seaplane*. Illustrated by James Walker. Toronto, McClelland and Stewart, 1965. 160 pp.

The plot revolves around bush-flying, but no feeling is conveyed of the unique characteristics of this occupation and there is no evocation of the northern setting. Three teen-agers—an Indian boy, a white boy, and a

French-Canadian girl—are lifelessly drawn, and things are not helped by a few painfully obvious references to their various cultural and racial backgrounds.

WOODWARD, LUCY BERTON. *Kidnapped in the Yukon*. Toronto, Burns and MacEachern, 1968. 112 pp.
Kidnapped by a 'mad' prospector, a young boy shows courage and resourcefulness as he is forced to elude the people who are trying to rescue him. The story is more simply (and therefore better) plotted and faster-paced than any other outdoor mystery-adventure by a Canadian.

WRIGHT, RICHARD. *Andrew Tolliver*. Illustrated by Lewis Parker. Toronto, Macmillan, 1965. 105 pp. ('Buckskin Books'.)
Young Andy Tolliver outwits a couple of bank robbers as the town of Harmony celebrates its hundredth anniversary. A pleasant, slightly tongue-in-cheek little story with attractive details of small-town Ontario life.

HORSE AND DOG STORIES

CALLAGHAN, MORLEY. *Luke Baldwin's Vow*. Illustrations by Stanley Turner. Philadelphia, Winston, 1948. 189 pp. Illustrated by Michael Poulton. Toronto, Macmillan, 1974. 187 pp.
Luke's love for his uncle's old and ailing dog seems unlikely to save it from being disposed of, for Uncle Henry has no use for anything that is not utilitarian. The story is blatantly didactic and has a rather cloudy ending. One can perhaps overlook the fact that it lacks the literary excellence of Callaghan's distinguished adult fiction, but that it has very little style at all must reveal the author's belief that only a moral is necessary in a children's book.

LEITCH, ADELAIDE. *The Blue Roan*. Illustrated by Charles Robinson. Toronto, Macmillan, 1971. 185 pp.
Roddy didn't know why he chose the little blue roan, but with her he won most of the competitions, until the day she threw him. There are dangerous moments and a dramatic climax before the boy and the horse understand one another again. A sensitive and well-written 'horse story'.

PERKINS, CHARLES. *Molly*. Toronto, Longman, 1966. 130 pp.
Molly was a lovable St Bernard as a puppy, but when she grew older and lost her puppies she caused serious trouble for her young master. While this is a 'love story' between a boy and his dog, it also vividly reveals a boy's life in a British Columbia town (Prince George) in the recent past—a happy and uncomplicated life by present-day standards.

WALKER, DAVID HARRY. *Big Ben*. Illustrated by Victor Ambrus. Toronto, Collins, 1969. 134 pp.
'Big Ben', the gentle, bumbling St Bernard, joins Farley Mowat's 'Mutt' as a genuine dog character. David Walker's firm grasp on reality does not fail him even when writing for younger children.

CAREER STORIES

BELL, ELEANOR. *New Salesgirl at Kendall's*. Toronto, Ryerson, 1963. ('Canadian Careers Library'.)
A highly glamourized account of clerking in a department store.

BRAITHWAITE, MAX. *The Cure Searchers*. Toronto, Ryerson, 1962. 173 pp. ('Canadian Careers Library'.)
The field of medical research offers built-in interest for a career book. The background in this one is authentic and the experiments in cancer research have considerable drama. One of the better books in this series.

BRAITHWAITE, MAX. *The Young Reporter*. Toronto, Ryerson, 1963. 148 pp. ('Canadian Careers Library'.)
A teen-age girl helps her mother run a small-town newspaper. Much of the glamour of the life of a reporter is debunked, while accuracy and responsibility—and crusading—are emphasized. The aspects of reporting are sufficiently detailed and interesting to compensate for a lack of characterization and style and for some fatuous incidents.

DENNIS, JUNE (pseud.). *TV Career Girl*. Toronto, Ryerson, 1964. 168 pp. ('Canadian Careers Library'.)
A reasonably interesting account of a radio station in a middle-sized Ontario city just as it is moving into television. The story includes the usual dosage of clothes, dating, and romance for the teen-age girl, and implies that these are more important than a career.

HAGELUND, WILLIAM A. *The Halibut Hunters*. Toronto, Ryerson, 1963. 179 pp. ('Canadian Careers Library'.)
The writer forgets the career and writes a stirring account of life on a commercial fishing boat. The hazards of the sea and fishing itself are contrasted with the daily routines aboard the *Stalvard II*. The cycle of the halibut fishing season and the nature of the men who risk their lives in this occupation are well described.

HARRIS, CHRISTIE. *The Confessions of a Toe-Hanger*. Drawings by Moira Johnston. Toronto, McClelland and Stewart, 1967. 209 pp.
An exuberant Canadian girl is dissatisfied with her role first as a 'middle' child and eventually as a wife and mother. She finally 'finds herself' when she decides simply to *be* herself and accepts a job with the CBC. The book lacks the spontaneity and humour of Harris's somewhat similar book about her eldest daughter, *You Have to Draw the Line Somewhere* (1964).

HARRIS, CHRISTIE. *Let X Be for Excitement*. Illustrated with photographs. Toronto, McClelland and Stewart, 1969. 236 pp.
The story of a young man's struggle to find out what he wants to be (a research engineer cum pilot) and eventually to fulfil his ambition. However, the protagonist is a curiously cold figure who in no way engages

sympathy as he struggles—perhaps because he exhibits a hard, logical drive and an ability to write letters to the right people at the right time. This is the third fictionalized biography of Harris's own children.

HARRIS, CHRISTIE. *You Have to Draw the Line Somewhere*. Illustrated by Moira Johnston. New York, Atheneum, 1964. 249 pp.
The heroine gives an account of herself from her unconventional home and school life near and in Vancouver to her career in fashion drawing in New York. An excellent light book that manages to have something to say.

MILLER, ORLO. *A Sound of Voices*. Toronto, Ryerson, 1965. 152 pp. ('Canadian Careers Library'.)
An introduction to the ministry (in this case Anglican) is a worthwhile theme for many young people, but this one is made ineffective by superficial characterization, banal dialogue, and diffuse ideas.

MILLER, ORLO. *The Water Savers*. Illustrated by Pat Gagnon. Toronto, Ryerson, 1962. 152 pp. ('Canadian Careers Library'.)
A boy at odds with his father over a career is persuaded to spend the summer on the South Saskatchewan River Development Project. He comes to see the importance of conservation engineering (he was at first interested only in astronomy and space engineering) and the problems with his father are ironed out. This story has the pedestrian writing that is too often found in career books.

SHIPLEY, NAN. *The Railway Builders*. Toronto, Ryerson, 1965. 150 pp. ('Canadian Careers Library'.)
A fifteen-year-old boy—a paper-thin character—is supposed to have his life 'irrevocably' settled. The purpose here is to inspire young boys to go to university and become engineers.

SWAYZE, FRED. *Manitoulin Manhunt*. Toronto, Ryerson, 1962. 171 pp. ('Canadian Careers Library'.)
The main purpose of this story is to interest young people in anthropology as a career. However, this aim gets lost in a rather pointless adventure that is complicated by the problem of the reservation Indian.

YOUNG, ASTRID and SCOTT YOUNG. *Big City Office Junior*. Toronto, Ryerson, 1964. 152 pp. ('Canadian Careers Library'.)
A seventeen-year-old girl leaves high school and the farm to get a job in an office in Toronto. Here she finds excitement, romance, and a life of her own. A stereotyped career story.

SPORTS STORIES

CHILDERHOSE, R.J. *Hockey Fever in Goganne Falls*. Toronto, Macmillan, 1973. 169 pp.
Even though the small-town kids even-out in a game with the city slickers

in traditional fashion, this is no run-of-the-mill sports story. Here kids play hockey admirably without the organized 'Junior Leagues', thus doing a lot for themselves and enjoying themselves too. The book also offers a delightful look at many aspects of a small Alberta town in the almost-recent past.

LONGSTRETH, T. MORRIS. *The Calgary Challengers*. Illustrated by William Wheeler. Toronto, Macmillan, 1962. 165 pp.

A high-school boy goes to Calgary to play non-professional hockey while he and his trained dog wait for an appointment to the R.C.M.P. A mediocre book in which the best scenes are played by the dog.

ORR, FRANK. *Buck Martin, Take Centre Ice: The Exciting Life in Junior 'A' Hockey*. Toronto, Musson, 1965. 197 pp.

As is usual with sports stories, the plot is contrived, but the background is treated more realistically and less 'rosily' than in the ordinary sports story and there is the occasional hint of verisimilitude in the character-ization.

YOUNG, SCOTT. *A Boy at the Leafs' Camp*. Illustrated by Doug Sneyd. Toronto, Little, Brown, 1963. 256 pp.

A high-school boy has a chance to try out at the Leafs' training camp. An attempt is made to interject drama by a rather artificial feud between the young hero and another player. A typical sports story—only the action of a game appears to have any validity. Two earlier books by Scott Young are *Scrubs on Skates* (illustrated by James Ponter; Toronto, McCelland and Stewart, 1952; 218 pp.) and *Boy on Defense* (illustrated by James Ponter; Toronto, McClelland and Stewart, 1953; 246 pp.).

And
All
the
Rest

7 | history and biography

Histories and biographies form the largest group of Canadian children's books. It is not strange that aspects of Canadian history should attract writers. Canadian history, some popular assumptions to the contrary, is anything but dull. 'How could a history full of grandiose projects, startling contrasts, stark antitheses, be dull? How could significance be lacking in the story of a country whose very existence consists in a never-ending battle to accomplish the impossible?' writes A.R.M. Lower in *Colony to Nation: A History of Canada*. The great motifs of Canadian history—exploration, endurance, war, pioneering—have a perennial and universal interest.

Canada's colourful past has great advantages for a writer in being available through the first-hand accounts of the actual participants in it. There are descriptions of Canada by Vikings, Spaniards, Portuguese, Italians, Frenchmen, Britons, and Americans; by little-known travellers as various as Jesuits and English gentlewomen. There are the journals of the great explorers—of Cartier, Champlain, Mackenzie, Hearne, and Vancouver. All of these accounts were written by people who were keen to observe and to share their observations with their insatiably curious contemporaries, and they are full of fascinating detail. They provide a wealth of possibilities for Canadian writers. Furthermore, no one exploiting these rich resources need do so unaided. Almost every aspect of Canadian history has been ably interpreted and clarified by scholars who rank with the best in any country—A.R.M. Lower, Donald Creighton, George Brown,

William Morton, William Eccles, to name but a few of the modern historians whose studies are now standard works.

How are these possibilities to be used in books for children? The basic choice lies in the determination of what share is to be given to the 'story' in 'history'. There must be some 'story' or the book will be merely a text for study. Conversely, a book that is mostly 'story' belongs in the realm of historical fiction.

Most Candian writers for children have taken a middle position. That is, they do not write history or fiction but adopt an in-between technique that can best be described as embellished history or fictionalized history. This is the knack of inventing conversations (that might have taken place) and manufacturing thoughts for historical personages. The basic intention of such fictionalized history is clearly readability. It seeks to make history bright and attractive for children, but it usually does so at the expense of essential truth.

Two examples may clarify the difference between straight history that has a story quality and embellished history that is difficult to tell from fiction. The first is taken from a notable book on Jacques Cartier by the American author Esther Averill. The second is from a Canadian treatment of the same subject.

In 1491 there was born in St. Malo a boy destined to take his place among the great sea captains of the world. His name was Jacques Cartier. Of Cartier's early life no trace can be found today. But the times in which he lived and the historical events that shaped his thoughts have been well recorded.

It was the period when men felt a pull toward the West— an urge to navigate the long-dreaded Atlantic. The urge was prompted by a new and exciting theory that the earth, instead of being flat like a table, is round like a globe.—ESTHER AVERILL, Cartier Sails the St. Lawrence.

A small group of men stood at the high sea-walls of the town, their hands shading their eyes as they looked westward to the Atlantic. . . .

Suddenly one of the men pointed out to sea and shouted, 'A sail! A sail!'

The others near him picked up the cry and in a moment it

was being echoed by dozens of voices within the town.
  'A sail! A sail!'
  'The fishing-boats are coming in!'
  'The men are home again.'
  —ROBERT FERGUSON, Man From St. Malo: The Story of Jacques Cartier.

In comparing these two opening paragraphs, it can readily be seen that Ferguson's invented conversation, of doubtful plausibility, has no advantage in the creation of interest and that Averill displays the greater historical imagination.

It is of some significance that the title-page of the Averill book notes that this account of Jacques Cartier is *retold*. Esther Averill makes effective use of the Cartier log books (having briefly mentioned the puzzle over the authorship), quoting extensively (for a short book) and uses her own narrative to link extracts from documentary evidence. The epidemic of scurvy that struck Cartier's crew was a significant event. Ferguson in *Man From St. Malo* takes four chapters of undistinguished writing to describe it. Averill begins her account with an imaginative image: 'Sickness entered the wilderness, stole across the snows of the forest and over the ice of the River and into the Indian village.' She closes the chapter four pages later with Cartier's entry in his log-book: 'God has had pity on us and sent us the knowledge and remedy for our cure.' As Averill makes clear to her readers, little or nothing was known of Cartier until he sailed on his first voyage at the age of forty. However, she builds up a convincing portrait of him that she says is based on a knowledge of the times. Ferguson, on the other hand, uses invented dialogue, at times both strained and mundane, and neither the times nor the man has any particular distinctiveness.

Even if it were somehow to be judged that Ferguson's approach had the greater appeal, there is still the telling point that embellished history runs the considerable risk of distorting the historical truth. This serious charge is very much apropos, for example, in the case of Joseph Schull's *Battle for the Rock: The Story of Wolfe and Montcalm* (1960). Schull states in his Foreword that 'the aim has been to treat people and facts with a certain imaginative freedom while still keeping the story within the framework of history.' Certainly this approach has produced an interesting book, but only some careful background reading can determine precisely what is fact and what is fiction. We know that Wolfe's army spent several frustrating months waiting for its general to decide on an effective way of attacking Quebec. We know also that, far from being the dauntless hero of legend, Wolfe at that time was ill, depressed, and practically unable to make a decision. What this meant to the men under his command is shown by the following description of the waiting camp:

> *The moody troops, still in the sprawling camps, greeted their returning mates with hard eyes. They had heard enough of scorchings, seen enough. The shores below the city were blackened too; they had their share of the work. 'Burn and destroy—take and kill'—they had ranged out over the green land, sullenly obeying. The wailing bands of the women had come back with them....*
>
> *The Indians howled in the woods at night, the screams of the pacing sentries choked in their throats as the knife plunged. Each day the lists of punishments grew; the sullen defaulters tramped to their floggings. Wrists dropped from the gunwheels, twisting in knotted cords, the lash ate at quivering backs. Deserters scuttled for the river, dived like rats and were gone. The men by the smoking campfires cursed and waited, coughed and died, the men of a headless army.*

This passage is not only considerably overwritten but it also muddles the facts by intermingling them with emotions. Schull appears to be referring in the first paragraph to Wolfe's policy of terror in burning the homes and parishes of the habitants. But this is never made clear, nor is his poetic reference to the army being headless, which it was not. Though it is an imaginative passage, it does not suggest the imagination of a historian.

Schull has used this same loose approach in portraying Wolfe and Montcalm. Commendably he makes them stand out as human beings with individual personalities and very human faults. Still, we could wish that in personalizing the heroes, he did not go so far as to have them engage in dialogue. It is obviously impossible to reconstruct the words of Wolfe, Montcalm, or Bigot, and such far-fetched attributions add nothing to the creation of atmosphere. Schull also presumes to tell us the thoughts of his principal figures. While some of the thoughts of these men might have been gleaned from letters, and while the device does aid in characterization, Schull has sacrificed historical accuracy to his particular literary style.

He [Montcalm] stirred in his saddle with a quick, impatient shrug, and the tall black horse which seemed an extension of his wiry body twitched beneath him in sympathy. The less one thought of the Governor the better and there was no point now in watching what could not be prevented. As he wheeled from the river the little knot of gold-laced horsemen wheeled with him and followed at a distance. Orderlies and staff were aware of the general's mood, glad enough to be separated from him by a respectful interval.

In essence this passage verges on historical fiction. Schull's 'imaginative freedom' might have allowed him to imagine that Montcalm's horse did in fact 'twitch' on June 26th, 1759, but common sense should have told him that flies and not sympathy would have been the reason.

Schull's novelistic approach to history means that any reader pursuing further the events of 1759 will have to unlearn some pseudo facts. He makes a fair amount of Wolfe's talking to a deserter before making his decision to scale the heights at Foulon, though the historian C.P. Stacey states in his *Quebec, 1759* that there is no evidence for such an assumption. Schull has not perpetuated the anecdote about Wolfe's reciting Gray's 'Elegy' aloud as he was rowed downstream on the eve of the battle, but without evidence he has the recitation take place in Wolfe's cabin. Small points, perhaps, but they indicate a weakness for historical myths and insufficient research. Schull's book—and in general all books of history for children that decorate the facts—suggests also a lack of respect for both the reader and the subject. Embellished history implies that the subject alone is not interesting enough to hold the reader or that the reader is incapable of appreciating it in its essential, unvarnished form.

Such an assumption is not justified, at least not when a writer of talent finds a topic of genuine appeal. A first-class example of how history can be written so as to appeal to children and yet adhere closely to verifiable facts is Pierre Berton's *The Golden Trail: The Story of the Klondike Gold Rush* (1954). Berton assures us that this 'is as faithful an account as the author can make it, of the events as they occurred between 1896 and 1899. Nothing has been invented and nothing has been fictionalized. Conversations and dialogue where they occur are reproduced as reported by people who were there, either in interviews with the author, in diaries or in published reports.'

Of course Berton's subject contains events worth recounting: high adventure, suspense, suffering and hardship, hopes of untold wealth, and memorable characters such as Robert Henderson, who sacrificed everything for the lure of sudden wealth and saw the wealth go to others. But the triumph of the book is due to Berton's judgement in selecting evocative details from the sources: the line of prospectors wending their way in a solid ribbon over the mountains; the German woman tramping along in full skirt and lace apron; haircuts costing $4.00; boots bought for $1.50 in Montreal and sold for $15.00 to the prospectors; the hungry men who stole food from an icebound ship, paid for it, and then paid themselves longshoreman's wages for unloading it! He simply tells us how it was. His account makes extensive use of the well-polished and carefully selected anecdote. This passage illustrates the food shortage in the boom town of Dawson City in the winter of 1897:

It was ironic that all over the north country men were clawing their way up frozen rivers and down forest trails and over mountain passes in tens of thousands to reach this town and the riches it contained. But in the town itself all the money in the world could not have bought a Christmas turkey. The following April, when a Dutchman brought a turkey in over the trail, ready cooked and stuffed, it was exhibited as an oddity in the Pioneer Saloon. Raffled off, it fetched $174.

Describing the suffering and desperation of man and beast during the trek inland from Skagway to the waterways leading to Dawson and the gold fields, Berton writes:

One horse was seen to walk to the edge of the precipice on Porcupine Hill, gaze at the boulders below for a moment, then jump head first onto them. The men who watched this incident were certain that the animal had committed suicide.

If Schull and Berton may be taken to represent the two poles in respect of the degree of invention that should be applied to a historical narrative, R.S. Lambert shows that an in-between position is tenable. His biography, *Franklin of the Arctic*, was published in 1949. Like Berton, Lambert had excellent material to work with. Franklin had an adventurous life: he fought at the Battle of Copenhagen and at Trafalgar under Nelson's command; he sailed with Captain Flinders to Australia and was on the Flinders expedition to the Arctic; and finally there was his last and tragic voyage to find the long-dreamed-of North West Passage. Like Berton, the author of *Franklin of the Arctic* shows great skill in the selection of detail and in its presentation. The major episodes in Franklin's life are isolated and told in 'close-up' form as separate stories. Short bridge chapters entitled 'The Story Moves On', confined solely to the narration of events, give the book its continuity. Although the major chapters are written in conversational style, including the part on Franklin's ill-fated voyage (which of course is based on the evidence of the search parties), *Franklin of the Arctic* is sound biography based on available information. Lambert in no way exceeds the evidence. For sheer excitement and vitality, *Franklin of the Arctic* is unmatched by any other Canadian biography for children.

Lambert's next two books—*North for Adventure* (1952), the story of Samuel Hearne, and *Trailmaker: The Story of Alexander Mackenzie* (1957)—are reasonably successful, but they do not have the intrinsic strength and literary quality of *Franklin of the Arctic*. They suffer from an overdose of detail. A case in point is the famous 1,000-mile trip from La Crosse Island to Grand Portage, made in a month by Alexander's cousin, Rory Mackenzie, to bring the news of the killing of John Ross. Lambert completely misses the dramatic opportunities of this striking episode, as he gives a page and a half of description—noting almost every waterway and every portage—that is not only dreary but could have been made clearer and more dramatic in a map.

Pierre Berton's *The Golden Trail* is probably the best book so far in a series called 'Great Stories of Canada', which is something of a phenomenon in Canadian publishing. It has provided more than thirty of the some seventy histories and biographies for children that have been published in Canada since 1950. The avowed purpose of the series is to provide 'historically sound' information and 'to recount history in story form, in a manner appealing to the young reader'. Commendably, the series shows no evidence of the hack writing that is so common in the United States, where a so-called professional writer is at one moment churning out a cutdown version of the *Odyssey* for children and at another a chewed-up treatment of science. Instead, most of the writers for the series are well-known and competent authors—Thomas Raddall, Marjorie Wilkins Campbell, and Kerry Wood are three. Roderick Haig-Brown, who has contributed a life of Captain George Vancouver (*Captain of the Discovery*), has long been noted for his books on British Columbia and the out-of-doors. Clifford Wilson, former editor of the Hudson's Bay Company magazine, *The Beaver*, was a first-rate choice for a book on the early colourful days of the Company, *Adventurers from the Bay*. T. Morris Longstreth (*The Scarlet Force*) and Fred Swayze (*Frontenac and the Iroquois*) are experienced writers for children.

The publishers must be praised also for their attempt (modest though it is) to explore the range of Canadian history. They have not always been content to restrict their series to the obvious subjects but have ranged widely—in time from Jacques Cartier (*Man From St. Malo*) to the Canadian Navy in the Second World War (*Ships of the Great Days*), and in space from British Columbia (*Captain of the Discovery*) to Nova Scotia (*The Salt Water Men.*)

It is a basically sound and reliable series as far as dates, places, and recorded events are concerned. The writers have drawn on some primary materials as well as on secondary sources and have often effectively included quotations from eyewitness participants (e.g. Longstreth's *The Scarlet Force* and Kerry Wood's *The Map-Maker*). Certainly the number of factual errors is minimal.

Within the general and rather conventional treatment that

Canadian history is accorded in this series, various viewpoints get recognition. Particularly in the group of books dealing with the Selkirk settlers—J.W. Chalmers' *Red River Adventure* (1950), Marjorie Wilkins Campbell's *The Nor'Westers* (1961), and Clifford Wilson's *Adventurers from the Bay* (1962)—various contemporary points of view are presented. Since Chalmers in *Red River Adventure* is primarily concerned to tell the story of the settlers, he naturally supports their position, while Marjorie Wilkins Campbell in *The Nor'Westers* attempts to show what the intrusion of the settlement at such a vital point in the North West Company's trade route meant to the Montreal firm. In the third book in this group, *Adventurers from the Bay*, Clifford Wilson relates the events from the viewpoint of the Hudson's Bay Company and the settlers. Of the competition with the North West Company's interests in the Red River area, Wilson says: 'The North West traders began a campaign of hostility. They forbade their half-breed servants to trade with the colony or to hunt buffalo for the settlers.' About the same situation Campbell points out, 'Even one thousand white settlers . . . would ruin the fur trade along the Red River.'

The two books on the Riel Rebellion—both by Edward Mc-Court—also offer a study in contrast. In *Revolt in the West: The Story of the Riel Rebellion* (1958), McCourt gives a fair and modern assessment of Riel that is not unlike that of Joseph Kinsey Howard's *Strange Empire. Buckskin Brigadier: The Story of the Alberta Field Force* (1955) is a tribute to the men who helped break the Rebellion: only incidentally (in the first one-and-a-half pages) does McCourt give any attention to the causes of the uprising. The emphasis is on the bravery of the Field Force, under its leader Tom Strange, and their astonishing five-hundred-mile march through 'rugged, hostile country'. The book is a valid attempt to bring to life some unknown and unsung heroes of Canadian history, but the resurrection is oddly incomplete because it is divorced from the main events of the Rebellion.

The series can also be commended for some interpretation of Indians as individuals and as a race. Because many of the books deal with the early days of the West, the Indians tend to be shown only as warriors. But even here there are differences in the understanding of Indian character. C.T. Ritchie, in *Runner of the Woods: The Story of Young Radisson* (1963), presents endless gory details of Indian warfare in which the Indians appear as savages with no redeeming features. Robert D. Ferguson, in *Fur Trader: The Story of Alexander Henry* (1961), is also naturally concerned with Indian warfare: Henry, after all, was at Michili-mackinac during the Pontiac uprising. The impression he gives of the Indians, however, is quite different. Although he does not blink at their brutality, he conveys his understanding of, and even sympathy for, the Indian point of view. Consider his comment on Indian tactics:

> To the British this Indian strategy was savage and cowardly. But for the Indian it was the only way to fight. Outnumbered and outdisciplined by the white man, he had to grasp a quick victory with as few casualties as possible. To trick an enemy into exposing himself, to make him believe a lie, to ambush, to massacre—these were the only tactics he could use against cannons and palisaded forts. And his native forests were made for his kind of fighting. To the Indian the most incredible sight was a regiment of white soldiers charging an unseen enemy in broad daylight. He recognized it as high courage, but he also saw it as madness.

Kerry Wood's *The Great Chief, Maskepetoon: Warrior of the Crees* (1957) takes Indian life and character as a basic theme. The interest of Maskepetoon's life springs from his conversion from a man of warfare to a man of peace and from the relevance of his situation to modern times: he could be a man of the 1970s. After a youth focused on traditional resentments, Maskepetoon became a leader in the cause of sanity and peace; in the end he was killed by one of his own group who felt he had betrayed its rights. While in no way a distinguished literary effort, the content, pace, action, and simplicity of *The Great Chief* make it almost an outstanding book. Certainly Maskepetoon himself is unforgettable.

A great number of writers in this series chose to reveal the past through the life of a great or representative man—an approach to history that has often proved rewarding, even if not everyone agrees with Carlyle that 'biography is the only true history'. It must be sadly noted, however, that the biographical form, with its concentration on one person, has not always resulted in a study of greater depth and perception than the volumes dealing with the broader aspects of history. For example, Ritchie's *Runner of the Woods* is a disappointing treatment of a promising subject, Pierre Radisson, who apparently made himself at home in such completely different settings as a Mohawk village and the English court. He must have been a fascinating man of great ability, but no attempt is made to examine and recreate his personality. Instead, Ritchie prefers to pack his book with repetitive detail, unbelievable dialogue, and preposterous incidents. This is biographical window-dressing at its worst.

One of the few examples in the series of the wholly unembellished biography is Roderick L. Haig-Brown's *Captain of the Discovery: The Story of Captain George Vancouver* (1956). Vancouver's voyages took him into the huts of the Hawaiian Islanders, the lodges of the West Coast Indians, and the galleys of Spanish men-of-war, and Haig-Brown takes full advantage of his opportunities for satisfying the child's natural interest in exotic settings, but never at the cost of distorting his subject. Vancouver was no swashbuckling explorer but a disciplined, skilled, conscientious navigator. Haig-Brown dares to show him as one, confident that solid achievement, however unspectacular in the accomplishment, is a theme that deserves and can hold an audience.

The real story of George Vancouver is not in one great voyage or in any one spectacular deed. It is in the hundreds of lesser voyages made by small boats . . . and in . . . the unfailing courage with which he carried out . . . three long years of exploration.

Another ordinary man in an extraordinary setting furnishes a rewarding subject for R.S. Lambert in *Mutiny in the Bay: Henry Hudson's Last Voyage* (1963). Abacuk Pricket may have been a spy on the voyage, paid by the men who financed Hudson's attempt to find the Northwest Passage. Lambert used Pricket's journal (Pricket was one of the few men who survived the terrible and ill-starred voyage), 'paraphrasing in many places, making his writing modern, and turning the bare narrative into dialogue where required'. If Lambert has taken a step away from strict historical veracity, he has nevertheless kept the flavour of the original journal to an unusual degree. In addition, he is able to give a vivid picture of the lives of ordinary seventeenth-century seamen exposed to scurvy, starvation, and shipwreck for little or no reward; of heartless merchants oblivious to all concerns but their own profit. And he is particularly successful in conveying Hudson's religious feelings and the skepticism of Harry Green, the leader of the mutiny. However, Lambert changes the name of Abacuk Pricket (used by all authorities with only one slight variant form) to Habakuk Pritchett. Such a change is hard to justify in the writing of history and biography, even if embellished. The young reader pursuing further information in this area and using the tools of research will be puzzled.

Alongside these accounts of individuals, the 'group narratives' form a neat counterpoint. Many of the most exciting and significant stories in Canadian history are the result of organized ventures, which the series amply represents. The explorers and fur-traders of the North West Company and the Hudson's Bay Company and the men of the North West Mounted Police have group personalities that are well reflected in such books as Campbell's *The Nor'Westers*, Wilson's *Adventurers from the Bay*, and Longstreth's *The Scarlet Force* and *The Force Carries On*. They show that many great stories were lived by nameless Canadians who had no titles or wealth, or who never experienced personal fame. The exploitation of group drama is best exemplified by *The Nor'Westers*. This is lively and fresh historical writing—an attempt to analyse events as well as to relate them. Campbell describes the challenge that faced each Nor'Wester: 'the potential danger and the potential wealth'; the irresistible promise of sudden riches blotting out the hardships and the isolation of the Canadian northlands. She discusses briefly what it would have meant to the livelihood of thousands of people if the furs had not flowed to Montreal and across the sea to England. And she includes a whole chapter on the role of Indian women (one of the few books in the series in which women appear) and their preparation of pemmican, the food that made the fur trade and the exploration of the West possible.

In sweeping across the history of the North West Company, however, Campbell leaves out some very basic questions and answers: Why was there a fur trade at all? What lasting effect did it have on Canada? What happened to the fur trade after 1821? What remains at the end of the book is a series of lively impressions. The reason why is missing.

The 'Great Stories of Canada' series does have serious weaknesses. Several spring from what appears to be a slightly defensive attitude towards the inherent interest of Canadian history, as though the editor of the series and some of the writers secretly thought it was dull. The books reflect the belief that the most suitable fare for children is physical struggle—exploration, the fight against environment, battles, and wars—and a rather lopsided view of Canadian history results, giving the impression that it is a succession of fights and adventures, just as some constitutional historians give the impression that it is only about politics.

The series can also be criticized for a certain dreary similarity— in format, in design, and in style. Presumably the economics of publishing force a certain amount of computer-like repetition, for no other publisher's series, whether Canadian or American or British, has avoided this. The books in the 'Great Stories of Canada' have a uniform format (binding, type, and illustration), although the jacket design changed with volume thirty. There is almost a uniform number of pages, whether the events took place in a few months, as in Joseph Schull's *Battle For the Rock*, or over a period of years, as in D.J. Goodspeed's *The Good Soldier: The Story of Isaac Brock*. Although the illustrations are by various artists, the standard format gives them a devastating sameness so that many could be transferred from volume to volume. With few exceptions this sameness can also be observed in the writing, whose steady monotony sometimes affects the impact of events it is not impossible to imagine a quick, partial shuffle producing a book called *The Story of Samuel Cartier* or *The Story of Jacques de Champlain*. The average book in the series, typified by D.J Goodspeed's *The Good Soldier: The Story of Isaac Brock*, is no more than competent—dull, crowded with events, places, and names, and with the main subject never rising from the pages as a person. Indeed, with the exception of the Berton and Haig Brown contributions, the majority of the books in the 'Great Stories of Canada' read as if the writers were amateur historian pilfering from a book for adults to make up a book for children; as though the author had written the book with his left hand while the right was engaged upon its regular occupation. Stories of 'real people' are a genuine interest of children that often develops from their interest in legendary heroes. It is true that many children need dialogue as much as they need pictures to keep the printed page from looking stark and forbidding. But in the book of a real writer who is also a conscientious biographer or historian, children will not notice the lack of invention.

'Great Stories of Canada' seems to have run its course as a series with Josephine Phelan's *The Ballad of D'Arcy McGee* (1967) and Marjorie Wilkins Campbell's *The Savage River: Seventy-One Days With Simon Fraser* (1968). These two books express, rather clearly, both the weaknesses and the strengths of the series. Phelan's book on D'Arcy McGee suffers from carelessness in both content and style. The title is misleading since the book is in prose, interspersed with McGee's own heavy verse (which is never actually attributed to McGee). The space so used might well have been assigned to bolster historical fact, since much is left unexplained and some points are misrepresented. For example, we are not told when McGee immigrated to the United States for the first time nor from where—although Ireland is implied. The Fenians and their relationship to Canada are not adequately explained. Joseph Howe's opposition to Confederation is dismissed as a result of his rivalry with and jealousy of Tupper, and Nova Scotia's very real dissatisfaction with the terms of Confederation is ignored. The assassination itself, with all its ingredients of mystery, is played down. The writing shows the same lack of care as the author's presentation of history:

It was always his ideas and words that brought about his success and failures.

He was a man of ideas and words.

The new land was growing fast. Action. Action.

The land offices in the new territories had been closed . . . Too late. Too late.

In *The Savage River* Marjorie Wilkins Campbell works within a narrow time span, the seventy-one days of Fraser's journey down the river that bears his name. The voyage is set in its historical context and there are frequent quotes from Fraser's journal. The limitations imposed by space may have prevented a close look at the Indian situation: the hostility of the coastal Indians would have been better understood if seen within the context of their previous experience with white traders. The concentration upon Fraser's major achievement, however, guarantees what many books in the series lack: a memorable presentation of a significant achievement. Campbell's writing is direct and simple; she wisely leaves the dramatics to Fraser himself, who unconsciously provided them in his remarkable journals.

The outstanding fault of the 'Great Stories of Canada' series is inherent in its title. It is both misleading and unimaginative to suggest to children that history is a series of plots. Though history does offer plenty of story material, the idea that everything can or should be turned into a conventional tale is unsound because it excludes the perceptive use of source material, the weighing of evidence, alternative interpretations, indeed all the facets that make the writing of history different from the writing of fiction. This common attitude towards the writing of history may in turn explain some observable phenomena in this country. First of all, there is the famous boredom that children are accused of having towards Canadian history and history books (some of which *are* boring). Many young people are poor students of history because they have been given no early insight into its significance and into the delights of research, the skills of interpretation and deduction that give the evidence and materials of history their meaning. This in turn may explain why we have so few young (under-fifty) scholarly historians who write and why there is a dearth in Canada of first-rate non-academic writing for both children and adults.

Should the whole history of Canada be handled in a series format? Will the end result be dullness and stereotype? Will a writer who is interested in presenting history to children be afraid or unable to 'go it alone' without the backing of a series? It is surely of some significance that only one outstanding history has been published outside this series since its inception in 1953. The notable exception, William Toye's *The St Lawrence*, published in 1959, stands alone in many respects. It tells the history of Canada in terms of the river. Quiet in tone, sensitive in its approach, the account begins with the physical facts themselves: 'It lay there massive, empty, inviting, awaiting with infinite patience the prow of its European discoverer.' From geologic history, the book moves on to portray the events that the river has seen and helped make, down to the Seaway of modern times.

Although the book depends heavily on quoted material (contemporary journals, documents, letters, etc.), such material is never used carelessly or gratuitously. With judicious selection, Toye ranges before the reader materials as diverse as the solemn 'Instructions for the Fathers of Our Society Who Shall Be Sent to the Hurons', issued by Father Brébeuf, to the words of the crusty captain of the English ship *Goodwill* who, when sailing his ship up the St Lawrence for the first time, refused to allow the captured French pilot to assist with the navigation. ' "Aye, aye, my dear," replied our son of Neptune, "But damn me, I'll convince you that an Englishman shall go where a Frenchman dare not show his nose." '

Toye's own narrative is no mere recital of plain facts. It exhibits historical imagination by interpreting a known fact; finding a particular detail that illuminates the whole; making the whole mean more than the collection of its parts.

The river was a self-contained world to some, with so many problems of its own that little thought or interest was spared for what lay beyond. But it beckoned others far afield over its tributary lakes and rivers towards . . . the Pacific? Cathay? That was the tantalizing question. Champlain had never lost sight of these fabled destinations (though he had no time to pursue them) and neither did Jean Nicolet, who carried a mandarin's robe on his journey to Lake Michigan in the hope that it would be of use. And other explorers after them—especially La Salle—were lured by the self-same goals.

Without obtrusive embellishments Toye preserves to a remarkable degree the intimate quality of history and indeed its 'story' aspect. He humanizes his narrative—we read about Roberval's niece marooned on the Isle of Demons, Madeleine de Verchères outwitting the Iroquois, and a dinner party given by Alexander Mackenzie—but never merely prettifies it. Inevitably there is a concentration upon the early history of Canada and complexity is sometimes sacrificed for vividness. But fifteen years after its publication *The St Lawrence* still represents our finest historical writing for children—the only important book to be published outside the series format—and it has a place with the best writing in this field from other countries.

Why is it so few professional historians and biographers wish to share their knowledge of Canada's past with the young? History is left to textbooks, with a resulting distaste for the subject on the part of young people. Were it not for some enlightened publishers who seek out writers to do set pieces, the books about our past would be slim fare indeed.

A recent outstanding publisher's series is 'Canadian Lives', with eight biographies published in 1971 and one in 1974: *James Douglas* by Dorothy Blakey Smith, *John A. Macdonald* by Donald Swainson, *Wilfrid Laurier* by Barbara Robertson, *William Lyon Mackenzie* and *John Strachan* by David Flint, *David Thompson* by James K. Smith, *Louis Riel* by Hartwell Bowsfield, *Alexander Mackenzie* by Roy Daniells, and *Lester Pearson* by Bruce Thordarson. They are brief (up to 160 pages, with *Pearson* 256 pages); the texts are reasonably authoritative; they have good contemporary photographs as illustrations and an index, bibliography, and a pleasing paperback format. This series has been automatically dubbed 'for older children' (meaning children in Grade 10 and beyond). This attitude may well derive from the impact of the 'Great Stories of Canada', in which fiction was all too frequently mixed with history. Yet all books in the 'Canadian Lives' series play it straight, giving the biographer's interpretation based upon findable evidence; they are clearly and simply written (there is most definitely no writing down: the books can be enjoyed by adults who don't want to read an exhaustive biography) and they do not neglect anecdotes and social background. A great many children can and do enter easily into historical material thus presented.

All the biographers deserve praise for keeping to a clear historical line while moving through the intricacies of events and acknowledging all viewpoints without creating confusion—not easy to do in political biographies. Riel caused a great deal of controversy in his time and continues to raise passions even today. Historians and biographers have tended to condemn him, praise him, or dismiss him as insane. Bowsfield presents a balanced view of Riel, the two rebellions, and the plight of the Métis. He examines the reasons, motives, and provocations on both sides, but not at tedious length and always with appropriate back-up material in the way of quotations. A very clear portrait of Riel emerges with the aid of such first-hand material as an interesting interview he gave to the *Winnipeg Daily Sun* in June 1883. One indication of the book's fairness and objectivity is that it has been translated and published in a French edition.

Plain, straightforward writing that yields facts is a minimum requirement in the writing of history and biography, and a valid interpretation based on those facts gives it strength and character. If the reading of history is to take place outside the demands of the school curriculum, a graceful and lively style is another requirement, though it is so rare in this kind of writing that it is accepted gratefully as an unexpected bonus when, as in Barbara Robertson's *Wilfrid Laurier: The Great Conciliator*, it does appear.

That Laurier's cabinet was not getting any younger struck Mackenzie King forcibly too, for he noted in his diary the many times he found ministers asleep during cabinet meetings.

The year before the First World War began, the strains of 'Rule Britannia' became fainter in Canada. The great questions of the Empire gave way to hard domestic ones as Canadians began to suffer from inflation and economic depression—fever and chills unpleasantly combined.

Robertson's quotable style does not mask poor biography. Most critics would probably quarrel with only a few minor points in the author's interpretations of the subject. Robertson also gives a bit of attention to Zoë Laurier as a person, not merely as the wife of Laurier, and to Laurier's friend, Mme Lavergne.

In *William Lyon Mackenzie: Rebel Against Authority* David
Flint shows that by his ideas Mackenzie was an agrarian conservative (or even reactionary) and a moral crusader rather than
a revolutionary or social reformer. Despite the sub-title, he was
not entirely a 'rebel against authority'—he even appealed to British
authority at times—and he was much too erratic to evolve a consistent plan or philosophy. The interesting political and economic
situation of the time, and the outrageous Mackenzie himself, are
treated fairly and in sufficient detail, with quotations from contemporary newspapers and correspondence.

These political biographies are the first of their kind for young
readers—a rather devastating measure of our interest in ourselves,
considering the number of American children's books there are on
Abraham Lincoln, for example. Some subjects have been covered
in the 'Great Stories of Canada', but the more recent 'Canadian
Lives' biographies—*David Thompson* by James K. Smith, *Louis
Riel* by Hartwell Bowsfield, and *Alexander Mackenzie* by Roy
Daniells—add a new dimension, if indeed they do not supercede
the older books: Kerry Wood's *The Map-Maker: The Story of
David Thompson* (1955), Edward McCourt's *Revolt in the West:
The Story of the Riel Rebellion* (1958), and Richard S. Lambert's
Trailmaker: The Story of Alexander Mackenzie (1957).

There is surely room for more than one good book on a topic.
There is an equally compelling need for the same topic to be
handled at different reading levels—from a stunning picture book,
to a fairly simple biography with only highlights, to a more
scholarly work of the 'Canadian Lives' type. (But would the
market support such variety? Alas, probably not.) Only Alexander Mackenzie has commanded the attention of more than two
biographers, but these books differ mainly in interpretation and
style, although Thomas Bredin's *From Sea to Sea: Alexander
Mackenzie* (1970) is intended for a slightly younger age group
than Richard S. Lambert's *Trailmaker: The Story of Alexander
Mackenzie* (1957), Roy Daniells' *Alexander Mackenzie*, published
in 'Canadian Lives' but first published in England in 1969, or
James K. Smith's *Alexander Mackenzie, Explorer: The Hero Who
Failed* (1973). Daniells is the most compelling biographer of the
four, not only because his book is so well written (as is to be

expected, considering the author's literary background) but because in so obviously admiring his subject he makes the reader sympathetic to Mackenzie—an important point in capturing the interest of the young, one that too many Canadian biographers have not considered. Daniells doesn't overdo it, however; he is critical of Mackenzie's opposition to Selkirk's scheme and sides with the colonists rather than with their fur-trading opponents. Daniells shows himself to be a genuine historian in extrapolating ideas from events. He sees Mackenzie's work not only as the opening up of the Canadian Northwest and the fur trade but as a parable of the Canadian experience, a foreshadowing of future history. There is rich commentary as well as description—on the role of women, Mackenzie's relationship to his men and so on. James K. Smith is less enamoured of Mackenzie than Daniells, as his sub-title indicates. For example he speaks of Mackenzie's low opinion of the Indians. (However, Daniells has recounted, with a speech, the story of Mackenzie carrying a wounded Indian through a rapid at a risk to his own life.) On the whole, Smith's account has a more academic feel to it than Daniells', although he has modernized the spelling and punctuation in the extracts from Mackenzie's *Journals*, while Daniells reproduces them authentically.

Outside of the life of John Strachan (and possibly William Lyon Mackenzie), the 'Canadian Lives' series has concentrated on men who are major to the history of Canada. 'Canadian Biographical Studies' was planned to 'fill a gap in our knowledge of men who seemed often to be merely secondary figures, frequently non-political contributors to our regional and national experience in Canada'. The series—which is allied to the *Dictionary of Canadian Biography*—includes *John Strachan* by J.L.H. Henderson, *Roland-Michel Barrin de la Galissonière* by L.A. Groulx, *Henry Alline* by J.M. Bumstead, *John Sandfield Macdonald* by B.W. Hodgins, and *The Denison Family of Toronto* by D.P. Gogan. These books were not aimed at children but at 'the general reader'. However, they are brief—100 to 150 pages—and although some are more scholarly in their approach than others, they certainly could be absorbed by older interested children.

Neither the 'Canadian Lives' series nor the 'Canadian Biographical Studies' has admitted a woman to the company of outstanding men. Some notable omissions are books on Agnes McPhail, Nellie McClung, Emily Murphy, L.M. Montgomery, Emily Carr, Helen Gregory MacGill, and Lady Simcoe—to mention only a few.

Another series is 'Adventures in Canadian History' edited by R.W.W. Robertson. These are booklets, with about 30 pages of text and 8 pages of photographs. For the most part they deal with events rather than people: the building of the Canadian Pacific Railway, early western settlement, the National Policy, the Royal Canadian Mounted Police, the execution of Thomas Scott and the birth of Manitoba. Together they are intended to 'give an overview of the decisive years 1867-85 during which the Canadian Nation was formed'. They do this in the way of a guide-book usefully but baldly.

Most individual books in this field lack good editorship, which could at least have cleared up some very obvious faults. John E Hood's *Hunters of the North* (1966) is not a continuous narrative but endeavours to emphasize various aspects of the fur trade—the Hudson's Bay Company, supplies, animals, Indians, etc. The simplistic and rather didactic style might be endurable if it were not for the writer's condescending attitude to the Indians and the Eskimos who were, after all, skilled and sensible hunters. His attitude towards the killing of wolves and the future use of electronic equipment in hunting should rouse the ire of environmentalists and conservationists.

Iris Allan's *Wop May: Bush Pilot* (1966) is one of numerous Canadian non-fiction books that make it difficult to judge the author's intention. Is the book absolutely based on fact or is it intended as fictionalized history and/or biography, or is it historical fiction? Based on actual events, it is told in story form:

> Violet smiled at him and then said seriously, 'Those planes didn't fly by themselves, Wop. It took courage and vision and ingenuity to fight against the odds you bush pilots encountered. But you had what it took and, among you all, you succeeded in opening up Canada's last frontier.

Wop May was first of all a *character* and his achievements were mportant and exciting: not even this badly written book can altogether destroy that. Vicky Metcalf's *Journey Fantastic: With he Overlanders to the Cariboo* (1970), although a better-written book than *Wop May*, presents the same mixture of fact and fiction. The story of the Overlanders' trek from Winnipeg to Kamloops in 1862 is told from the point of view of the only woman among some 200 men, Catherine Schubert. Pregnant and with three children to look after, she survived the trip across the prairies and through the mountains, arriving in Kamloops just in time to bear her child—'the first white child born in Kamloops'. The author has used, among other sources, accounts and diaries of some of the Overlanders (McMicking's is perhaps the best known). But since Catherine presumably kept no diary, one must assume that her thoughts and observations and some of the dialogue are re-creations by the author.

Many books are enjoyed by the young that are not written specifically for them and this applies in the fields of history and biography as in other fields. Fast-paced books with a touch of the violent and the macabre have appeal almost regardless of subject matter. Dick North's *The Mad Trapper of Rat River* (1972) is a fast-moving account of 'true crime', the life of Albert Johnson who was the subject of a 48-day police hunt near the Arctic Circle over forty years ago. North includes a considerable amount of information about the locale of the hunt and the people who live there. (The inclusion here of such a book as *The Mad Trapper of Rat River*, which is more adventure than biography or history, serves only to point up the appalling lack of material that is both interesting and well written.)

1066 and All That by Sellar and Yeatman is the classic humorous spoof of British history. Every year some children discover it with joy and it is still as fresh and timeless as when it was first published. Stanley Burke's *Frog Fables and Beaver Tales* (1973) could be appreciated by children with some knowledge of Canadian history and politics of the last ten years, but it is not a funny book in the sense that *1066* is funny. It is rather political satire about French-English troubles, regional troubles, and Canadian-American relations. The setting is a swamp called Canada inhabited and run by the Beavers (Central Canadian English). In and around the swamp also live the Frogs (French), the Turtles (Indians), the Gophers (Westerners), the Otters (British Columbians), and others. The Americans are, of course, the Eagles. The tone veers almost constantly towards cynicism. Here is Burke on Canada's peacekeeping role:

It was very noble, but the Beavers were modest—they said it was simply that they were more sensible than other animals.

However, *any* note of humour is welcome in the almost unbroken round of dullness of our histories for children.

FOR YOUNGER READERS

It is not easy to write sound history that is readable for children under ten—this is presumably why we have so few books worthy of one's attention—but it can be done by presenting facts simply, and especially by concentrating on anecdotes and atmosphere. William Toye's *Cartier Discovers the St Lawrence* (1971), illustrated by Laszlo Gal, is a brave and successful attempt to recount an important event in our history as well as to lavish the utmost visual attractiveness on it in the form of large picture-book illustrations. With admirable simplicity and brevity the narrative includes all the significant (and colourful) incidents associated with Cartier's voyages and something of the atmosphere of them as well.

William Toye is the co-author with Ivon Owen of another good picture-book on Canadian history, *A Picture History of Canada*, with four-colour pictures by the English artist Clarke Hutton on every page. Colourfully illustrated, tastefully designed so as to link text and pictorial material, concisely and plainly written, full of vivid details, it comes off very well. First published in 1956, it was revised (to include Expo 67) in 1967. It is still the best simple overview of Canadian history for young children.

Two runners-up for excellence (although perhaps for slightly older children) are *The Story of Canada* (1960), with text by S.J. Totten and illustrations by B. Biro, and *O Canada!* (1964) by Isabel Barclay, illustrated by Cécile Gagnon. *The Story of Canada*, while an attractive publication, is much more an abridgement than ither *A Picture History of Canada* or *O Canada!*, which wisely prefer to concentrate on a few selected events rather than attempt to cover the whole of Canadian history. *O Canada!*, although the more recent publication, ends with Confederation. *The Story of Canada* brings the history up to modern times.

Still another worthy candidate for the youngest readers' attention is Mary Graham Bonner's *Canada and Her Story*, first published in 1942 and issued in a revised edition in 1950. It is a general history of Canada that is brief and simple without being merely a bald recital of dates and deeds. Bonner's style combines liveliness with dignity.

The measure of these writers' success in making a straightforward presentation of history interesting can be seen by comparing their books with *My First History of Canada* (1958) by Donalda Dickie. Though some allowance must be made for the disadvantage this book suffers in having been written in a textbook format, its chief deficiency is clearly intrinsic—the matter of style. The author has written in a childish rather than a childlike way, and what should be simplicity often is merely cloying cuteness. Sentences such as, 'For several years Governor Simpson dashed round the west building up the fur trade,' and 'Prince Edward Island invented fox farming' subtract from, rather than add to, the intended effect.

Four recent books of some historical and strong graphic interest that will appeal to younger readers are autobiographical: *Grandmother Came from Dworitz* (1969) by Ethel Vineberg, *A Child in Prison Camp* (1971) by Shizuye Takashima, *Pitseolak: Pictures Out of My Life* (1971), and *A Prairie Boy's Winter* (1973) by William Kurelek. They are all discussed elsewhere in this book.

IN SUMMARY

History is scholarship and interpretation. These two elements assume knowledge and sensibility. To present history in an entertaining, simple, and yet undistorted way calls for an exceptional combination of skills. Instances of such talent are not numerous, so it is not surprising that even among the wealth of children's histories and biographies published in Great Britain and the

United States, very few spring to mind as being distinguished or of enduring quality.*

The extent of historical knowledge is so vast that it is possible to give a child only an introduction to history, a taste of what it offers. Simplified though it is, however, this experience can be a significant one and can provide a sense of satisfaction and an understanding of the 'real' that other forms of literature do not offer.

ALLAN, IRIS. *Wop May: Bush Pilot.* Illustrated by William Wheeler. Toronto, Clarke, Irwin, 1966. 170 pp.
The bush pilots are the heroes of the North and none was more of a hero than the first of them all, Wop May. However, this brief story-biography, sentimental in tone, hardly does him justice.

BARCLAY, ISABEL. *O Canada!* Illustrated by Cécile Gagnon. Toronto, Double-day, 1964. 96 pp.
A simple and sprightly introduction to Canadian history, attractively illustrated, for children under ten.

BERTON, PIERRE. *The Golden Trail: The Story of the Klondike Rush.* Illustrated by Duncan Macpherson. Toronto, Macmillan, 1954. 147 pp. ('Great Stories of Canada'.)
The author captures the tremendous excitement engendered by the discovery of gold in the Yukon. This is lively and authentic historical writing.

BONNER, MARY GRAHAM. *Canada and Her Story,* 2nd rev. ed. New York, Knopf, 1950. 182 pp.
In age level this general history of Canada falls between Barclay's *O Canada!* and Toye's *The St Lawrence.*

BOWSFIELD, HARTWELL. *Louis Riel: The Rebel and the Hero.* Toronto, Oxford, 1971. 160 pp. ('Canadian Lives'.)
No one in Canadian history, either in the past or the present, has raised more passions than Louis Riel. Bowsfield's brief but scrupulous and fair examination of the man and the events that surrounded him is all the more welcome.

---

*Some outstanding examples in this field from the United States and Great Britain are Carl Sandburg's *Abe Lincoln Grows Up*; Geoffrey Trease's *Sir Walter Raleigh*; Anna Hall's *Nansen*; Mary Renault's *The Lion in the Gateway* (about three famous Greek battles); Leonard Cottrell's *The Last of the Pharaohs*; James Playford Wood's *The Snark Was a Boojum*, a life of Lewis Carroll; and *Child O'War* by Leon Garfield and David Proctor.

BREDIN, THOMAS. *From Sea to Sea: Alexander Mackenzie.* Toronto, Longman, 1970. 117 pp. ('Canadian Pageant Series'.)

An episodic, textbook approach to Mackenzie's work. Its value as information intended for younger readers than the other biographies may well be superceded by the style and conviction of the Daniells biography.

BREDIN, THOMAS. *River of Canada.* Illustrated by J.L. Patterson. Toronto, Longman, 1962. 134 pp. ('Canadian Pageant Series'.)

This history of Canada, which draws seriously on contemporary documents, ends with Champlain. Although a worthwhile addition to our history books, it in no way approaches the distinction of Toye's *The St Lawrence* in content, style, or format.

BROWN, GEORGE W., ELEANOR HARMON, and MARSH JEANNERET. *The Story of Canada.* Illustrated by Virginia Byers and Margaret Salisbury. Toronto, Copp Clark, 1950. 434 pp.

This general history of Canada, written as a textbook, gives importance to trends rather than events. While similar in format to Donalda Dickie's *The Great Adventure*, the writing is less sprightly. It does, however, complement the Dickie book and is intended for the same 'middle-aged' children.

BURKE, STANLEY. *Frog Fables and Beaver Tales.* Illustrated by Roy Peterson. Toronto, James Lewis & Samuel, 1973. 45 pp.

A political satire of Canada well within the range of those children who have some historical background. A few more such amusing books would relieve the aura of dullness and solemnity that has been made to surround Canadian history.

BUTLER, KENNETH C. *Igloo Killinek.* Illustrated by William Wheeler. Toronto, Longman, 1963. ('Canadian Pageant Series'.)

Dr Butler was only nineteen years old in 1920 when he helped set up the first R.C.M.P. detachment in the Eastern Arctic at Port Burwell in Labrador. This account of his exciting and sometimes tragic experiences is more thrilling than many a work of fiction.

CAMPBELL, MARJORIE WILKINS. *The Nor'Westers: The Fight for the Fur Trade.* Illustrated by Illingworth Kerr. Toronto, Macmillan, 1961. 176 pp. ('Great Stories of Canada'.)

This history of the North West Company concentrates on the struggle for supremacy in the fur trade. A complex subject is handled in an interesting manner with attention to the colourful figures in the trade.

CAMPBELL, MARJORIE WILKINS. *The Savage River: Seventy-One Days With Simon Fraser.* Toronto, Macmillan, 1968. 146 pp. ('Great Stories of Canada'.)

Although this book confines itself to one aspect of Fraser's life—his journey down the river that bears his name—the expedition is firmly set within its historical framework. Apt quotations from Fraser's *Journal* add considerably to the interest.

CHALMERS, JOHN W. *Red River Adventure: The Story of the Selkirk Settlers.* Illustrated by Lewis Parker. Toronto, Macmillan. 1956. 158 pp. ('Great Stories of Canada'.)

Caught between the rivalries of the Hudson's Bay and North West Companies, the Selkirk settlers struggled for existence in the early nineteenth century. A tense, complex period is for the most part depicted with admirable clarity.

COSGROVE, EDMUND. *Canada's Fighting Pilots.* Illustrated by the author. Toronto, Clarke, Irwin, 1965. 190 pp. ('Canadian Portraits Series'.)

The achievements of the Royal Canadian Air Force are recounted through the deeds of individual pilots in the First and Second World Wars. The writing is vivid, and documentary in style.

CREIGHTON, LUELLA B. *Tecumseh: The Story of the Shawnee Chief.* Illustrated by William Lytle. Toronto, Macmillan, 1965. 159 pp. ('Great Stories of Canada'.)

The tragedy of the American Indians in the face of westward encroachment is reflected in the life of Tecumseh. This sympathetic and forceful picture of the Indian chief, who was allied with the British in the War of 1812, is sometimes submerged in a maze of small details.

DANIELLS, ROY. *Alexander Mackenzie and the North West.* Toronto, Oxford, 1971. (First published by Faber in 1969.) 219 pp. ('Canadian Lives'.)

'I admire Alexander Mackenzie,' this biography proclaims; but Daniells' admiration is tempered not only with judgement, but with historical fact. By virtue of his writing style, his perceptive interpretation of Mackenzie, and his ability to link a seemingly narrow aspect of history to larger events, Daniells has produced what could be called a definitive biography for young people.

DICKIE, DONALDA. *The Great Adventure: An Illustrated History of Canada for Young Canadians.* Illustrated by Lloyd Scott. Toronto, Dent, 1950. 470 pp.

The history of Canada, simply told, informative, and dramatic, emphasizing the social and economic aspects. It was written on the theory that the discovery, colonization, and development of Canada have been sufficiently exciting to appeal to boys and girls without any literary colouring or heroics. It remains, however, a textbook.

DICKIE, DONALDA. *My First History of Canada.* Illustrated by Lloyd Scott. Toronto, Dent, 1958. 204 pp.

An uninspired history of Canada for younger readers in textbook format.

FAIRLEY, THOMAS C. and CHARLES E. ISRAEL. *The True North: The Story of Captain Joseph Bernier.* Illustrated by James Hill. Toronto, Macmillan, 1957. 160 pp. ('Great Stories of Canada'.)

By virtue of his assiduous exploration of the Polar Seas, Bernier assured Canada's sovereignty over the Arctic. An adequate presentation of the work of this too-little-known Canadian.

FARRAR, FREDERICK S. *Arctic Assignment: The Story of the St. Roch*. Edited by Barrett Bonnezen. Illustrated by Vernon Mould. Toronto, Macmillan, 1955. 180 pp. ('Great Stories of Canada'.)

The hardships and dangers that faced earlier Arctic explorers were not far removed as the R.C.M.P. schooner, *St. Roch*, began a two-year voyage from Vancouver to Halifax via the Northwest Passage in 1940. Interest and drama are often stifled by the pedestrian writing.

FERGUSON, ROBERT D. *Fur Trader: The Story of Alexander Henry*. Illustrated by Douglas Sneyd. Toronto, Macmillan, 1961. 159 pp. ('Great Stories of Canada'.)

How the British victory on the Plains of Abraham affected the Indians and the fur trade is the basic theme running through this dramatic life of Alexander Henry the elder. The book loses its very strong impact and its continuity after the end of the Pontiac uprising.

FERGUSON, ROBERT D. *Man From St. Malo: The Story of Jacques Cartier*. Illustrated by Douglas Sneyd. London, Macmillan, 1959. 160 pp. Revised 1974. 123 pp. ('Great Stories of Canada'.)

The exploits of the man who claimed Canada for the French are recounted here in a lively enough manner but without the distinction and authenticity of Esther Averill's *Cartier Sails the St. Lawrence*.

FLINT, DAVID. *John Strachan: Pastor and Politician*. Toronto, Oxford, 1971. 160 pp. ('Canadian Lives'.)

This clergyman, teacher, politician, and founder of two universities—a man of mainly local interest in the early history of Ontario—would not seem to be the ideal subject for a biography for young people. Yet Bishop Strachan *was* influential and Flint has examined his long career lucidly and interestingly. A useful companion to the same author's *William Lyon Mackenzie*.

FLINT, DAVID. *William Lyon Mackenzie: Rebel Against Authority*. Toronto, Oxford, 1971. 192 pp. ('Canadian Lives'.)

Only Louis Riel has provoked more controversy than William Lyon Mackenzie. In spite of his sub-title, Flint shows (quite correctly) Mackenzie to be a man who fundamentally respected *constitutional* authority and was even rather right-wing in some of his views—though always most erratic. The events of 1837 are depicted with the utmost clarity, with interesting details, and with a commendable fairness towards the protagonists on both sides.

GOODSPEED, DONALD J. *The Good Soldier: The Story of Isaac Brock*. Illustrated by Jack Ferguson. Toronto, Macmillan, 1964. 156 pp. ('Great Stories of Canada'.)

Brock's defence of Upper Canada refuted Jefferson's prediction that the conquest of Canada would be 'a mere matter of marching'. A straightforward, competent biography and history of the War of 1812.

HAIG-BROWN, RODERICK L. *Captain of the Discovery: The Story of Captain George Vancouver.* Illustrated by Robert Banks. Toronto, Macmillan, 1956. 181 pp. ('Great Stories of Canada'.)

This is a plainly written but interesting account of the far-flung explorations of Vancouver, particularly his survey of the British Columbia coast, made from 1792 to 1794.

HAIG-BROWN, RODERICK L. *The Farthest Shores.* Toronto, Longman, Green, 1960. 127 pp. ('Canadian Pageant Series'.)

The explorers of British Columbia, from Bering to Thompson, are presented in a combination of the narrative and dramatic forms. While it does not have much drama, this history, based on a series of radio broadcasts, is a product of Haig-Brown's usual careful research and direct presentation.

HARRIS, JOHN N. *Knights of the Air: Canadian Aces of World War I.* Illustrated by William Wheeler. Toronto, Macmillan, 1958. 160 pp. ('Great Stories of Canada'.)

An account of Canada's flying heroes told in unimpassioned and undistinguished prose.

HOOD, JOHN EDWARD. *Hunters of the North.* Illustrations by Jerry Lazare. Toronto, Ryerson, 1966. 159 pp.

The fur trade forms the connecting link in a series of chapters dealing with hunting in the North. Hood's remarks on hunting are anti-conservationist.

LAMBERT, RICHARD S. *Franklin of the Arctic.* Maps by Julius Griffith. Toronto, McClelland and Stewart, 1949. 354 pp.

This life of Franklin from his early experiences as a midshipman under Nelson to his explorations and death in the Arctic is presented with liveliness and authenticity.

LAMBERT, RICHARD S. *Mutiny in the Bay: Henry Hudson's Last Voyage.* Illustrated by Joe Rosenthal. Toronto, Macmillan, 1963. 160 pp. ('Great Stories of Canada'.)

The dramatic and shocking events of Hudson's last voyage lose none of their impact as they are related by an eye-witness. Based on the journal of Abacuk Pricket.

LAMBERT, RICHARD S. *North for Adventure.* Illustrated by Vernon Mould. Toronto, McClelland and Stewart, 1952. 208 pp.

Samuel Hearne was the first white man to reach the Arctic overland from Hudson's Bay. This is a lively account of his adventurous journeys and his contacts with the Indians, but in spite of a wealth of detail and a conversational approach, Hearne does not emerge as the fascinating, unforgettable character he was.

LAMBERT, RICHARD S. *Redcoat Sailor: The Adventures of Sir Howard Douglas.* Illustrated by Adrian Dingle. Toronto, Macmillan, 1956. 160 pp. ('Great Stories of Canada'.)

Douglas (1776-1861) began his Canadian career by being wrecked on the coast of Newfoundland and ended it as Lieutenant-Governor of New Brunswick. In between he had little link with Canada. The events of his life are recounted in simple story form.

LAMBERT, RICHARD S. *Trailmaker: The Story of Alexander Mackenzie.* Toronto, McClelland and Stewart, 1957. 160 pp.
This emphasizes Mackenzie's two chief voyages as a Nor'Wester—to the Arctic by way of the Mackenzie River and to the Pacific, the first crossing of North America north of Mexico. Although based solidly on fact, this is a fictionalized account, overladen with detail.

LEITCH, ADELAIDE. *Canada: Young Giant of the North.* Toronto, Nelson, 1964. 223 pp.
In this uneasy combination of geography and history, the writer only manages to promote a pathetic, self-conscious Canadianism.

LONGSTRETH, T. MORRIS. *The Scarlet Force: The Making of the Mounted Police.* Illustrated by Ruth M. Collins. Toronto, Macmillan, 1953. 182 pp. Revised 1973, 1974. 154 pp. ('Great Stories of Canada'.)
The achievements of the North West Mounted Police are related clearly to the settlement of the West, but individuals and individual achievements are given their due. The sequel, *The Force Carries On* (illustrated by Clare Bice; Toronto, Macmillan, 1954, 'Great Stories of Canada') continues the work of the Royal Canadian Mounted Police until the fifties. The author could have relied on built-in glamour and sensationalism, but instead he writes with restraint and knowledge.

MC COURT, EDWARD. *Buckskin Brigadier: The Story of the Alberta Field Force.* Illustrated by Vernon Mould. Toronto, Macmillan, 1955. 150 pp. ('Great Stories of Canada'.)
A view of the North West Rebellion of 1885 is given through the comparatively little-known efforts of the Alberta Field Force, under the leadership of the retired British general, Tom Strange. The writing shows a laborious striving for effect.

MC COURT, EDWARD. *Revolt in the West: The Story of the Riel Rebellion.* Illustrated by Jack Ferguson. Toronto, Macmillan, 1958. 159 pp. ('Great Stories of Canada'.)
This straightforward account of the stirring events of 1885 does not lose sight of the tragedy of the Métis.

MC CREADY, LOUISE G. *Famous Musicians: MacMillan, Johnson, Pelletier, Willan.* Toronto, Clarke, Irwin, 1957. 140 pp. ('Canadian Portraits Series'.)
Because it provides information not readily available elsewhere, this is a valuable contribution to modern Canadian biography. Unfortunately the style is generally dull, over-simplified, or encyclopaedic.

METCALF, VICKY. *Journey Fantastic: With the Overlanders to the Cariboo.*
Toronto, Ryerson, 1970. 159 pp.
The story of Catherine Schubert, the only woman on the Overlanders' expedition to the Cariboo (whose child was the first white child born in
Kamloops), is told with a mixture of fact and fiction. As there are so few
books about Canadian women, it is regrettable that those we have should
present their subjects no more than adequately, as Catherine Schubert is
presented.

MILLER, ORLO. *Raiders of the Mohawk: The Story of Butler's Rangers.* Illustrated by John MacLellan. Toronto, Macmillan, 1954. 182 pp. ('Great
Stories of Canada'.)
'By a succession of military feats of an almost superhuman character
[Colonel Butler and his corps of Rangers] kept the armies of the rebellious
colonies from seizing the basin of the Great Lakes.' This is a fictionalized
story stressing action rather than a historical look at, or justification of,
causes.

NORTH, DICK. *The Mad Trapper of Rat River.* Toronto, Macmillan, 1972. 144
pp.
The greatest manhunt in the history of the RCMP took place forty years
ago, lasted forty-eight days, and led north to the Arctic Circle. In discussing the mystery surrounding Albert Johnson ('the mad trapper'), the author
reveals much of the way of life of those who live in the North.

OWEN, IVON and WILLIAM TOYE. *A Picture History of Canada.* Illustrated by
Clarke Hutton. Toronto, Oxford, 1956; second edition 1968. 64 pp.
Bold and colourful four-colour pictures by an English artist convey a sense
of Canada's dramatic past for readers under ten, as well as something of
the vastness of the natural environment. The text highlights the significant
details of this past.

PHELAN, JOSEPHINE. *The Ballad of D'Arcy McGee.* Illustrated by David Craig.
Toronto, Macmillan, 1967. 132 pp. ('Great Stories of Canada'.)
A rather dull presentation of the life of McGee that is made even duller
by the inclusion of passages from his florid poetry. There is certainly room
for another biography of this vocal and vivid Irish-Canadian.

PHELAN, JOSEPHINE. *The Bold Heart: The Story of Father Lacombe.* Illustrated
by Jerry Lazare. Toronto, Macmillan, 1956. 182 pp. ('Great Stories of
Canada'.)
A straightforward account of the life of the great missionary of the prairies
whose work spanned the development of the West from 1853 to 1916.

PRATT, VIOLA W. *Famous Doctors: Osler, Banting, Penfield.* Toronto, Clarke,
Irwin, 1956. 160 pp. ('Canadian Portraits Series'.)
The lives of three brilliant and dedicated men are here reduced to a weary
round of minuscule detail that tends to obscure the genuine drama of their
major accomplishments.

RADDALL, THOMAS H. *The Rover: The Story of a Canadian Privateer.* Illustrated by Vernon Mould. Toronto, Macmillan, 1958. 156 pp. ('Great Stories of Canada'.)

The Nova Scotia privateer, *The Rover*, fought and defeated a Spanish schooner and two gunboats in the Spanish main on September 12, 1800. This fictionalized account of the encounter precedes a plain recital of events that linked Nova Scotia to the West Indies in peace and war during the Napoleonic period.

RITCHIE, CICERO T. *The First Canadian: The Story of Champlain.* Illustrated by William Wheeler. Toronto, Macmillan, 1961. 155 pp. ('Great Stories of Canada'.)

Champlain's main accomplishments in Canada are covered in all their aspects, but the emphasis is on events rather than on the man.

RITCHIE, CICERO T. *Runner of the Woods: The Story of Young Radisson.* Illustrated by William Wheeler. Toronto, Macmillan, 1963. 160 pp. ('Great Stories of Canada'.)

Radisson's exploits among the Iroquois, his captures, escapes, and his partnership with Groseilliers make him one of Canada's most exciting characters, but he never comes alive in these pages.

ROBERTSON, BARBARA. *Wilfrid Laurier: The Great Conciliator.* Toronto, Oxford, 1971. 160 pp. ('Canadian Lives'.)

Laurier is one of the few colourful and charismatic prime ministers of Canada and Robertson supports this view with a sound interpretation of historical fact. The succinct, light, graceful style is a pleasure to read.

SANDERS, BYRNE HOPE. *Famous Women: Carr, Hind, Gullen, Murphy.* Toronto, Clarke, Irwin, 1958. 145 pp. ('Canadian Portraits Series'.)

These lively accounts of four remarkable women—an artist (Carr), an agricultural expert (Hind), the first woman doctor trained in Canada (Gullen), and the first woman magistrate (Murphy)—show that Canada has produced fascinating and courageous personalities in modern times.

SCHULL, JOSEPH. *Battle for the Rock: The Story of Wolfe and Montcalm.* Illustrated by Lewis Parker. Toronto, Macmillan, 1960. 158 pp. ('Great Stories of Canada'.)

This is a fast-paced, intense account of the events leading up to the Battle of the Plains of Abraham and of the battle itself. Unfortunately a colourful imagination in reconstructing atmosphere and events sometimes overpowers adherence to historical evidence.

SCHULL, JOSEPH. *The Salt-Water Men: Canada's Deep-Sea Sailors.* Illustrated by Ed. McNally. Toronto, Macmillan, 1957. 144 pp. ('Great Stories of Canada'.)

This is a sketch of the great days of the Canadian wooden ships and the 'Bluenose' sailors. There are a few interesting stories, but the book has little cohesion.

SCHULL, JOSEPH. *Ships of the Great Days: Canada's Navy in World War II.* Illustrated by Ed. McNally. Toronto, Macmillan, 1962. 156 pp. ('Great Stories of Canada'.)

Technical or informational details provide this book's greatest strength. The heroes, while never underplayed, are left to speak for themselves.

SHAW, MARGARET MASON. *Bush Pilots.* Illustrated by John Young. Toronto, Clarke, Irwin, 1962. 178 pp. ('Canadian Portraits Series'.)

The important and dramatic role of the bush pilots in the development of the North almost becomes dull through the pedestrian writing and the author's lack of ability to select pertinent detail from valuable and original source material.

SHAW, MARGARET MASON. *Geologists and Prospectors: Tyrrell, Camsell, Cross, LaBine.* Toronto, Clarke, Irwin, 1958. 190 pp. ('Canadian Portraits Series'.)

These biographies are not without interest, but it is the documentary material, particularly on the prospectors Cross and LaBine, rather than the 'portraits' of the men that gives this book what virtue it has. These accounts are too solemn and contain too much trivia to be of much interest as general reading.

SMITH, DOROTHY BLAKEY. *James Douglas: Father of British Columbia.* Toronto, Oxford, 1971. 128 pp. ('Canadian Lives'.)

A sound brief biography of 'Old Square Toes', the autocratic man who was responsible for leading Canada's far-western province from mountain wilderness through the first stages of civilization.

SMITH, JAMES K. *Alexander Mackenzie, Explorer: The Hero Who Failed.* Toronto, McGraw-Hill Ryerson, 1973. 190 pp.

A rather dry though accurate account of Mackenzie's life and achievements —Mackenzie is not even allowed to speak for himself.

SMITH, JAMES K. *David Thompson: Fur Trader, Explorer, Geographer.* Toronto, Oxford, 1971. 128 pp. ('Canadian Lives'.)

Mainly a record of Thompson's experiences from 1784 to 1812, which included his exploration of the Columbia River. A workmanlike short biography that uses interesting quotations from Thompson's *Narrative.*

SWAINSON, DONALD. *John A. Macdonald: The Man and the Politician.* Toronto, Oxford, 1971. 160 pp. ('Canadian Lives'.)

The events of Confederation form a considerable portion of this biography, and occasionally Swainson simplifies events; but this is inevitable because it is intended as a brief review of Macdonald's life. Swainson is highly sympathetic to Macdonald's domestic problems but does not avoid noticing the flaws in his character.

SWAYZE, FRED. *Frontenac and the Iroquois: The Fighting Governor of New France.* Illustrated by Huntley Brown. Toronto, Macmillan, 1959. 158 pp. ('Great Stories of Canada.')

Of course throughout this dismal period Canadian children took what they wanted from the adult world and made it their own. This can be seen in the popularity of Pauline Johnson's *Flint and Feather* (1912). For many Canadian children 'The Song My Paddle Sings', encountered in textbooks, was their first pleasurable entrance into poetry. The first anthology—made up of Canadian poetry likely to appeal to children—seems to have been John W. Garvin's *Canadian Verse for Boys and Girls* (1930), containing poems by Pauline Johnson, Arthur Bourinot, Archibald Lampman, W.H. Drummond, and others. Over thirty years later *The Enchanted Land* (1967), an anthology of Canadian poetry compiled by Thelma Reid Lower and Frederick William Cogswell, himself a poet, had the same dull tone, both in the choice of verse and in the book's textbookish appearance. It does, however, include some good poems by modern poets such as Miriam Waddington, A.M. Klein, and Irving Layton. But many of the selections are merely facile and sentimental literary equivalents of calendar art:

> *What can we say to you, Running Wolf,*
> > *little brother?*
> *Will you tell us what the wind means when it*
> > *blows in the autumn?*
> *Will you show us the ways of the forest?*
>
> *You are all Canada's children now, you, Ileana,*
> > *you, Matsumoto, you, little Loyze,*
> *You, Ellaf, you, Margarita, you, John and Michael.*
>
> *You are all Canada's children now:*
> *What do you bring to her in your small warm hands?*
> > > (FRANCES SHELLEY WEES)

To add to the general blandness, each poem is surrounded by a sepulchral black line; the illustrations, in dark purple and black, are depressing.

A welcome and celebratory riot of colour surrounds the well-chosen poems in *The Wind Has Wings: Poems from Canada* (1968), which were imaginatively selected from the whole range of Canadian poetry by Mary Alice Downie and Barbara Robertson. The first poem in the book—'Orders', by A.M. Klein, which ends 'Let me sit silent/Let me wonder'—establishes the atmosphere of the book, which is maintained from beginning to end in the carefully contrived succession of moods and subjects expressed by the poems and in the illustrations of Elizabeth Cleaver. In choosing poems that were not necessarily written for children but that had qualities that they thought might appeal to them, the compilers found seventy-seven, ranging from Eskimo chants to poems by Irving Layton and James Reaney, and including the good old 'Shooting of Dan McGrew'. The popularity of the book is an indication of how good their judgement was—and of how an appealing collection for children can be compiled without deference to childish, empty stereotypes of what is considered suitable for them. The collages and black-and-white linocuts won for the illustrator international distinction.

The Canadian poet Louis Dudek has compiled an anthology of poetry for young people, *All Kinds of Everything* (1973), which, as its title suggests, has a wide range—from poetry written by young people, to standard poems such as 'The Walrus and the Carpenter', to concrete poetry. It is a tempting little book for browsing that is somewhat spoiled by Dudek's gratuitous homilies on poetry at the beginning of each section, which makes it more didactic than enjoyable.

Walter de la Mare has probably been the only genuine *poet* for children; he has been called the 'children's poet', not only for his *Peacock Pie, Bells and Grass*, and *Collected Rhymes and Verses*, but also because of the variety of his work, which included humour and mystery. Some of his poems are touched with a delicious fear and offer a vision of a world that seems caught between sleeping and waking. But a de la Mare is a rarity in any literature.

Poetry deliberately written for children usually comes in the form of lighthearted versifying, but even this has been scarce in Canada. It was seen at its first modern best in two collections by Desmond Pacey, *The Cow With the Musical Moo* (1952) and *Hippity Hobo and the Bee* (1953), which were brought together with additions under the title of *The Cat, the Cow, and the Kangaroo* (1968). For many years these were the only verses by a Canadian that could be offered to young children. The content was in no way Canadian, however, being derivative of A.A. Milne, but it had its own brand of originality. Pacey is able, like a child, to clothe the everyday and the mundane with magic. A boy named Hippity met a cow:

> *It had silver horns and a platinum nose,*
> *A pure white skin and scarlet toes.*
> *Around its neck was a string of pearls*
> *And the hair on its head was a mass of curls.*
> *Its eyes were blue and its tail jet-black,*
> *And a golden blanket covered its back.*

Many of his poems tell a story. Regrettably the narrative form, like rhyme, is unpopular with modern poets who write for children; this may explain why, in spite of the numerous books published for children, especially in the United States, poetry no longer seems very attractive to them for leisure reading.

Desmond Pacey is a man of letters, as is Dennis Lee, winner of the 1972 Governor General's Award for poetry and creator of the newest entrants into the world of rhythm and rhyme for children. The verses from his first book, *Wiggle to the Laundromat* (1970), are now included in his new book, *Alligator Pie*, which was published simultaneously with his collection for slightly older children, *Nicholas Knock*, in 1974. Dennis Lee makes considerable use of things Canadian. His avowed intent has been to give Canadian children (his own at first) a sense of their particular time and space—a feat that obviously cannot be accomplished in writing from other countries, no matter how excellent it is. Northrop Frye once pointed out that 'In what Canadian poets have tried to do there is an interest for Canadian readers much deeper than what the achievement itself justifies.' Fortunately Lee can hold his own with the best of the modern nonsense versifiers, as is shown by these quotations from *Alligator Pie*:

> *In Kamloops*
> *I'll eat your boots.*
>
> *In the Gatineaus*
> *I'll eat your toes.*

> *In Napanee*
> *I'll eat your knee.*

> or

> *Yonge Street, Bloor Street,*
> *Queen Street, King,*
> *Catch an itchy monkey*
> *With a piece of string.*

Much of the appeal of the poems is due to Lee's colloquial diction, his sense of the incongruous, and to the internal rhyme and strong beat:

> *So my dad he got snarky and barked at the shark*
> *Who was parking the ark on the mark in the dark.*
> *And when they got back they had ants in their pants,*
> *Dirt in their shirt, glue in their shoe,*
> *Beans in their jeans, a bee on their knee,*
> *Beer in their ear and a bear in their hair,*
> *A singer in each finger; a stain in the brain*
> *A small polka-dot burp, with headache tablets,*
> *And a ship on the lip and a horse, of course,*
> *So we all took a bath in the same tub and went to bed early.*

Nicholas Knock has a wider range than *Alligator Pie*. The title poem is a drama in seven parts—a celebration of the youthful imagination in the face of adults and their institutions. Amoral Harry in the cautionary 'Oilcan Harry' is a modern Struuelpeter. The collection ends with a gentle 'Song for Ookpik':

> *Ookpik,*
> *ookpik*
> *Dance with*
> *Us,*
> *Till our*
> *Lives*
> *Go*
> *Luminous.*
>
> . . .

Ookpik
  Ookpik
By your
   Grace,
Help us
   Live in
Our own
   space.

The drawings by Frank Newfeld, many of them in four colours, and the attractive layout, make *Alligator Pie* and *Nicholas Knock* two of our few thoroughly delightful illustrated books.

Nonsense verse such as that of Dennis Lee can be deceptively simple. That it requires skill, sensitivity, and a kind of controlled playfulness is often apparent only when these qualities are missing, as they are in Susan Musgrave's *Gullbrand Thought Measles Was a Happy Ending* (1974). Thrum is a creature whose

> *. . . breath smelled of*
> *Laundry powder and*
> *Old socks.*
> *His teeth were*
> *Weight less as*
> *Flowers.*

Susan Musgrave has attracted considerable interest with her adult poetry, but this book is spoiled by a misunderstanding of children. On one hand the verse is pretentious. On the other it spurns logic and coherence, and it is perhaps for this reason that children will resist it.

James Houston's *Songs of the Dream People* (1972) is a sensitively chosen collection of 'chants and images from the Indians and Eskimos of North America'. May have the delicacy of the Japanese haiku and others express with extraordinary neatness an aspect of the Eskimo character that is often overlooked:

> *I want to laugh, I, because my sledge is broken.*
> *Because its ribs are broken I want to laugh.*

> *Here at Talviuyaq I encountered hummocky ice, I*
> *   met with an upset.*
> *I want to laugh. It is not a thing to rejoice over.*
>
> (CENTRAL ESKIMO)

Songs of the Dream People is not specifically a book for children; but the poems are a part of the Indian and Eskimo oral traditions and are as closely related to their legends as the English ballad is to English folklore. Their appeal therefore spans the gap between adulthood and childhood.

Chief Dan George's *My Heart Soars* (1974) is original poetry, and much of it *is* directed towards children, but it is a question whether they will rejoice in it:

> *Perhaps there will be a day*
> *you will want to sit by my side*
> *asking for council.*
> *I hope I will be there*
> *but you see*
> *I am growing old.*

or

> *Little things*
> *are important,*
> *because they are little*
> *we see them*
> *but do not understand them.*

In general Chief Dan George writes epigrammatic platitudes that are expected to take on significance because a few lines of what is chiefly prose are set in poetic form on a large expanse of paper (accompanied by meditative illustrations by Helmut Hirnschall).

In the last fifteen years we have become acquainted with a great deal of poetry written by children and young people. The most famous anthology of this work is probably *Miracles* edited by Richard Lewis, containing poems chosen from around the world. *All About Us—Nous Autres* (1973) is a small Canadian collection and contains about forty-five poems (in English, some in French) selected out of thousands of entries, with the young writers ranging in age from seven to eighteen. (Like most collections of verse by children, this book gives not only the name of the young writer but also his age and location. The last two bits of information seriously detract from one's enjoyment of a poem simply as poetry; it is information that belongs in an appendix.) The book is attractively illustrated with children's art. A book such as this has two chief values. Children themselves may—but most do not—enjoy reading poems by their own contemporaries. More important, for adults they represent an opportunity to discover what children are thinking. There are too few poems in this collection to make any generalization about them—though one cannot be resisted: the younger the child, the better the poem.

PLAYS

Drama for children has never been a strong part of children's literature as it has been in literature for adults. Not many children's plays have been written; few are read and even fewer have been performed. Since publication usually follows performance, the lack of children's theatres almost everywhere in the world— except, perhaps, in the U.S.S.R. and Czechoslovakia—may be the simplest and most obvious explanation of the dearth of children's plays. Indeed the traditional Christmas eagerness to give children a treat in addition to Santa Claus seems to have been about the only consistent spur to children's theatre.

Because children's spoken and listening vocabulary is far superior to their reading one, they can and do enjoy some adult plays; children from theatre-going families may be seen at all kinds of performances, from musical comedies to Bunraku, with Shakespeare somewhere in the middle. Adult theatre, then, may actually inhibit the development of a children's theatre except for very young children.

As there have been until recently so few Canadian plays for adults, it is hardly to be expected that there will be many Canadian plays for children. In recent years there has been some activity in children's drama, chiefly in the area of what is called 'creative dramatics', due mostly to OFY and LIP grants. But such efforts tend to be 'come and go' affairs: when the money stops flowing the leaders and the children go.

In some countries—Czechoslovakia, Sweden, and Great Britain—television can be a substitute for live drama, both for writers who have an outlet for their talents and for children who can see some good plays on film. But in North America, where children's programming is chiefly confined to Saturday morning cartoons, few such opportunities exist. And the films that are used (in the CBS Children's Film Festival, for example) consist chiefly of imports. Moreover, cartoons, by their very nature, are more likely to deaden a child's interest in theatre rather than stimulate it. What playwright can compete with the cartoon's ability to go beyond reality at every conceivable step—when the hero can be squashed by a steamroller in one second and be seen flying in the next? Yet countless children have made folktales, most of which are largely dialogue, a part of their lives and they react most favourably to the near relatives of children's theatre: storytelling and puppet shows. They are certainly not inimical to dramatic values and performance when opportunities present themselves. But the opportunities are rare.

Most published children's plays are versions of folktales usually lengthened from their perfect short-story form to tedious three-act plays and distorted out of all proportion to the original material. The writers indulge their creative talent by changing the characters of the people in the stories or by adding satirical and love elements that have no appeal to children, as Nicholas Stuart Gray does in *New Clothes for the Emperor*, his version of Hans Christian Andersen's *The Emperor's New Clothes*. Only a few plays yield the emotional power of an outstanding children's novel, but they have evidently never become widely known as a reading experience to children or as an inspiration to those few who produce live theatre for them. Outside of *Peter Pan* (1904), the most notable children's play of the early twentieth century was Maurice Maeterlinck's *The Blue Bird*, first published in 1909. In this the Belgian dramatist of the symbolist school expounded his philosophy of happiness for children: it is to be found, after a search, in one's own backyard. The characters, including the two child protagonists, Mytyl and Tyltyl, children of a poor woodcutter, are personifications of ideas, but they are galvanized into life by humour and sincerity. *The Blue Bird* has some elements of the folk and fairy tale, but these are not as deeply pervasive as in Walter de la Mare's *Crossings* (1923). A family of children locked into the harsh discipline of an aunt and the forbidding surroundings of a Bayswater home are granted unexpected freedom in a cottage in the country. Here they are surrounded by the seasonal and mythic realities of folk life and the presence of a beautiful ghostly spirit. The play has all the marks of de la Mare's genius as it is shown in his poetry and in his stories for children, and because of its timeless quality and dramatic power it can hold interest by reading alone, although one longs to see it in production. The play has original music and songs by C. Armstrong Gibbs and one critic has pointed out that the 'Lullaby' sung by Sallie is an example of the madrigal at its finest. For Walter de la Mare, and for his composer, only the rarest kind of best was good enough for children.

Lucy M. Boston's *The Horned Man; or, Whom Will You Send to Fetch Her Away?* (1970) seems to have been unnoticed in both the world of children's literature and that of children's theatre. At least there is no record of an actual production. It is about witchcraft in the reign of James I and the participation of two easily influenced young girls in the dreadful events. The play is far more than a youthful version of *The Crucible*; indeed, in terms of sheer dramatic skill and chill, it outranks Arthur Miller's lauded work. It is played out in terms of the old nursery rhyme: 'Whom will you send to fetch her away/Fetch her away/Fetch her away?/Whom will you send to fetch her away/All on a frosty morning?'/ And someone is sent!

These plays represent drama in the traditional sense—an aspiration to create the illusion of reality for an audience that gains thereby a cultural, social, or literary experience. The trend in recent years has been for *creative drama*, which means primarily self-expression. In adult theatre the difference between the two forms can be seen perhaps in a superb performance of Ibsen's *The Doll's House* by trained and disciplined actors and actresses who probably do not give a hoot about women's rights, and in an exuberant performance of *Hair*, which can mean so much personally to the mostly young and untrained participants. Children, with their natural flair for the dramatic, have taken easily and successfully to this form of expression.

Two recently published plays for children in Canada, Eric

Nicol's *The Clam Made a Face* (1972) and James Reaney's *Appl
Butter & Other Plays for Children* (1973), exemplify the creativ
rather than the literary aspects of drama and therefore do no
read well as plays; their elements of mime and audience participa
tion obviously have to be seen in performance before they ca
be enjoyed. The setting for *The Clam Made a Face* is a potlatc
ceremony in a West Coast Indian longhouse. This gives an op
portunity for the presentation of various Indian legends, whicl
are chiefly carried out in mime, and for some slight interpretatio
of the old Indian way of life in juxtaposition with the new. Th
legends are the standard ones—the flood, the Cannibal Ogre, an
the 'Legend of Siwash Rock', although here Nicol has used A.M
Stephen's poetic version rather than the far more mythic on
retold by Pauline Johnson in *Legends of Vancouver*. The introduc
tion of a Fool in the early scenes seems out of keeping with India
tradition; at least there is no mention of such a personage i
George Clutesi's study of the great Indian ceremony in *Potlatch*

Reaney's *Apple Butter & Other Plays for Children* develope
out of his experience in directing his Listeners' Workshop in th
1960s. His children's plays are an expression of his belief in wha
drama should be: 'the delight of listening to words, the deligh
in making up patterns (scribbling with your body/bodies) o
movement for fun and in play.' With the exception of *Appl
Butter*, which is a strongly crafted marionette play, the othe
three plays—*Geography Match*, *Names & Nicknames*, and *Igno
ramus*—follow the loose format that Reaney prefers. The scrip
is kept to a minimum and what little there is does not have to b
followed word for word. It is often just words rhythmically chant
ed—'Abenaki, Montagnais, Oneida, Beothuk' and on throug
other Indian groups, or 'Chip, Soak, Digest, Cook, Pulp-pulp'
ending with 'A plate of hamburger!' There is no need for stag
props as all the actions are mimed. The settings are Canadia
and the themes are openly didactic. Indeed, Reaney wanted t
call the collection *Schoolplays*, although not for the reason th
title suggests. They were usually produced in schools—'public
nursery, private and high'. But whether the theme is a race acros
Canada to prove the physical fitness of Canadian children (*Geog
raphy Match*) or fun with names (*Names & Nicknames*) or th
great debate on education sparked by Hilda Neatby's *So Littl*

or the Mind (*Ignoramus*), they are all characterized by great good un and exuberant spirits. Reaney has not only a strong historical ense but an even stronger mythic one, which is seen in his expert se of the lore and language of schoolchildren, bits of nursery hymes, and his own lively verse.

Eric Nicol's *The Clam Made a Face* bears the imprimatur 'New Drama C4', which brings up the most important point about plays, whether for adults of children: there has to be a theatre or production. Plays can be produced successfully in barns and choolrooms, but the establishment of a theatrical group with a permanent theatre has obvious implications for the encourage-ment of the art. Dramatists as well as poets and novelists want o be heard; plays must be performed and revised and performed again before they can be considered final. Susan Rubes' Young People's Theatre in Toronto was the acknowledged proving ground not only for Eric Nicol's play but also for three plays by Dodi Robb and Pat Patterson: *The Dandy Lion, The Popcorn Man, and Red Riding Hood*. These three entertainments are one-hour musical comedies (with music by Pat Patterson) and were most attractively published in 1972. They are children's versions of such light-hearted musical comedies as *Finian's Rainbow, Guys and Dolls*, and *Up in Central Park*, where memorability lingers n the songs rather than in the plots. In this context the plots are beyond criticism—light, fast-moving and forgettable vehicles for the music—while the songs are bright, tuneful, and gay and allow for audience participation. The settings are likely to appeal to young children: a circus in *The Dandy Lion* and a park in *The Popcorn Man*. However, a few things do strike a discordant note. A song such as

> Girls like things that are pretty—
> Butterflies, lullabies,
> Boys like noise,
> But girls like pretty things.
>
> . . .
>
> Girls like things that are proper:
> Nice clean knees, 'thanks' and 'please'—
> Boys lack poise,
> But girls like proper things.   (The Dandy Lion)

seems old-fashioned to say the least in 1974. It is also hard to believe that a kangaroo, once back home in Australia, would really
want to return to the confines of the zoo (*The Popcorn Man*). The
language seems at times too simplified, considering the fact that
children's spoken and listening vocabulary is far superior to their
reading vocabulary. After all, the high point of the musical film
Mary Poppins is produced by one word: 'supercalifragilistic-
expialidocious'! An introduction to each book gives some professional tips in describing how the writers worked, but it reads as
if their methods were the be-all and end-all of children's theatre
and unfortunately suggests at times a Madison Avenue analysis
of the toy market. However, the humour and the comedy are well
sustained on the whole. *Red Riding Hood* concludees with a hilarious slapstick scene, and since the mythic element of the story has
been ignored, the ending is good comedy. If adults can have escape
entertainment, why not children?

Henry Beissel's *Inook and the Sun: A Play for Masks and
Marionettes* was performed in 1973 at the Stratford Festival.
Beissel has drawn on mythological and realistic elements of
Eskimo life to create a strong poetic drama.

There are probably hundreds of unpublished children's plays.
It is to be hoped that the present upsurge of interest in children's
theatre will not wane but will go on to greater strength— and that
more plays will be made widely available by publication. Whether
watching or participating, children too deserve to know that
breathless and magic moment of 'Curtain going up!'

POETRY

All About Us—Nous Autres. Creative Writing, Painting, Drawing. Montreal,
Content Publishing, 1973. 36 pp.
A collection of poems (English and French) and art by young Canadians
from 7 to 18.

DOWNIE, MARY ALICE and BARBARA ROBERTSON (eds). *The Wind Has Wings.
Poems from Canada.* Illustrated by Elizabeth Cleaver. Toronto, Oxford,
1968. 96 pp.
The poetry is judiciously chosen, covering a wide range and reflecting both
literary quality and children's interests. Almost every poem has its own

illustration in full-colour collage or black-and-white linocut. A visually brilliant book—the first really impressive illustrated book to be published in Canada.

DUDEK, LOUIS (ed.). *All Kinds of Everything: Worlds of Poetry*. Toronto/ Vancouver, Clarke, Irwin, 1973. 150 pp.
The anthology choices of a distinguished Canadian poet should be of great interest, if not agreement, among readers. Dudek provides much variety in this collection, yet there is an overall sense of conservatism in that many of the poems he has chosen are readily available in other standard antholo- gies. Dudek's introductions to the various sections make it more of a teaching book than a collection to enjoy for itself.

HOUSTON, JAMES. *Songs of the Dream People: Chants and Images from the Indians and Eskimos of North America*. Edited and illustrated by James Houston. Toronto, Longman, 1972. 83 pp.
Here Indians and Eskimos speak for themselves in highly affective brief poems. They are representative of various cultures and are reinforced by drawings of artifacts in muted colours.

LEE, DENNIS. *Alligator Pie*. Pictures by Frank Newfeld. Toronto, Macmillan, 1974. 64 pp.
An attractive collection of nonsense rhymes and verses that have—as all good nonsense should have—an underlying ring of sense. The joyful atmosphere of this book is partly created by Frank Newfeld's appealing drawings and design.

LEE, DENNIS. *Nicholas Knock and Other Poems*. Pictures by Frank Newfeld. Toronto, Macmillan, 1974. 64 pp.
The title storytelling poem, 'Nicholas Knock'—rhymed verse and playfully satirical in its look at 'the establishment'—is a welcome change from modern unrhymed poetry or poetry that is not really distinguishable from prose. A companion volume to *Alligator Pie*, this has a wider range of verse and is for slightly older children. Frank Newfeld, in his illustrations and design, has made the book irresistible visually.

LITTLE, JEAN. *When the Pie Was Opened*. Toronto/New York, Little, Brown, 1968. 83 pp.
A collection of highly sentimental and inept verse about growing up by the author of *Take Wing* (1968) and other problem fiction for children.

LOWER, THELMA REID and FREDERICK WILLIAM COGSWELL. *The Enchanted Land: Canadian Poetry for Young Readers*. Illustrated by Peggy Steele. Toronto, Gage, 1967. 150 pp.
An uneven anthology—some poems are very good and some are very bad. The illustrations are gloomy, stylized block prints in purple and black; the key one is repeated six times.

PLAYS

BEISSEL, HENRY. *Inook and the Sun: A Play for Masks and Marionettes.* Toronto, Playwrights Co-op, 1974. 76 pp.

Drawn from mythological and realistic aspects of Eskimo life, this play was successfully performed at the Stratford Festival in 1973, and will be produced in Europe.

NICOL, ERIC. *The Clam Made a Face.* Toronto, New Press, 1972. 36 pp. ('New Drama C4'.)

West Coast Indian legends as told at a potlatch are re-created for a modern audience. Much of the action is based on mime.

REANEY, JAMES. *Apple Butter & Other Plays for Children.* Vancouver, Talonbooks, 1973. 195 pp.

The contents consist of a marionette play (*Apple Butter*) and three plays *Geography Match*, *Names & Nicknames*, and *Ignoramus*—written to match Reaney's concept of theatre. This means almost a bare stage and a flexible script that will accommodate inventive contributions from the actors. Reaney's poetic imagination and creative understanding of the child mind should be warmly welcomed in children's theatre.

ROBB, DODI and PAT PATTERSON. *The Dandy Lion.* A One-Act Musical Play for Children. Music: Pat Patterson. Toronto, New Press, 1972. 56 pp. ('New Children's Drama 2'.)

The setting of a small circus provides plenty of opportunity for mime on the part of the actors and for laughs on the part of the audience. The two lions and their owners—a fierce lion and his villainous owner and young Andrew and his 'Dandy Lion'—provide the dramatic contrast. As in all the plays in this series, audience participation is invited.

ROBB, DODI and PAT PATTERSON. *The Popcorn Man.* A One-Act Musical Play for Children. Music: Pat Patterson. Toronto, New Press, 1972. 51 pp. ('New Children's Drama 1'.)

The new park superintendent doesn't think that parks are for people. However, the Popcorn Man, with the help of the park's habitués, manages to reform him. A light-hearted entertainment.

ROBB, DODI and PAT PATTERSON. *Red Riding Hood.* A One-Act Musical Play for Children. Music: Pat Patterson. Toronto, New Press, 1972. 49 pp. ('New Children's Drama 3'.)

An extended version of the old folktale, with considerable slapstick comedy.

9 illustration and design

In children's books generally, particularly those from the United States, there is some cause for alarm in the flood of over-illustrated books. Today the impact of the visual is so strong that many children cannot cope with a book that is not illustrated. Pictures are asked to be substitutes for words—beyond the age when such a role is valid. Too many educationalists seem to assume a kind of disassociation between the audio-visual and print worlds. Language and visual imagery are both essential tools of human perception and response. While the impact of pictures in this visual age is indisputable, the creative and liberating power of words must not be forgotten. Verbal communication should not be made secondary because the skills to perceive and express this power are not easy to acquire. If the genius of language is not forever recognized and nurtured, its neglect could lead to the cataclysmic destruction of meaning itself. ' "When I use a word," Humpty Dumpty said, in rather a scornful tone, "it means just what I choose it to mean—neither more nor less." '

However, art in children's books is a part of all art, just as the best writing for children is part of all literature. The venerable tradition of book illustration stretches across time, from illuminated manuscripts to children's picture-books, encompassing all those forms of illustration that are contained in the etymology of the word itself—to illustrate: to light up, illuminate, make bright, adorn. Pictures do not merely take the place of words; they extend and illuminate them; they enrich and interpret the story with 'bright adornment'. We need only look at the work of John Tenniel, N.C. Wyeth, Ernest Shepherd, and Arthur Rackham—and of Garth Williams, Maurice Sendak, and Charles Keeping today— to see such a fulfilment.

Anyone who has ever seen a child entranced with TV cartoons or absorbed in an illustrated book—it can be anything from an Eaton's Catalogue to an illustrated history of the American Civil War—cannot doubt the power of pictures. How many of us do not carry some indelible visual image picked up in childhood, often from a book that carries a wealth of past sensation, which we call nostalgia, or have had Stravinsky's *Rite of Spring* ruined forever by Walt Disney's *Fantasia*? Although visual sensitivity— the ability to see rather than merely look—is a mysterious correlation of genetic coding and experience, most children seem to have a remarkable capacity for intense visual concentration and perception (which unfortunately often deteriorates with age). They relate images immediately to their daily experience. Images for them are powerfully connotative symbols and each picture has both informational and storytelling significance, in the tradition of early man's picture-writing in which the symbols of pictographs, hieroglyphics, and ideographs spelled out the world. Pictures are indeed windows on the world that allow children to discover new directions in building upon their limited, self-contained experience of life. They can lead a child to a richness of informative, emotional, and imaginative experience that stimulates and exercises the faculties of both imagination and intelligence. In this context times have not changed since 1658 when Bishop Comenius wrote in his *Visible World* (the first picturebook): 'Pictures are the most intelligible books that children can look upon.'

The perennial question of what children like in illustration and design, their preferences and prejudices, is perhaps basically unanswerable. The old contention that children prefer naturalistic drawings and bright, lively colours is not nearly so compelling now that major talents have made effective use of black-and-white pictures and highly stylized formal designs. Actually, children can enjoy many different styles and types of illustration: realistic, abstract, stylized, impressionistic, caricature, full colour, black-and-white. What is essential apart from artistry in the illustration of children's books, as in any books, is that the style be appropriate to, and work with, the text. Illustrations can vary in their legitimate purpose. They can explain; they can characterize and animate in a storytelling sense; and they can interpret mood or meaning by playing creatively with colour and form. Whatever their purpose and their artistry (or lack of it), their success with children will ultimately depend on the artist's ability to see and feel with the eyes and heart of a child, to tap the unconscious reservoir of childhood perception and even memory.

'What is the use of a book,' thought Alice, 'without pictures or conversations?' Alice wanted double security in her reading, but it is only in fairly recent times that she would have found much comfort in Canadian children's books. While overladen with conversations, they have been conspicuously lacking in pictures, or at least in pictures having much artistry. The child of 1865 might have settled for *any* pictures, but in the highly charged visual world of 1975 an adult has reason to expect the best in visual imagery for children, which is what a child deserves. While there have never been many Canadian children's books that provided this, the fact that *some* do, and that the last few years have seen the débuts of several truly gifted artists who work in full colour, is cause for rejoicing.

With its history of insufficient population and halfhearted interest in things artistic, typical of a frontier and pioneer society, Canada has had no real tradition of book illustration; the work done here was inspired on the whole by non-Canadian forerunners. It was obviously felt that the local market would absorb books of Canadian content without any expert attention to the possibilities of their visual aspect. Economy could have been one reason for poor or indifferent illustrations, but economy does not have a great deal to do with *quality* in art work. In any case Canadian book illustration, with some notable recent exceptions, is undistinguished. We can see this in the dreary round of old-fashioned textbook formulas in books for older children (ages ten to thirteen), whether fiction or non-fiction. The apparent indifference to illustration has resulted in anonymity for the few artists and designers who have been permitted to exercise their talents on behalf of children. Because of the lack of literary possibilities, and possibly of editorial judgement, they have had no opportunity to build up a body of work that is recognized and appreciated. Those illustrators who *are* known tend to be picture-book artists (Elizabeth Cleaver, Frank Newfeld) rather than illustrators. Theo Dimson, Leo Rampen, and Donald Grant have done very few books, and none at all in recent years.

For many years the best-known author-illustrator was Clare Bice. *Jory's Cove* (1941) and *Across Canada* (1949) were certainly the most effectively illustrated and produced books of the 1940s. Most of his writing has been set in the Atlantic provinces—Nova Scotia and Newfoundland—and his realistic illustrations express a deep feeling for this part of the country. Bice is the only one of our illustrators who has produced a considerable body of work over a long period. There was *The Great Island* (1954), *A Dog for Davie's Hill* (1956), and he illustrated books for other writers, notably Catherine Anthony Clark, most of which came out in the 1950s. The illustrations for these books are undistinguished compared with those for *Jory's Cove*; nor does his work show any development either in the traditional style or in attempts at new trends. Bice did not work in the 1960s and has so far illustrated nothing in the seventies.

Until recently most Canadian illustrators worked in black-and-white line drawings, but it was only in the late 1950s that this technique got out of the stereotyped, realistic, schoolbookish category and displayed a combination of graphic skill and imagination. Theo Dimson, the illustrator of James McNeill's *The Sunken City* (1959) and *The Double Knights* (1964), has given distinction to stories that are not in themselves outstanding. The dense black in his Beardsley-like drawings for *The Double Knights* (achieved by a double run) adds far more to the effectiveness of the illustrations than would an uninspired use of colour. Dimson superbly translates into pictorial terms the primitive, mysterious past from whence these stories came. His drawings for *The Sunken City* are lighter in style and humorously impressionistic. They represent an unusual and even a daring approach to illustration for children's books; their non-figurative qualities do not seem to have made them inaccessible.

That design and illustration can contribute immeasurably to

non-fiction as well as to more imaginative works is shown by Toye's *The St Lawrence* (1959). Leo Rampen's illustrations are informative, as they should be in a book of information, but they are also ornamental, and include stunning decorative maps. Although the drawings are slightly stylized, they convey an uncanny feeling for the period and certainly could represent no other country but Canada.

Leo Rampen adopted an entirely different style in the next book he illustrated: Anne Wilkinson's *Swann & Daphne* (1960), which is a serious fantasy with a strain of satirical humour. Rampen has illustrated it in a serious and realistic manner. The pencil sketches only seem soft; they have an angular hardness that is quite suited to the idea of man's inhumanity to man implicit in the story. There is one exceptionally charming drawing, reproduced on the cover, in which the angular body of Swann is surrounded and caressed by the graceful, long-necked swans, the whole making an oval on the page. Swann is to find his happiness with the swans, not with people.

Rampen's drawings for James Reaney's *The Boy with an R in His Hand* (1965) have something in common with those for *The St Lawrence* in that they successfully achieve a contemporary look. The book deals mainly with the type-riot at William Lyon Mackenzie's printing office in 1826 and gives a picture of the political and social life of York. The drawings are in the style of contemporary woodcuts and give both charm and meaning to the story. In these illustrations one can see, perhaps even more clearly than in the story, both the crudities and the refinements of that period.

For Dorothy Reid's *Tales of Nanabozho* (1963), a collection of Ojibway legends, Donald Grant distorted the figures of the characters; the style of his black line drawings captures the primitive nature of the stories and the unpredictable trickster qualities of Nanabozho. The strong, graphic drawings and the type, space, decoration, binding, and jacket of this book are unified in a pleasing whole. Overall integrated design is also a feature of Robert Ayre's *Sketco the Raven* (1961). The illustrations by Philip Surrey also have a primitive look, with the sweep of sky and water in several illustrations recalling the fact that these are stories of when the world was young. They have less impact, however, than the illustrations for *Tales of Nanabozho*. The illustrator of Kay Hill's *Badger, the Mischief Maker* (1965), John Hamberger, has taken a far more conventional and realistic approach and therefore fails to capture the mythic quality of the stories.

In the main, James Houston's illustrations for his *Tikta'Liktak* (1965), *The White Archer* (1967), *Akavak* (1971), and *Wolf Run* (1971) resemble the sculptures for which the Eskimos are famous, and almost demand to be lifted from the page and handled. Their formality suits the legend-type stories. In *Kiviok's Magic Journey* (1973) Houston uses a softer style to match the simple folktale with its European flavour.

The appearance in the last few years of new and gifted artists and of several books illustrated, with great beauty and distinction, in colour may have signalled the beginning of a productive and distinctive Canadian tradition of book illustration. Elizabeth Cleaver, Laszlo Gal, Ann Blades, William Kurelek, and Frank Newfeld (in two 1974 books that mark a great advance on his previous work) have produced the kind of illustrated books that we hardly dared hope for ten years ago.

In 1968 a colourful breakthrough was made in illustration with *The Wind Has Wings: Poems from Canada* illustrated by Elizabeth Cleaver. All Cleaver's art work has a splendid royal magnificence—whether in this poetry anthology or in her Indian-legend picture-books, *The Mountain Goats of Temlaham* (1969) and *How Summer Came to Canada* (1969), or in *The Miraculous Hind* (1973), a Hungarian legend that she both illustrated and retold. Beginning with densely coloured and textured monoprints, she does paper cut-outs and linocuts and assembles them in collages, creating a rich and beautiful style of illustration. In *The Mountain Goats of Temlaham* the rhythmic, rippling strips of collage paper capture the mountainous folds of earth and the tactile feel of rock and cliff in British Columbia. The figures of people, animals, and birds are stylized in the totemic silhouette shapes of Indian art; they are frozen and static in a ceremonial, ritualistic sense. This aura of Indian mystery is also present in the linocuts of totem poles and longhouses, which are sombre, black, and dramatic against the white pages. *How Summer Came to Canada* is set in

By ELIZABETH CLEAVER for *The Wind Has Wings* edited by
Mary Alice Downie and Barbara Robertson (Oxford, 1968)

By ELIZABETH CLEAVER for *The Mountain Goats of Temlaham* retold by William Toye (Oxford, 1969)

he Eastern woodlands, and forest greenery is immediately, tan-
gibly present in the striking use of cedar leaves, ivy, moss, and
grass in the collages. However, collage is not everything here: new
intricacies of line and brush work are used in the details of snow,
costume, loon feathers, and faces. The landscape changes—from
north to south, in winter and summer—and receives a sparkling
representation in scenes of icy desolation and sunny, flowering
splendour. *The Miraculous Hind*, in keeping with its lavish theatrical style, was originally prepared as a film strip for the National
Film Board, and in spite of the foreign subject matter it has many
technical similarities to her previous books. Cleaver's visual
imagery, though beautiful, might change with advantage in the
future, for we would not like to see her work become monotonous
and overfamiliar (as Brian Wildsmith's has done, despite the richness and mastery of *his* technique). Her latest illustrations—a further treatment of Indian subject matter—are attractive linocuts
for Cyrus Macmillan's *Canadian Wonder Tales* (1974) that show
a definite advance on her earlier black-and-white work. They suggest that, given the opportunity, she will continue to grow as an
illustrator.

Besides Cleaver's two Indian-legend books, 1969 saw the publication of another illustrated book, *Sally Go Round the Sun: 300
Songs, Rhymes and Games of Canadian Children*, that has become
very popular, and with reason, for the content is enchanting. The
gay, decorative drawings by Carlos Marchiori are a feast for the
eye.

In William Toye's *Cartier Discovers the St Lawrence* (1970)
Laszlo Gal interestingly imposes a European sensibility on a famous Canadian subject. (Hungarian by birth, Gal has illustrated
several children's books for Mondadori in Italy.) He creates a
variety of surface textures, from flat, shadowy skin and cloth to
swirling breadths of ocean, land, and sky. A strong spatial sense
pervades the landscape. The people are firmly rooted in this background of earth and water; they are statuesquely posed, Giotto-
like, as sculptural figures having the same stately massive grace
as the trees. The features of the faces are understated, anony-
mously inexpressive, and the figures are interchangeable in their
stylistic simplicity. However, this impersonal quality does not de-

tract from the book; rather it is the perfect complement to the history-making events described in the narrative, which would be reduced by the gratuitous injection of 'personality' into scenes that require no artistic dramatization. Attention to the spirit of the time is evident in the precise details of costume and in the archaic tone of the maps. This is a large, lavish picture-book of a kind that is unique in Canada but taken for granted in other countries.

Gal did the illustrations for Nancy Cleaver's *How the Chipmunk Got Its Stripes* (1973) and they have the same sculptured quality as those in *Cartier*. They are in brown only. Nevertheless they are remarkably effective, particularly in suggesting animals and the clothing of the Indians: Gal has given his pictures a delightful furry softness.

Ann Blades' watercolour illustrations of life in the far northern Mennonite and Indian communities of Mile 18 and Taché have a dream-like calm. In *Mary of Mile 18* (1971) and *A Boy of Taché* (1973), which she both wrote and illustrated, there is an effect of poignant clumsiness in her asymmetrical compositions—as if life has been caught and held in the primitive toy world of childhood art: houses look like toy boxes, children like wooden dolls. But if the figures are posed, geometrically stiff as statues or dolls, the subtle texture of layered washes, the wet and dry brush techniques, the rich, pebbly watercolour paper, the skilful blending of colours and tonal variations all convey a remarkable impression of weather, seasons, night and day in the lonely northern landscape.

The noted artist William Kurelek both wrote and illustrated *A Prairie Boy's Winter* (1973). With meticulous realism, but with more conviction and emotion than a photograph could convey, he depicts nostalgic boyhood scenes of farm and school life, work and play, against a prairie winter background. The illustrations have a youthful spirit of curiosity, and of wonder and faith in the natural world—a world not frozen in memory but alive. The active figures that people his farmyards and fields, with their playful vitality and buoyancy, and his round sculptured animals, small in scale against the landscape, are drawn with lively humour; the children are full of mischievous teasing and quarrelling. More than the text or the pictures as a whole, these are the

By LASZLO GAL for William Toye's *Cartier
Discovers the St Lawrence* (Oxford, 1970)

By ANN BLADES for *Mary of Mile 18* (Tundra, 1971)

By WILLIAM KURELEK for *A Prairie Boy's Winter* (Tundra, 1973)

By FRANK NEWFELD for Dennis Lee's *Alligator Pie* (Macmillan, 1974)

things that the young will respond to. Kurelek has a strong compositional sense of colour, using tones that are subdued and shadowy-soft, as for the gauzy snow, sometimes dusted with delicate tones of red and blue; at other times he achieves a crisp freshness with blue sky, red barns, and colourful clothing, which provide a translucent warmth against the sea of snow. In 1974 Kurelek produced another pictorial autobiography, *Lumberjack*, in which the text also describes the pictures. As in his previous book, the visual details are irresistible.

William Kurelek is a mature artist of international reputation; so is Shizuye Takashima, who illustrated and recounted, without emotion, her memories of her life as a child internee in British Columbia during the Second World War. In *A Child in Prison Camp* (1971) her eight full-page watercolours give a soft, impressionistic view of the magnificent surroundings of the camp in New Denver, B.C., and of the cultural life that persisted under unusual circumstances. Even more than the text, the pictures express a recollection that suggests the harsh circumstances only slightly, as in the inclusion of a military figure standing against a campfire.

Frank Newfeld was the illustrator of an early four-colour picture-book, *The Princess of Tomboso* (1960), which has long been popular with children, thanks partly to the story and partly to the playful illustrations. Newfeld has also illustrated and designed two books of verse by Dennis Lee, *Alligator Pie* and *Nicholas Knock* (1974), which must rank with the best illustrated books in Canada. The pictures have a wonderful storytelling quality; Newfeld has come through (literally) with flying colours in satisfying an imaginary child who might have said, 'Please, draw me that rhyme.' This quality can be especially seen in the pictures for 'Homage to Moose factory, Ont.', 'I Found a Silver Dollar', and 'In Kamloops'. He illustrates the details of a poem most satisfactorily, but always with a slight and amusing overstatement. Many artists faced with the eating of limbs, as in 'In Kamloops', would have included a touch of the macabre, but Newfeld's literalness is in no way frightening. Each page is a journey of exploration. Only occasionally do a poem and a picture seem mismatched, as in 'The Friends', which surely should have depicted comfort rather than fright for this Milne-like poem. As the verses are by one person, both books are more of a piece than the anthology *The Wind Has Wings*, and so are the illustrations.

Recently some Indian illustrators have brought their stylized art, much of it in colour, to the interpretation of their own legends. George Clutesi began the trend when he did illustrations for his own *Son of Raven, Son of Deer* (1967). Frances Kagige enhanced Patronella Johnston's *Tales of Nokomis* (1970) with vivid colour. However, the most fluid, dramatic, and poetic interpretation of Indian legends are the illustrations of Norval Morriseau for Herbert T. Schwartz's *Windigo and Other Tales of the Ojibways* (1969). Morriseau's striking drawings, filled with symbolic Indian imagery and a curious but effective x-ray depiction of figures, convey the spirit rather than the actual events of the stories.

Drawings, stonecuts, and engravings by one of the finest graphic artists at Cape Dorset illustrate the autobiography *Pitseolak: Pictures Out of My Life* (1971). They are haunting, imaginative images of mythical nightmare monsters, spirits, and demons, combined with naively realistic depictions of Eskimos living the 'old ways', enacting the traditional ceremonies of life, work, and play—'the things we did long ago before there were many white men'. There is a playful spontaneity and energy in the shapes and silhouettes of human, animal, bird, and demonic figures. The felt-pen drawings are buoyant with bright colours—deep blue, bright turquoise, canary yellow, gold, pea-green, moss-green, and purple.

With such books as these we can take pleasure in the knowledge that there *are* good book illustrators in Canada. With encouragement more will appear. But what we do not seem to have is a ready market for those artists who do their best work in large, full-colour illustrations. By this I do not mean a lack of encouragement and appreciation, but the lack of a dependable and considerable buying public for books that are expensive to produce and must be able to justify long print-runs. Today that buying public mainly means institutions. If every elementary-school library in English Canada bought one copy of a good new children's book, our publishers would have little difficulty in extending and enriching with illustration our body of children's reading.

10 | picture-books and picture-storybooks

PICTURE-BOOKS

While the illustrated book is the product of centuries of artistic enterprise, the picture-book is a more recent and independent development in children's book illustration; it is, in fact, a separate genre. The creator of a picture-book may be an author-illustrator, such as Jean de Brunhoff, Ezra Jack Keats, or John Burningham; or, less usual, the book may represent the work of a writer and an artist, such as the happy combination of Marjorie Flack and Leonard Weisgard in *The Story About Ping*, or more recently of Eugène Ionesco and Étienne Delessert in *Story Number 1*. But, whether crafted by one or by two, the genius of the picture-book lies in its balance of words and pictures, neither of which is complete without the other: together they form a perfect whole. Many picture-books are visually beautiful but lack a honed and disciplined text. A case in point is the widely acclaimed *Tiger Flower*, in which Robert Vavra's text is a pallid companion to Fleur Cocole's jewel-like paintings. In the perfect picture-book no line or word is out of place.

From the beginnings of the picture-book as we know it in late nineteenth-century England, its great illustrators developed individual styles, immediately recognizable as their signatures, that reflected not only their originality but also their vision of a child's world. The works of such artists have a timeless quality and it is in children's response to such 'classics'—their choice of favourite picture-books—that they express *their* criteria of what is good.

These chosen books include works by Randolph Caldecott, Beatrix Potter, Leslie Brooke, Wanda Gag, Jean de Brunhoff, Ludwig Bemelmans, H.A. Rey, and more recently Tomi Ungerer, Maurice Sendak, Brian Wildsmith, and many others.

Recently picture-books have become one of the most sophisticated forms of expression in either art or writing, often seemingly produced for the delight of adults rather than children. But in any form they are a rarity in Canada; only in the last few years have we had anything that even approaches the 'lively art of the picture-book'.

What has been called Canada's earliest picture-book was published in 1966. This is *An Illustrated Comic Alphabet,* drawn and lettered by an Englishwoman, Amelia Frances Howard-Gibbon, in 1859, probably for the teaching of her little scholars in Sarnia, Ont. The text—even when Miss Howard-Gibbon knew it—is hundreds of years old.

> *A was an Archer and shot at a Frog,*
> *B was a Butcher who kept a great Dog.*

The children, who are focal points of the pictures, are clothed as Victorian adults and are posed in what we now consider typical Victorian attitudes. The book strikes the modern eye as something of an unintentional parody of Victorian manners and customs; nonetheless it is charming and childlike. The pictorial background is not of Canada but combines the soft English countryside and glimpses of the castle home (Arundel) where Miss Howard-Gibbon grew up.

Picture-books with a Canadian background did not come until the 1930s and, with the exception of the work of Elizabeth Cleaver, Ann Blades, and William Kurelek, they attract very few publishers—mostly, one gathers, for reasons of cost, but also perhaps because the genre has not attracted artists with exceptional imaginative and graphic talents. In England Charles Keeping gives us powerful glimpses of a London slum; Ezra Jack Keats does the same for New York. Surprisingly enough the Canadian environment, whether rural or urban, has provided very little real inspiration.

A Canadian Child's ABC (1931), with verses by R.K. Gordon

nd drawings by Thoreau Macdonald, and *French Canada: Pic-ures and Stories* (1938) by Hazel Boswell, both made effective use f Canadian content. *French Canada* conveyed by far the more aluable and interesting look at a particular Canadian environ-nent. The illustrations are soft full-page watercolours that are lmost tactile in their portrayal of French-Canadian scenes and andicrafts. The book retained its popularity and usefulness for s long as it was in print and the first edition is now a collector's tem. Fortunately a new edition was published in 1967. (Some-vhat similar illustrations are in Boswell's *Legends of Quebec*, a 966 publication.)

The verses of *A Canadian Child's ABC* are doggerel, although s far as 'Canadianism' goes, they have a modern ring, almost of unconscious parody.

> *To Ottawa from coast to coast*
> *The chosen come to make the laws.*
> *For weeks they talk about a lot*
> *Of different things with scarce a pause:*
> *The railway line to Hudson Bay,*
> *Taxes and tariff, immigration,*
> *The great St Lawrence waterway,*
> *And whether we are yet a nation.*

The drawings have more charm that the verses, even though they are baldly realistic. 'O for Ottawa', for example, is a plain pen-and-ink sketch of the Parliament Buildings. M, of course, is a blackly inked Mountie with a suggestion of prairie and sky behind him. With simplicity and factualness, though with no artistic flair, these drawings do manage to convey scenes that are typically Canadian.

The best examples of picture-book art in Canada can be seen in the work of Elizabeth Cleaver, the young Montreal artist. For *The Mountain Goats of Temlaham* (1969) and *How Summer Came to Canada* (1969) William Toye provided satisfying retellings of West Coast (Tsimshian) and East Coast (Micmac) Indian legends. In *The Miraculous Hind* (1973) Elizabeth Cleaver, herself of Hungarian descent, retold one of the most famous legends of Hungary, that of Hunor and Magyar who helped to form the

Hungarian nation. Her collage technique is the same as in her illustrations for *The Wind Has Wings*, but in the three legend books the pictures are more illustrative. With the Indian legends Cleaver and Toye have achieved that integration of text and pictures found in all the best picture-books: the stories stand on their own, the pictures tell the stories without the text, yet when used together the two complement each other perfectly. As in her Indian books, Cleaver enriches the theme of *The Miraculous Hind* —the Hungarian spirit—with details of landscape, customs, and dress. The attention to cultural tone as well as to meticulously researched details of costume is certainly an Elizabeth Cleaver signature: the book is a visual *tour de force*. The placement of the minimal number of lines of text on each page is primarily aesthetic and is only secondarily concerned with ease of reading. A fascination with typographical effect is chiefly seen in the change from a modest modern typeface to bold, decorative cut-out letters on a brightly coloured ground, which disrupts the flow of the story and at times makes the text difficult to read. In the Indian books there is no such dichotomy.

The outstanding artists of the picture-book have tended to use precise and lively detail. The storytelling capacity of pictures has not been fully realized in any Canadian attempt at a picture-book. *Jolly Jean-Pierre/Voyage Extraordinaire de Jean-Pierre* (1973) by Lyn Cook and Mary Davies succeeds almost perfectly in its pictorial aspect but is marred by a poor text. Jean-Pierre is a happy-go-lucky voyageur who loves to regale his companions with a 'tall tale' as they camp for the night. This time he tells them of a giant fish that refused to be caught but pulled Jean-Pierre and the island he was on down the Chaudière Falls, along the St Lawrence, and off to sea. The story is told in rhymed verse that is often strained and inconsistent in its Drummond-like patois:

> But suddenly I wake up fast!
> My boat, she jump and spin;
> I cry, 'Oh ho, you big fish there!
> Just wait, I bring you in!

The French text is longer and seems more skilfully handled. The illustrations by Mary Davies are colourful and robust, catching the gay and insouciant spirit that is associated with the voyageurs. However, it is too bad that the artist chose to portray the fish in a cartoon manner—a 'tall tale' should be taken very, very seriously! Another flaw may well be the book's bilingualism, which was no doubt intended to be a strength. But with the French version considerably longer than the English and with the lines on the page often positioned awkwardly, it is sometimes difficult to pick up the correct line in either language.

Humour is a fundamental quality in *Jolly Jean-Pierre*, as it is in the work of most of the great picture-book artists. Little children tend to have a comic view of life rather than a tragic one and through first-rate humorous picture-books they can come to terms with their own realities. And more often than not they can catch glimpses of the adult world, which at once protects them and controls them. Often, too, a picture-book can be a kind of sublimation. What child does not really want to ring the fire department as George does in *Curious George* or fool everybody as the brothers do in *Five Chinese Brothers*? But as yet no Canadian picturebook-maker has succeeded in offering such laugh-begetting experiences to a child.

However, Hugh McClelland *almost* succeeds in *The Bold Bad Buccaneers* (1968). The buccaneers were very fierce pirates until they attacked a ship and found a crowd of children who had been sent off by adults to search for a new land because their own country was too small to support all the children in it. The buccaneers are horrified by such cruelty and take steps to remedy the situation. The illustrations are not outstanding—they verge on cartoons—but they are bold and gay, and the red on black and white produces quite a piratical effect. This book lacks the neatness and humour of Tomi Ungerer's *The Three Robbers*, which has much the same theme.

There has been a marked attempt in recent years to provide books for Indian children with settings more natural to them than the artificial world of *Dick and Jane*, the closeness of city streets, or the strangeness of circuses and zoos. Two such books, whose intentions can be lauded, are *Normie's Goose Hunt* and *Normie's Moose Hunt* (1968) by Vi Cowell who (according to the dedication) taught Indian children in Moosonee, Ont. The one- and two-line sentences apparently aim to be no more than descriptive, as do the flat, primitive drawings, somewhat in the style of Ann Blades but without her artistry—though pictures of the huge brown moose do have some power.

As if to make up for a great lacuna—an actual scarcity of picture-books, good and bad—and as if to compensate for an adult lack of imagination and joy and surprise, the field has been invaded by children, in groups and individually, and compared with their Canadian elders they have shown far more verve. *Alphabet Book* (1968) was prepared by a group of Indian children on a reserve in southwestern Ontario, who seem instinctively to have created it out of their own environment. While most alphabet books start with 'A' either for 'Apple Pie' or for 'Ardvaark', these children rather sensibly started with airplane and went on to 'M' for 'Sir John A. Macdonald' and 'P' for 'Plants'. 'Y' (usually for Yak) takes a nice twist for 'Lesser Yellow Bird'. The childish drawings are in black-and-white and somehow are more appealing than many lavishly coloured alphabet books we import from Great Britain and the United States. The success of *Alphabet Book* led to publication of a counting book—the only Canadian one—that was also done by Indian children. *The One to Fifty Book* (1973) edited by Anne and Alex Wyse is charming, graphically interesting, and very popular in libraries.

It would be rather helpful to the adult ego to think that Kendall James MacDonald (aged nine) and Joey Hildes (aged ten) had actually read or looked at picture-books before they produced *Patrick the Diesel* (1974) and *How the Pelican Got Its Baggy Beak* (1974). At any rate these young author/illustrators have grasped the secret of the combination of pictures and words that, with imagination and fun added, makes for a real picture-book. In *How the Pelican Got Its Baggy Beak* (Hildes), the Pelican gets a fish struck in his throat, then his beak is caught in a wooden buoy and swells from the salt water. The young writer believes in the theory of the inheritance of acquired characteristics, for 'the Pelican's wife and children . . . they had bags, too. From that time, all generations of pelicans have baggy beaks.' The illustrations are lively crayon drawings in pastel shades. *Patrick the Diesel* (MacDonald) is a 'handsome red diesel engine' who moved so fast hat he 'whipped the caboose right off the tracks'. The most interesting point about young Kendall MacDonald, to an adult at least, is that he is such a moralist. Or is it that the nature of trains is righteous? (Two of the most famous creators of train stories, Virginia Lee Burton in *Choo Choo* and Watty Piper in *The Little Engine That Could*, also make sure at the end that the trains do their duty.) Patrick, for example, 'got a safety prize . . . for going the whole next year without an accident!' The illustrations are flat, highly simplified, and indeed childlike, with none of the flair of those in *How the Pelican Got Its Baggy Beak*. Another child author is William Robson who was nine when his three illustrated fantasies—*The Magic Mailbox*, *The Boronian War*, and *Trouble Underground*—were published in 1970 (see page 88).

Christmas often brings out the worst in writers. In Lyn Cook's *Toys from the Sky* (1972) two Eskimo children chatter about the birth of a Baby long ago and the love it brought to the world, and the impression conveyed is that the children approve of this love because it produces toys. The attractive charcoal-wash illustrations cannot make up for a poor text. Chip Young in *Honkey the Christmas Goose* (1972) uses the 'Rudolf the Rednosed Reindeer' theme, but his story does not have its polish and appeal. Honkey was first called Henry because he was born in a Model-T Ford. He eats so much that for a time he cannot honk; indeed, he would be far more appropriately served up for Christmas dinner than, after his diet, moving space debris out of Santa's way. The pictures change jerkily from page to page in both colour and technique and so are far from making with the text a perfect whole.

Johann in *Johann's Gift to Christmas* (1972) by Jack Richards was a mouse who lived in a church because he loved to hear the beautiful music; but in a time of hunger he nibbled away the leather on the bellows of the church organ. Out of this disaster came 'Silent Night', first sung in a little church in the Tyrol over 150 years ago. The pictures are by the well-known cartoonist Len Norris, who keeps a slight but masterly touch of caricature in his mice and human figures (they are mostly coloured in sepia) and also provides the sweep of the Tyrolean Alps in two full-colour pages. All in all it is a successful combination of humour and sentiment and a welcome addition to the sparse supply of genuine Christmas picture-books (that is, such books as Ezra Jack Keats' *The Little Drummer Boy* and Ruth Robbins' *Baboushka and the Three Kings*). However, perhaps it is more accurately described as a picture-storybook.

A prominent trend in recent publishing for children in the United States is the 'non-sexist' book that has resulted largely from the women's liberation movement. The editors of women's presses know that stereotypes are formed early in life, so it is no surprise that picture-books figure largely in their efforts to re-dress, reverse, or somehow overthrow the stereotyped images of femininity. Certainly there is some reason for these efforts. Al-though many would argue that girls have obviously chosen the better part and have themselves wisely perpetuated the older image, there is no doubt that a statistical enumeration of male figures as against female (including animals!) in picture-books would come out strongly in favour of the male. But in such a count is it fair to include second- and third-rate titles unlikely to engage a child's sustained attention or affection? Can the rash of boy-heroes and coy girls in the latest pot-boilers be equated with the (un-feminine?) logic of Alice in *Alice's Adventures in Wonder-land* or the metaphysics of Charlotte in *Charlotte's Web* or the mature understanding of the little girl in Helen Cresswell's *The Pie-Makers*? Or, staying in the picture-book field, can a character like Ludwig Bemelmans' Madeline really be statistically over-whelmed by more numerous and forgettable little boys? A quan-titative evaluation is likely to produce a misreading of the situa-tion, while a qualitative one would be nearer the truth: taking the great books of children's literature as a whole, there is surely a very good balance of female and male figures.

In any case Canada now has its own offerings in the field of 'non-sexist' picture-books published by the Women's Press in Toronto, but it would be rash to take them as the standard of what is wanted in books for young children. They are very few in num-ber (perhaps because Canadian picture-books of any type are scarce), but they follow standard ultra-feminist practice, as can be seen in two examples that have won some recognition. In *Mandy and the Flying Map* (1973) by Beverly Allinson, with illustrations by Ann Powell, a girl who likes maps takes off (either in imagination or by some kind of undeclared magic) to fly over her town. Various townspeople think she needs rescuing, but Mandy assures them that 'I'm flying and I'm safe and I'm free.' In a story such as this there is a strong suspicion that the author and illustrator have simply made a substitution: a few years ago the protagonist would have been a boy. Here the gender is changed, but virtually nothing else. *Fresh Fish . . . and Chips* (1973) by Jan Andrews, illustrated by Linda Donnelly, is concerned with mutual role-reversal: mother goes out to fish and father stays home to make the chips. The story has some humour in the fact that both parents overdo it—father's pile of chips would feed an army and mother's fishing would stock a first-rate aquarium. The little text is pathetic: 'She reeled the reel and reeled it hard,/She played her catch with skill. She badly wanted nice fresh fish/her family to fill.' On the other hand the black-and-white line drawings are marvellous action pictures of the denizens of the deep and are filled with sly and inventive touches of humour. The artist deserved a text by Edward Lear, though her pictures are somewhat spoiled in all their black-and-white activity by the intrusion of an orange-coloured cat, which eventually produces the feeling that the book is merely intended as a child's colouring book.

The scorned stereotype 'Boys do, girls are' summons up the Cartesian priority of 'doing' and the Scholastic priority of 'being'. The absolute 'rightness' of either pole has yet to be demonstrated in philosophy and the very divergence of the views has enriched modern thought. Whenever *good literature* is written on the role of the sexes—from whichever viewpoint—it too will enrich our children's heritage.

Of course *purpose* has plagued children's literature from its beginnings. Writing for literary merit alone came late to books for children, and spirited and independent women were among the foremost creators: Edith Nesbit, Louisa May Alcott, Mrs Molesworth, and Mrs Ewing wrote well when it was not 'fashionable' for them to write at all. Now, after a hundred years of relative freedom from the most blatant religious or moral dictation to the young, the pendulum may be swinging away from literature of aesthetic quality back to literature that is designed to impose some social value. This is welcome when it is done well and effectively, but not when it is done with a jack-boot.

PICTURE-STORYBOOKS

Not a step up from the picture-book but rather a step to the side is the picture-storybook. It is generally recognized by its more formal arrangement of text and pictures—usually one page of text with matching picture—and so lacks the fluidity of the picture-book. Because the picture-storybook is usually intended for beginning readers, its vocabulary is often restrained—not controlled as in school readers, but usually lacking the word-magic of the great picture-book stylists: 'There were hundreds of cats, thousands of cats, millions and billions and trillions of cats' (Wanda Gag, *Millions of Cats*) or 'You hear a snorting sound from out of nowhere and you know that no, you are not alone. A family of porpoises is nearby, rolling over and over, having an acrobatic breakfast of herring under the bay' (Robert McCloskey, *Time of Wonder*). Very few picture-storybooks achieve any kind of memorability; they come and go like the average best-seller, their fall as rapid as their rise. Two Canadian picture-storybooks will probably have more staying power—Ann Blades' *Mary of Mile 18* (1971) and William Kurelek's *A Prairie Boy's Winter* (1973)— chiefly because of their intense and loving portrayal of the Canadian landscape.

Mary of Mile 18 reveals the daily life of a little Mennonite girl in northern British Columbia (north on the Alaska highway for 73 miles then right for 18). It is a monotonous, hard-working existence whose pattern is broken only when she acquires a wolf-pup for a pet. Mary is an earnest miniature adult going about the serious business of living—all work and little play. The simple text has an inner rhythm that supports full-page watercolours that are warm, still, unsentimental evocations of a bleak yet glowing northern scene.

One clear night in February the temperature drops to forty degrees below zero and the northern lights flash across the sky. Mary Fehr gets out of bed and goes to the window to watch and listen. She hears a crackling sound and smiles, excited. Mary likes to pretend that if she hears the music of the lights, the next day will bring something special.

In both the text and illustrations of *Mary of Mile 18* the simplicity achieved is perfectly suited to the subject. Blades' *A Boy of Taché* (1973) strives for the same quality in the text but it lacks polish, while the inherent dramatic possibilities in the little plot are not fulfilled. On an Indian reserve in northern British Columbia a young boy is preparing to accompany his grandfather on the annual hunt to trap beaver. The grandfather falls ill with pneumonia and Charlie goes for the help that will summon a rescue plane. While the illustrations show Ann Blades' great talent as a landscape artist and as an interpreter of Indian life, the text is little more than short, jerky sentences put together in 'readerlike' fashion:

> Camille turns to Charlie. 'Za will get better, Charlie. He never gives up. But this will be his last trip. You will hunt and trap for Za and Virginia now. I know you can do it, Charlie.'

As a teacher in the communities she describes, Ann Blades intended to give the children she knew a book about themselves; but the children in her book emerge as little stereotypes of social history rather than as characters that other children will take to their hearts. Her illustrations are a great contribution to the Canadian picture-storybook, however; the picture in *Mary of Mile 18* of the girl trudging through the silvery northern woods is memorable.

So far Ann Blades and William Kurelek have shown themselves as artists rather than as writers, but they both have the saving grace of unpretentiousness that allows their art to play upon the imagination. Kurelek's text for *A Prairie Boy's Winter* (1973) is chiefly a word picture of the paintings—like personal notes in an art catalogue:

> The next morning, all the outside was a howling whiteness that took his breath away when he stepped out. There would be no school for sure, because children had been known to lose their way and freeze to death in such a blizzard. Farmyard chores were kept to a minimum, but some had to be done. William raised his mackinaw collar as high as possible, shielded his face with his

hands, and plunged through the snow to the chicken coop to gather eggs and give the chickens water.

The full-page painting shows a swirling landscape of snow, the prairie skyline blotted out, and William bending, like the bushes, into the slant of the wind.

In *A Prairie Boy's Winter* William Kurelek is recalling his own boyhood of the 1930s and many adults will find in it a re-creation of their own experience. Today's children, without the stimulus of nostalgia, are likely to see it only as winter portraits, or as a record of themselves at play, since the Canadian winter has not changed, nor have the games of winter (and perhaps not even the work in some parts of Canada). Many authors and illustrators do draw on their own childhood experiences, but the greatest of them manage to distil them and transform them into the universal experiences of childhood. Robert McCloskey, the American picturebook-maker who has drawn the towns and buildings he knew as a child in the mid-western United States of the 1930s, also draws himself as a child so that he somehow becomes an archetypal boy of his time and place. William Kurelek presents himself in a literal fashion. He has produced a documentary, which has its own kind of artistry, rather than a creative picture-book or picture-story-book.

In 1974 Kurelek produced another pictorial autobiography, *Lumberjack*, in which the text also describes the pictures. They do not in any way suggest the roistering tradition one associates with lumberjacking. Nevertheless, as in his previous book, the pictorial details are irresistible.

The pictorial treatment of history for young children, with a reliable and interesting text generously illustrated in colour, can provide a valuable introduction to important historical subjects. Unfortunately there is only one such book in Canada, William Toye's *Cartier Discovers the St Lawrence* (1970) illustrated by Laszlo Gal. It is a simply written but not superficial account of Cartier's three voyages that makes effective use of the journals. With Gal's superb illustrations in full colour (described on page 226), it is both a picture-storybook and a history book.

Adventure at Moon Bay Towers (1974) by the novelist Marian

Engel, with illustrations by Patricia Cupples, is a slight but charming bit of fantasizing. Two affluent and protected children escape from their sterile city apartment to seek adventure in the great outdoors. In a 'tall tale' atmosphere they are both helped and hindered by a remarkable crocodile and a quartet of northern-Ontario lakeside animals—a beaver, a skunk, a raccoon, and a porcupine. The animals keep to their natural habits and instincts while participating in a kind of nonsensical extravaganza. The illustrations are highly reminiscent of the humorous and realistic work of Robert McCloskey. It's all great good fun.

Chip Young may well have created a legend in *The Little Hen of Huronia* (1971). Out of the momentous days of the seventeenth-century Huron Missions he has invented a charming little incident that gives more of the atmosphere of those fateful days than many a volume of history. Shipped from Montreal to Huronia, Madame Poulette provides an egg a day for the missionaries—a treat that becomes a necessity when illness strikes. Thus at this particular time the Mission was saved. It might well be true. The illustrations are simple, bold, and colourful. Canadian publishers can rarely afford the high cost of colour and other production expenses necessary to produce the kind of lavish picture-books that are issued in such numbers by American and English publishers (many of them over-illustrated and with texts that are flat and cold). *The Little Hen of Huronia* is far less pretentious and much more warm-hearted than most of these imports.

Madame Poulette is a figure of consequence, but she remains very much a hen. The animals in Chip Young's *Foxy Grandpa* (1971) are no more than dull caricatures of hockey players and so a good idea—animals playing hockey—degenerates into a kind of slapstick 'Hockey Night in Canada' but without any genuine fun or satire. The small line drawings by Chip Young and Tye Palleck are as cartoon-like as the text.

Thomasina and the Trout Tree (1971) by Joan Clark, with pictures by Ingeborg Hiscox, has the advantage of bright, colourful pictures but that is about all. A little girl's search for a 'trout tree' is probably meant to be a symbolic search for art and so provides a vehicle for spatters of colour and a great deal of 'pop art'. The book is an exercise in confusion, although the author and illustrator probably thought they were encouraging children to consider art in its various modern forms.

In recent times the picture-storybook format has been enriched by the advent of the illustrated single folk or fairy tale. Almost all the great illustrators have tried their hand at an interpretation of the world's great stories from the oral tradition: for instance, Evaline Ness's *Tom Tit Tot*, Nancy Burkert's *Snow-White*, Edward Ardizzoni's *Dick Whittington*, and Marcia Brown's *Once a Mouse*. The major publishers of children's books in most countries have a strong list of such publications that appear to provide continuing revenue. The first such illustrated folk tale in Canada was *The Princess of Tomboso* (1960), taken from *The Golden Phoenix*, the well-known book of French-Canadian folktales collected by Marius Barbeau and retold by Michael Hornyansky. The single fairy tale was illustrated by Frank Newfeld in bright but subtle colours contrasted with alternate pages of strong, humorous drawings in black-and-white. The idea remained dormant in Canadian publishing until it was resurrected in 1969 by the same publisher in two Indian legends retold by William Toye and illustrated by Elizabeth Cleaver—*The Mountain Goats of Temlaham* and *How Summer Came to Canada*—which are more strictly categorized as picture-books (as is Elizabeth Cleaver's *The Miraculous Hind*, a Hungarian legend).

Indian legends, however, continue to provide most of the material for the illustrated folktale or legend. *How the Chipmunk Got Its Stripes* (1973), retold by Nancy Cleaver, has illustrations by Laszlo Gal. The flatly told story of how Squirrel learns from Manitou how to help the people when they are sick is strengthened by the sepia illustrations, which seem to take on the actual feel of fur, birchbark, and skins. *Nanabozho and His Brother* (1970) is a collection of Nanabozho stories put together by Ed Alton and illustrated by Doreen Foster. The illustrations redeem the simple and prosaic text to a considerable degree. With their fluid lines and soft colours (a gentle meld of blues and browns and pinks), they cast an aura of romantic beauty over the tales that has not been seen in the illustrations of Indian legends since the 1920s with the work of George Sheringham for Cyrus

Macmillan's *Canadian Wonder Tales* and that of Marcia Lane Foster for Macmillan's *Canadian Fairy Tales*.

The European folktale is represented in Canadian illustrations by Alan Suddon's *Cinderella* (1969) and Carel Moiseiwitsch's *The Sleeping Beauty* (1973) with text by Michael Macklem. *Cinderella* was first written down in France against a background of royal seventeenth-century splendour, but she has ended up in Canada as a Victorian spoof. Suddon has used cut-outs from magazines, newspapers, coloured paper, pieces of cloth, and has often juxtaposed the old and the new (a Victorian statue holds a parking sign) to create an extravaganza of fun. Frequently in the middle of the calculated bad taste there are simple, charming touches—Cinderella in her dress made of newsprint, the horses of silver paper, the cats and the mice at the wedding. Unfortunately the publisher chose to fit the story to the pictures rather than allowing the illustrations to embellish the story, thus giving an air of unreality to a story that in its original form is told with conviction:

> Below she could see one of the Duchesses in a dress made of chocolate cake and behind her a man from the Press, who was wearing an angry scowl to show he disapproved of balls. Farther up the stairs there was a woman with a bowl of fruit on her head and another with an ace of spades in her hair.

Michael Macklem adds some distracting and gratuitous details to the Perrault version of *The Sleeping Beauty*, but the clear mythic line of the story is not destroyed. The illustrations were first prepared for a National Film Board filmstrip, which probably accounts for the framing of the pictures on each page. Carel Moiseiwitsch has given the story a medieval setting, with stylized frozen pictures that make the free-flowing portrayal of the witch all the more alive and powerful with evil.

Sheila Burnford, well known for *The Incredible Journey*, has tried her hand at an illustrated book, *Mr Noah and the Second Flood*, that is neither a picture-storybook nor a full-fledged fantasy. Pictures there are—attractively drawn by Michael Foreman—but they are not prominent. There is humour in the account of the Noahs' preparing to escape a flood caused by pollution, but the lesson in ecology and conservation rather spoils the little story.

PICTURE BOOKS

ALLINSON, BEVERLY. *Mandy and the Flying Map*. Illustrated by Ann Powell. Toronto, Women's Press, 1973. 32 pp.
Mandy gets a glimpse of her town and the townspeople—portrayed in realistic line-drawings—as she flies over it on a map. Since this is published by a 'Woman's Press', it must be presumed that the intent was to produce a 'non-sexist' picture-book by portraying a girl on an adventure rather than a boy. This is its only claim to originality.

Alphabet Book. Designed by Alan Fleming. Toronto, University of Toronto Press, 1968. 60 pp.
The texts of most alphabet books are rather conventional—'A' is for 'Apple', etc. Here Canada and the environment meant something to the Indian children who 'prepared' it in touchingly childlike black-and-white drawings, with 'M' for Sir John A. Macdonald and 'Y' for Lesser Yellow Bird.

ANDREWS, JAN. *Fresh Fish . . . And Chips*. Illustrated by Linda Donnelly. Toronto, Women's Press, 1973. 32 pp.
Mother goes out to fish while Father stays home and prepares the chips. The rather trite little story—an exercise in role-reversal—is enhanced by swirling line drawings that depict the denizens of the deep with marvellous humour. It is to be hoped that the illustrator does not fade into oblivion.

CLEAVER, ELIZABETH. *The Miraculous Hind: A Hungarian Legend*. Illustrated by the author. Toronto, Holt, Rinehart and Winston, 1973. 64 pp.
Hunor and Magyar, who helped found the Hungarian nation, have long been invested with the aura of legend. Here the author/illustrator has charged it with a new cultural vitality through brilliant use of her now-famous collage technique. The French version, translated by Irène E. Aubrey, is entitled *La Biche miraculeuse: Une Légende hongroise*.

COOK, LYN. *Toys from the Sky*. Illustrated by Mary Davies. Toronto, Clarke, Irwin, 1972. 32 pp.
Two Eskimo children discuss in Dick-and-Jane language the birth of a Baby long ago and the toys that arrive each December in a 'shining Bird'. The attractive charcoal-wash illustrations cannot compensate for the trite and ill-conceived text.

COOK, LYN and MARY DAVIES. *Voyage Extraordinaire de Jean-Pierre: Jolly Jean-Pierre*. Toronto, Burns and MacEachern, 1973. 36 pp.
A French-Canadian 'tall tale' with coloured pictures of great vitality and

a genuine and humorous storytelling quality. The text is told in French and English—a strained English. It is fortunate that pictures require *no* language skills!

OWELL, VI. *Normie's Goose Hunt*. Pictures by the author. Toronto, Copp Clark, 1968. 24 pp.
A simple, descriptive story of a modern Indian family near James Bay who hunt geese for food. The colourful, primitive pictures neatly mesh the old ways with the new. A companion book is *Normie's Moose Hunt* (1968).

DE ROUSSAN, JACQUES. *Au-delà du soleil/Beyond the Sun*. Illustrated by the author. Montreal, Tundra, 1972. 28 pp.
Peter's dream voyage 'beyond the sun' is depicted in hand-silkscreened collages. Peter never appears, however. The art represents the plants and stars in simple bold cut-outs, which are given luminescent strength by the silkscreen process but which, by their very simplicity, reduce the heavens to cold, boring abstractions. This is a sterile graphic exercise that cannot be taken seriously as a children's book.

HILDES, JOEY. *How the Pelican Got Its Baggy Beak*. Winnipeg, Peguis Publishers, 1974. 32 pp.
The trying but amusing adventure of a pelican, written and illustrated by a ten-year-old boy. The pictures—crayon drawings in pastel shades—exhibit verve, humour, and some skill. So does the text: 'Big belowing clouds rumbled in. The young pelican could not see a foot in front of him.'

HOWARD-GIBBON, AMELIA FRANCES. *An Illustrated Comic Alphabet*. Toronto, Oxford, 1966. 32 pp.
Although a fairly recent publication, this is a genuine product of the Victorian age with all its conventions and charm. Drawn by Miss Howard-Gibbon, an Englishwoman, when she lived in Sarnia, Ont., in 1859, it will delight adults as well as children.

MCCLELLAND, HUGH. *The Bold Bad Buccaneers*. Toronto, Macmillan, 1968. 58 pp.
Some bloodthirsty pirates are promptly reformed when they find a boatload of children cast adrift by adults who have 'too many children'. The cartoon-like drawings in black, white, and red have a suitably bold, piratical look.

MACDONALD, KENDALL JAMES. *Patrick the Diesel*. Winnipeg, Peguis Publishers, 1974. 24 pp.
Patrick the diesel inconveniences everybody by whipping the caboose right off the track. However, he becomes repentent and reforms. The story was written and illustrated by a nine-year-old boy. The pictures in black and red are bold and childlike.

RICHARDS, JACK. *Johann's Gift to Christmas*. Illustrations by Len Norris. Vancouver, J.J. Douglas, 1972. 34 pp.

Few people know that a churchmouse was really responsible for the world
best-loved carol, 'Silent Night'. Len Norris, the famous Vancouver car
toonist, turns his pen to drawings of Tyrolean scenery and charming mic
in full colour and sepia.

TOYE, WILLIAM. *How Summer Came to Canada*. Illustrated by Elizabet
Cleaver. Toronto, Oxford, 1969. 32 pp.
A companion to *The Mountain Goats of Temlaham*, this appealing, roman
tic Micmac legend receives from Cleaver rich, brilliantly coloured collag
illustrations that extol the Canadian landscape as it changes from ic
blue-white winter to blazing summer. A beautiful picture-book.

TOYE, WILLIAM. *The Mountain Goats of Temlaham*. Illustrated by Elizabet
Cleaver. Toronto, Oxford, 1969. 32 pp.
The combination of a famous West Coast Indian legend (Tsimshian) simpl
told and glowing collages by one of Canada's outstanding illustrator
makes this an outstanding picture-book. A companion volume to *How
Summer Came to Canada*.

WYSE, ANNE and ALEX (eds). *The One To Fifty Book*. Toronto, University o
Toronto Press, 1973. 108 pp.
This, our first home-grown counting book, is by children from the Indian
reservation that gave us *Alphabet Book*. It has the same charming child
like drawings (a few in colour) and, more importantly, childlike concepts
in the simple, everyday objects they chose to represent the numbers.

YOUNG, CHIP. *Honky the Christmas Goose*. Toronto/Vancouver, Clarke, Irwin,
1972. 32 pp.
Honky, who was first called Henry because he was born in a Model-T Ford,
eats himself into such fatness that he cannot honk. The pictures are so
varied in style that they do not show his transformation into Santa's
helper, nor do they make an artistically unified picture-book.

PICTURE-STORYBOOKS

ABELL, KATHLEEN. *King Orville and the Bullfrogs*. Illustrated by Errol Le Cain.
Toronto/Boston, Little, Brown, 1974. 48 pp.
A sophisticated court fairy tale in the tradition of Thackeray's *The Rose
and the Ring* and A.A. Milne's *Once Upon a Time*, but much shorter and
not as neatly funny. For such a short tale the plot is quite complicated.
It involves two kings, three queens, three princesses, and three princes who
are changed into frogs by a witch for no reason at all. The story has some
humorous details, which are nicely played upon by the colourful pictures
by a well-known English illustrator.

BLADES, ANN. *A Boy of Taché*. Illustrated by the author. Montreal, Tundra,
1973. [24 pp.]
On the reserve of Taché in northern British Columbia a young boy rushes
for the help that will bring a relief airplane to his ailing grandfather. The

watercolour illustrations, portraying brilliant autumn, are different in atmosphere from, but just as effective as, those in Blades' *Mary of Mile 18*. However, the text, with its short, jerky sentences, lacks the rhythm and polish that helped to make her first book so gently appealing.

BLADES, ANN. *Mary of Mile 18*. Illustrated by the author. Montreal, Tundra, 1971. [40 pp.]
A little Mennonite girl in a northern British Columbia community is allowed to keep a pup when it proves itself of value as a watchdog. With a rhythmic text and quiet, memorable full-page watercolours, the author/illustrator re-creates the daily round of life against a subtly changing winter background. A distinguished picture-storybook.

BURNFORD, SHEILA. *Mr Noah and the Second Flood*. Illustrated by Michael Foreman. Toronto, McClelland and Stewart, 1973. 63 pp.
The world is drowning in its own pollution and Mr and Mrs Noah set about building a second Ark to escape the flood, but many species of animals are now extinct. There are wonderfully humorous touches—such as Mrs Noah calculating the food needed—in this picture-storybook, but the idea is gracelessly overpowered by a lesson in ecology and conservation.

CLARK, JOAN. *Thomasina and the Trout Tree*. Illustrated by Ingeborg Hiscox. Montreal, Tundra, 1971. 40 pp.
One suspects a purpose beneath Thomasina's search for the 'trout tree', which may be the symbol of art itself. The gaudily brilliant illustrations, representing different techniques in modern art, give the book a brilliant but facile look.

CLEAVER, NANCY. *How the Chipmunk Got Its Stripes*. Illustrated by Laszlo Gal. Toronto, Clarke, Irwin, 1973. 36 pp.
The stripes really came from the claw marks of a bear as the chipmunk tried to save the humans from a serious sickness. The use of sepia only in the illustrations is an exercise in dramatic simplicity; the soft brown fuzzy colour is highly appropriate for the skins of the animals and the buckskin of the Indian clothes.

ENGEL, MARIAN. *Adventure at Moon Bay Towers*. Illustrated by Patricia Cupples. Toronto, Clarke, Irwin, 1974. [34 pp.]
When two city children escape to the country, all sorts of zany things begin to happen in the animal world. The lively line drawings, more than the text, convey a 'tall tale' atmosphere in a seemingly normal Ontario resort.

KLEIN, MARNIE. *The Stanley Saucer*. Illustrations by Patrice Parkinson. Toronto/Vancouver, Clarke, Irwin, 1972. 32 pp.
Stanley is a turtle from Lake Nipissing and a great fan of the Maple Leafs, whom he visits in Toronto. A graceless little story with tasteless pictures.

KURELEK, WILLIAM. *Lumberjack*. Illustrated by the author. Montreal, Tundra, 1974. [50 pp.]

The famous Canadian artist continues his pictorial recollections, begun in *A Prairie Boy's Winter*. Each page of descriptive text is matched by a full-page illustration. The lumberjacks themselves are bright, static midgets against the overpowering trees. An intense and pictorially beautiful glimpse of the lumberjack trade.

KURELEK, WILLIAM. *A Prairie Boy's Winter*. Paintings by the author. Montreal, Tundra, 1973. 42 pp.

The writer/painter looks back on his life as a boy on the Canadian Prairie (southern Alberta) of the 1930s. The landscapes in the appealing paintings seem frozen in time and space, but Kurelek's little figures move through a round of work and play with astounding vitality. A beautiful book and a valuable bit of Canadian social history for children.

MACKLEM, MICHAEL. *The Sleeping Beauty*. Illustrated by Carel Moiseiwitsch. Ottawa, Oberon, 1973. 48 pp.

The old fairy tale is presented against a pictorial medieval background; the figures (with the exception of the witch) are as one-dimensional as those in a 'book of hours'. The book as a whole is distinguished for illustration rather than for the text which, although following Perrault's traditional plot, sacrifices his style.

SUDDON, ALAN. *Cinderella*. Including a French translation of the text by Claude Aubry. Illustrated by Alan Suddon. Ottawa, Oberon, 1969. 60 pp.

The age-old story is retold with extravagant additions based on Suddon's collage illustrations—a glorious spoof on the bad taste of the Victorian age and yet with occasional endearing touches. Cinderella herself is charming in a little newsprint dress. The book as a whole would have been more effective without the modern embellishments to the Perrault text.

TOYE, WILLIAM. *Cartier Discovers the St Lawrence*. Illustrated by Laszlo Gal. Toronto, Oxford, 1970. 32 pp.

Lavishly illustrated with large full-colour paintings on every page, this well-told narrative of Cartier's three voyages is a splendid picture-story-book approach to history for young children—unfortunately almost the only one in Canada.

VINEBERG, ETHEL. *Grandmother Came from Dworitz: A Jewish Story*. Sketches by Rita Briansky. Montreal, Tundra, 1969. 64 pp.

In all cultures, grandparents are the link between the past and the present and it is to them that children say: 'Tell me about when you were little.' Here a grandmother tells, in a gentle, factual way, the background of the Polish-Russian-Jewish society of her forebears, ending with her mother's arrival in Springhill, N.S., as a young bride. These quiet reminiscences are given considerable atmosphere by the soft drawings of the Polish-Canadian artist Rita Briansky.

YOUNG, CHIP. *Foxy Grandpa.* Illustrated by Tye Palleck. Toronto, Clarke, Irwin, 1971. 56 pp.

Hockey night among animals behaving like humans is, unfortunately, not as exciting as the real thing. The cartoon-like drawings are only slightly amusing.

YOUNG, CHIP. *The Little Hen of Huronia.* Illustrations by Christiane Duchesne. Toronto/Vancouver, Clarke, Irwin, 1971. 32 pp.

Madame Poulette plays her part in the seventeenth-century Huron Mission by laying an egg a day, a delicacy that is particularly useful when the missionaries fall ill. This delicate and humorous side-look at Canadian history has considerable charm and is enhanced by colourful, stylized, full-page illustrations.

11 early canadian children's books

The first Canadian book deliberately written for children is as unimportant as the first English book, whatever that may have been. It is safe to assume that it would have been written for their instruction rather than for their delight. The English Puritans produced their 'good Godly books' for children and the writers of the eighteenth and early nineteenth centuries lectured to them through the 'moral tale'. Although there came a glimmering of levity about the middle of the nineteenth century, it was not until Lewis Carroll caused a 'spiritual volcano' with *Alice's Adventures in Wonderland* (1865) that books which merely stirred the imagination were considered entirely suitable for children.

When the British immigrants in Canada first turned from logging to literature, they naturally chose as their models the literary style of their mother country. The first Canadian books are thus almost indistinguishable in manner, mood, and emphasis on morality from English books of the day. There was, however, one significant addition: the Canadian scene. This gripped writers' imaginations perhaps more than they knew, and if the style was English—often at its worst—the setting was Canadian. And not merely superficially. The immigrants' knowledge of their new land had been won through personal travail and their observations were impressively accurate and fresh. In the midst of their problems of transferral and adjustment, and with the hardship that went with pioneer life—even for those who were in more 'gentlemanly' circumstances—the transplanted Britishers came to know Canada both in its breadth and in its miniscule detail of plant and flower life. They observed the Indians, the woodsmen, and the trappers as well as their neighbours on the next farm. And they wrote with affection and appreciation of the 'thousand wild graces which mock the cultivated beauties of Europe' (Frances Brooke, *The History of Emily Montague*).

This combination of English subject matter and Canadian background is best seen in Frances Brooke's *The History of Emily Montague*, first published in England in 1769 and considered to be the first Canadian, indeed the first North American, novel. Brooke spent five years in Quebec and certainly used her time in Canada to good advantage. *Emily Montague* is written in the epistolary form of Richardson's *Pamela* and, like it, is a novel of manners at the upper levels of society. Pioneer life itself is hardly glimpsed, but descriptions of Quebec—its beauties, grandeurs, and lushness, its severe winters and hot summers—dominate the book and are made all the more telling by minute detail. The setting is no mere backdrop; indeed Quebec might almost be considered the protagonist and the problems of the various lovers appear at times to be simply bridges between the descriptive passages—for example, as a convenient way to get the reader from a rhapsody on the beauties of the Montmorency River to a narrative account of an Indian-style picnic.

An examination of printing in Canada before 1800 reveals only a few alphabets and catechisms published in Montreal. The first Canadian children's magazine, *The Snow Drop; or, Juvenile Magazine*, which began publication in April 1847, is typical of its period and could have been published in London rather than in Montreal. The first issues contain the obligatory moral and religious tales (including stories of deaths of young children), indifferent verse, some interesting snippets of information and anecdotes on natural history, and a riddle or two. Canadian content is provided in some of the early numbers by means of sketches of Canadian history that were continued in later issues. These are quite good historical accounts, written directly and with a warmth and personal involvement that sprang, one suspects, from a genuine desire to instruct. Moral edification was also provided in liberal doses. The unknown writer of the following paragraph does not hesitate to point out the misdemeanour, and a serious one at that, of one of our early explorers:

I am sorry to feel obliged to tell you that Cartier committed an act of great injustice towards the poor natives, in this expedition which was long remembered by them, and operated greatly to the disadvantage of succeeding adventurers. He invited the chief Sachem and several of his warriors to an entertainment in his ship, and while they were feasting, the anchor was raised and the vessel sailed with the unfortunate captives. Thus treacherously deprived of their native freedom, and subjected to the restraints of civilization, the poor Indians pined away and died, only one, a young girl, lived to return with Cartier on his following voyage. Cartier who it was said was a man of principle and humanity, was not probably aware, till too late, of the injustice he committed. (The Snow Drop, *vol. 1, no.4, New Series.*)

The *Snow Drop* was basically instructional, and the books that followed it were rarely free of this element, no matter how many Indians were biting the dust, no matter how many grizzlies were killed or how many rapids skilfully navigated.

The first distinctively Canadian note in a children's book was provided by the well-known immigrant writer, Catharine Parr Traill (1802-99). In *The Backwoods of Canada* (1836), about her life in Upper Canada, she gives an indication of the attitude to Canada that permeates her writing, whether for adults or children:

Not to regret my absence from my native land, and one so fair and lovely withal, would argue a heart of insensibility; yet I must say, for all its roughness, I love Canada, and am as happy in my humble log-house as if it were a courtly hall or bower; habit reconciles us to many things that at first were distasteful.

Curiously enough, Traill wrote a book about Canada for children before she came to this country: *The Young Emigrants; or Pictures of Canada. Calculated to Amuse and Instruct the Minds of Youth* (1826). The preface tells us that many of the scenes and events were communicated to the writer by a family who immigrated to America in 1821. Traill came from both a writing and an immigrating family, the famous Stricklands, who

contributed as much to our pioneer life as they did to our literature. She was the sister of Susannah Moodie, whose *Roughing It
in the Bush* (1852) has become a Canadian classic, and of Samuel
Strickland, the author of *Twenty-Seven Years in Canada West*
(1853). She had an impressive list of children's publications to her
credit before coming to Canada in 1832, but none with the
strength and maturity of her first Canadian children's book. This
was significantly titled *Canadian Crusoes* and was published in
1852. It was later republished as *Lost in the Backwoods* and republished again as late as 1923 with its original title. We can presume that the choice of the title *Canadian Crusoes* was deliberate,
for it gave the Canadian book a link with two proved popular titles,
Daniel Defoe's *Robinson Crusoe* (1719) and Johann Wyss's
Swiss Family Robinson (1813). Traill's book is no mere imitation
of them and in most respects it is far less dated (but less endear-
ingly ridiculous) than *Swiss Family Robinson*. At least the grandeur and originality of her setting for a long time saved Traill
from the fate of those writers who produced what came to be
called 'Robinsonnades'—deliberate imitations of the plot of
Defoe's work without its 'sense and sensibility' and good writing.
The Canadian work has a feeling of danger and excitement and
also genuine irony. When the children are discovered by an old
trapper three years after they have been lost, they are only seven
miles from their home. Consider, then, instead of Crusoe's desert
island, a vast and unknown wilderness inhabited by Indians,
spreading to the north and west behind the town of Cobourg,
Ont.; consider, instead of a mature adult, three young cousins
(two fourteen-year-old boys and a twelve-year-old girl); consider
also, however, the flowery style of the nineteenth century rather
than the plain words of the eighteenth. Nevertheless, this contains the irresistible stuff of the isolation story—the procuring of
food, shelter, and clothing; the need for protection against wild
animals; and in addition the young girl's capture by unfriendly
Indians. The children conduct themselves with the same equanimity as the 'great Crusoe' and look to the same spiritual guidance. Above all, the Canadian wilderness is reduced to something
that can be handled:

They now turned all their attention to drying huckleberries (or whortleberries). Catherine and Louis (who fancied nothing could be contrived without his help) attended to the preparing and making of the bags of birch bark; but Hector was soon tired of girl's work, as he termed it, and, after gathering some berries, would wander away over the hills in search of game, and to explore the neighbouring hills and valleys, and sometimes it was sunset before he made his appearance.

In spite of the high potential she showed in *Canadian Crusoes*, Traill failed to attain its standard in her succeeding children's books. In *Lady Mary and Her Nurse; or, A Peep into Canadian Forests* (1856), Lady Mary questions her nurse about life in the Canadian woods (a typical ploy of the period) and must at times have received far more information than she wanted. We suspect an unintentionally pathetic note at the end of the second chapter, when Lady Mary says, 'Indeed, nurse, I have learned a great deal about squirrels, Canadian rice, otters and Indians; but, if you please, I must now have a little play with my doll.' This book was later republished as *Afar in the Forest* and *In the Forest. Cot and Cradle Stories*, edited by Traill's great-niece and published in 1895, is a mish-mash of nature stories, heavily larded with anthropomorphism.

The land of ice and snow and the Eskimo, of forest and lake and mountain and the Indian, was bound to provide attractive themes for writers, particularly British ones, even though some of them had never been to Canada. Titles such as *Lost in the Wilds of Canada* and *Three Boys in Beaverland* by British and American writers are commonplace. The prolific and well-travelled George Alfred Henty *appears* to have written *With Wolfe in Canada* (1887) without setting foot in the country, although he did get as far west and south as California. The well-known Captain Frederick Marryat (1792-1848) had earlier added to the store of travellers' tales about Canada. His tour of the United States and Canada in 1837 provided material for his book for young people, *The Settlers in Canada* (1844).

R.M. Ballantyne (1825-1894), on the other hand, entered the service of the Hudson's Bay Company at the age of sixteen and spent six years in Canada. Of his many books, *Snowflakes and*

Sunbeams; or, The Young Fur Traders (1856)—later published as *The Young Fur Traders*—*Ungava: A Tale of Esquimaux Land* (1858), *The Wild Man of the West: A Tale of the Rocky Mountains* (1863), *The Red Man's Revenge: A Tale of the Red River Flood* (1880), among others, were all solidly based on the Canadian scene. It is possible that much of the detailed and explicit information he provided was borrowed by other and lesser writers. Certainly there was a Ballantyne 'style' running through most of the Canadian books that came later. To a modern reader much of Ballantyne would appear heavy-handed, moralistic, and full of circumlocutions. But he had a lively pen and a good eye; his stories always move at a brisk pace and the descriptions of life in the wilds, the fur-trading posts, and the early settlements are full of striking details. Above all, as he was familiar with the Canadian wilderness, he could escape the hackneyed view of it as a vast unknown and show it in all its guises and even as a friendly playland.

All nature was joyous and brilliant, and bright and beautiful. Morning was still very young—about an hour old. Sounds of the most cheerful, light-hearted character floated over the waters, echoed through the woods, as birds and beasts hurried to and fro with all the bustling energy that betokened preparation and search for breakfast. Fish leaped in the pools with a rapidity that brought forcibly to mind that wise saying, 'The more hurry, the less speed'; for they appeared constantly to miss their mark, although they jumped twice their own length out of the water in the effort.
—The Young Fur Traders.

So too his knowledge of boys enabled him to create characters that went beyond the standard stiff-lipped 'young adventurers'. Here, for example, is the way Ballantyne caught the mood of exuberance and deviltry:

Yes, Charley, I'm going with you! I upset the stool, tilted the ink bottle over the invoice-book, sent the poker almost through the back of the fireplace, and smashed Tom Whyte's best whip on the back of the 'noo 'oss as I galloped him over the plains for the last time: all for joy, because I'm going with you, Charley, my darling!—The Young Fur Traders.

Although it can be seen that, except for a few phrases, Ballantyne's books still have quite a modern ring, his Canadian stories have not had the 'staying power' of his desert-island adventure story *Coral Island*, which is still frequently reprinted. It is as didactic as anything else he wrote, but the desert-island theme appears to have a more universal appeal in the long run than Indians and forests and furs and floods.

Ballantyne exemplifies the new English stream of writing of this period: the contemporary adventure story for boys. Books of instruction were designed for children, both boys and girls, but once the idea of an *adventure* story for children took hold, it chiefly turned into a body of writing specifically designed for boys; it did not draw on the past but on life that was close at hand and accessible to those who read about it. The whole world was made real and open to those who had the fortitude to investigate it personally.

While the cult of the boy's book was developed in the 1860s and 1870s in England, there also came a great wave of enduring fantasy that has come to be called the 'Golden Age of Children's Literature'. John Ruskin's *The King of the Golden River* was published in 1851 and William Thackeray's *The Rose and the Ring* in 1855. Then came in fairly rapid succession Kingsley's *The Water Babies* (1863), Carroll's *Alice's Adventures in Wonderland* (1865), Mrs Ewing's *The Brownies and Other Stories* (1870), and the works of George MacDonald, Mrs Mulock, and Mrs Molesworth. Books of sheer imagination had arrived.

Canadian writers stood aloof from this trend. It is not surprising that outstanding books of fantasy were not written in Canada at this time. In fact, nothing of a richness comparable to the English productions occurred in *any* other country, least of all in a frontier society such as Canada.

It is less understandable that there is little or no improvement in style in the books for children that followed those of Traill and Ballantyne. Acceptable as they must have been in respect of plot and background, they are quite dead now. They lacked what gives a book staying power—that glow that shines beyond the particular period in which a book was written, even if it is markedly of that period. In speaking of the years of the 1870s and 1880s in

Canadian writing for adults, Fred Cogswell in *The Literary History of Canada* points out that 'Seldom has any literature been so exclusively the province of the amateur.' This was also true of writing for children.

At this time there was an unusual note in Canadian writing for children that is ignored in several surveys of Canadian literature and should be mentioned, if only to regret that some original talent never sparked a further development. It was provided by the New Brunswick author, James de Mille (1833-80). He was a professional writer, turning out some twenty-seven books between 1869 and his death in 1880, about eleven of them for boys. Most notable is his 'B.O.W.C.' (Brethren of the White Cross) series. *B.O.W.C.: A Book for Boys* was published in 1869, *The Boys of the Grand Pré School* in 1870, *Picked Up Adrift* in 1872, *Treasure of the Sea* in 1873. Not only was this the first series by a Canadian author, but the books had a Canadian schoolboy approach before the British school story became a popular and highly commercialized venture. The famous *Boys' Own Paper*, which came to glorify the school boy (and manliness), did not begin publication until 1879. De Mille drew upon his own experiences as a boy for his stories, and as a result they were noticeably free from didacticism, both religious and instructional. He did, however, indulge in stereotypes common to the life of the period: the stupid but good-natured 'darky' who was the boys' flunkey, who always had to be rescued but who could produce a delectable meal under the most adverse conditions. The boys' other companion in adventure is the equally obtuse sea captain who is always at their beck and call in his most unseaworthy boat, *The Antelope*. But for the most part these are gay, insouciant stories of boy life, recounted in staccato conversational style. They display none of the schoolboy cruelty—or intellectualism—that later characterized Kipling's famous *Stalky and Co.* (1899); for their time, and for Canada, they were startlingly original. De Mille's description of the maritime coast and coastal waters in the 'B.O.W.C.' series is as impressive as any Canadian background found in adult books of this period. He was, after all, describing his native waters. His later series, 'The Young Dodge Club', involved a group of Canadian boys (with an ineffectual adult) travelling abroad. Although these books could represent a remarkably good tourist guide of the period, the incidents and crises, the conversation, and the general tone are far less convincing than in his books with Canadian settings.

On the whole, until well into the twentieth century Canadian writing for children concentrated on the outdoor adventure story or the historical romance. The only difference among dozens of these books is in the degree to which they indulge in moralizing.

Little of this appears in the work of James Macdonald Oxley (1855-1907), of Halifax, who wrote more than twenty boys' adventure stories. *Fife and Drum at Louisbourg* (1899), one of his better efforts, is quite lively historical fiction, with interesting details of the siege of Louisbourg. The twin boys who accompany the American army under General Pepperell are effectively contrasted, and, unlike the boys in much modern historical fiction, they remain boy-like and are not credited with greatly changing the course of history. Oxley also sought locales outside of Canada. His 1902 publication—entitled *L'Hasa at Last*—describes a boy's journey with his father to the forbidden city. Oxley had a sense of realism: after the painfully long and hazardous journey the expedition is summarily expelled from L'Hasa.

Although writing twenty years apart, De Mille and Oxley had more in common than their maritime background. They were professional writers of children's books who wrote to an extent that is unknown in Canada today. Volume of publication, of course, is in no way related to excellence and is probably a hindrance to it (unless the writer is a Trollope or a Scott). These Canadians, however, demonstrated that money could be made by writing for the young. De Mille wrote to supplement his university teaching salary; Oxley gave up his legal and business career and turned almost exclusively to the writing of boys' books. Both wrote to entertain.

Egerton Ryerson Young (1840-1904), on the other hand, mainly used his books, even his boys' books, to further missionary endeavours. The son of a Methodist minister, Young served as a missionary in the North and later earned his living as a writer and a lecturer. The evangelical tone is quite apparent in his *Three Boys in the Wild North Land* (1897)—in which an English boy, a Scottish boy, and an Irish boy (artful conjunction) spend some time in Canada as the guests of a former member of the Hudson's Bay Company—although it does not detract from the spirited adventures. The boys' host had, at age thirty, fallen in love with a twelve-year-old Indian girl. Being a man of culture and refinement, he sent her off to school in England to become a woman of culture and refinement and married her eight years later upon her return to Canada. This is reminiscent of the life of the English educational theorist, John Day (the author of *Sandford and Merton*), who, taking Rousseau's theories literally, educated two girls in the hope that one would prove suitable for his wife. The Canadian and fictional Ross was more successful than the real Day.

It is hard to tell whether some of Young's other books were intended for children. It is probably safe to assume that, with the scarcity of reading material, many of them would have been put into the hands of children and would have had appeal for them, perhaps in spite of parental approval. *Children of the Forest: A Story of Indian Love* (1904) may serve as a fair example of Young's approach. It tells of the tribulations and romances of four Indian young people; it has a kind of Romeo and Juliet motif, implausibly romanticized but still vivid. Things go along reasonably well until Young remembers that he is a missionary and hastily converts a tribe or two, to the detriment of the story.

Canadian children read a British magazine of the time that had a strong connection with Canada: *Wee Willie Winkie*, which was started by Lady Aberdeen and carried on mainly with the editorial assistance of her daughter, Lady Marjorie Gordon. Lord Aberdeen became Governor-General of Canada in 1893, and soon after he and Lady Aberdeen took up residence at Government House in Ottawa, she embarked on the same kind of ambitious program of benevolent reform for which she had been noted in Great Britain. Children were part of her plan, and by 1894 there was a *Wee Willie Winkie* editorial office in Montreal and a Canadian edition was under way; it was published until 1897. *Wee Willie Winkie* was not intended to contain literature for chldren. It was designed 'to amuse' children, to give them something to do 'out-of-school-hours and during the holidays'. To this end it concentrated on competitons (then the rage in English magazines for children), puzzles, correspondence, and on encouraging children to send gifts of clothing and toys for the poor, especially at Christmas time. That one or two good pieces of writing turned up in its pages during the seven years of its publication was, one feels, an accident. Canadian content was certainly provided by the correspondence of a good many Canadian children who wrote enthusiastically for a magazine that obviously captured their affection.

This was also the era of Seton and Roberts (who have been discussed in the chapter on the realistic animal story). Their influence on the animal story came to be great and lasting, but they apparently did little to change the general outlook or style of their Canadian contemporaries. The stream of outdoor adventure in northern and western Canada continued much as before. Books such as C. Phillipps-Wolley's *Gold, Gold, in Cariboo; A Story of Adventure in British Columbia* (1894) and John Burnham's *Jack Ralston; or, The Outbreak of the Nauscopees: A Tale of Life in the Far Northeast of Canada* (1901) were realistic enough in setting, but marred by the woodenness of their characters and the conventionality of their plots. Only Seton in *The Two Little Savages* (1903) and Norman Duncan in *The Adventures of Billy Topsail* (1906) were able to create believable boys in natural surroundings, thus giving to children's literature of the period its only genuine realism. Both books became instantly popular and gained a hold on the imagination of generations of Canadians; indeed, they are still read. (These books are discussed in Chapter 6).

By 1900 the heavily sentimental 'sweetness and light' school of writing for children, which was disappearing in the mother country, was entering Canadian writing in books for both adults and children through the works of Ralph Connor, Nellie McClung, Marshall Saunders, and L.M. Montgomery. Although Connor and McClung cannot be considered writers for children, their books were not only read by them but, owing to the scarcity of Canadian books that could interest children, they were used in children's departments of some public libraries as late as the 1930s and 1940s.

Ralph Connor (the pseudonym of the Rev. Charles William Gordon, 1860-1937) wrote *The Man From Glengarry* (1901) and

Glengarry School Days (1902), which offered a sentimental look backwards to the pioneer days in Glengarry County in Ontario. Most of the neighbourly and social customs are described, as well as the rougher life in the Ontario lumber camps. Schooldays, the swimming-hole, 'sugaring off', church services, barn-raisings, tests of physical skill, wakes, and revival meetings are all included. The ultra-goodness of the chief characters is at times almost cloying; nevertheless Connor in his many books had an understandably spellbinding effect upon his generation, both in Canada and abroad. Arrant proselytizer though he always was, he had narrative skill and wrote with force and emotion. He can even make the modern reader suspend disbelief.

In most cases the sentimentality and moralizing of the time can hardly be swallowed now, even momentarily. Nellie McClung (1873-1951) wrote quite accurate observations of life in Manitoba, but they are outweighed by the falseness of the emotions she sought to arouse. For example, her *Sowing Seeds in Danny* (1908) has as heroine twelve-year-old Pearlie Watson, who is more closely related to Pollyanna and Elsie Dinsmore than to any normal child. Like *Glengarry School Days*, it is told in a series of loosely connected episodes rather than as a continuous plot; Pearlie supplies whatever link there is. The daughter of a poor section hand, she goes into domestic service to repay her father's debt and in the process conquers, by her lovable nature, all whom she meets. She also helps to solve their problems: thanks to her, a young doctor faces up to his responsibilities and the old doctor is rescued from habitual drunkenness. Yet Nellie McClung had an eye for environment and was able to reveal both its harshness and the ability of people to enjoy themselves simply in the small town and on the farms of the Manitoba she knew. Even her militant attitude towards temperance was part of the social fabric of the time. Equally apparent is her strong belief in the importance of Sunday School, which the children were enticed by gifts of candy to attend, with the cunning rider that they would not be told on which Sunday the candy would be distributed.

As much as we may now scorn Ralph Connor and Nellie McClung, they provided an insight into Canadian life that was unobtainable in other books of the period that were written specifically for children. Particularly revealing was their insight into the adult world, which is so seldom more than shadowy in the average children's book. Connor and McClung also provided a rare opportunity to see Canada as something more than a wild west and frozen wastes.

Fewer redeeming qualities can be found in the works of Marshall Saunders (1861-1947). A popular and prolific writer, she turned out twenty-six books between 1894 and 1927, most of which were animal stories for children and all of which were several degrees worse than her famous and sentimental *Beautiful Joe* (1894). Her motive was laudable: the attempt to persuade children (and adults) to be kind to animals. Unfortunately she simply turned animals into human beings who provided an occasion for moralizing in every sentence.

Canada's best-seller, *Anne of Green Gables*, burst upon the scene in 1908. To denigrate the literary qualities of *Anne of Green Gables* is as useless an exercise as carping about the architecture of the National War Memorial. Anne arrived and she has stayed. There is no doubt that the first book in the twenty-two titles by L.M. Montgomery (1874-1942) was an improvement on what little was being written for children at the time. The spirited redhead from Prince Edward Island added a note of girlishness and mischief to Canadian children's books that was hitherto lacking. But when we have mentioned the Prince Edward Island setting, which is lushly described, there is little else to comment on. Montgomery belongs to that breed of writers who give themselves away in their second and succeeding books. Of Anne, we are inclined to say, 'Her I can accept,' but the increasingly sentimental dishonesty of the succeeding books tends to destroy the first. Only the most avid Anne fans will refuse to admit that the appealing qualities of the first book are soon dissipated. It is sad but true that the Anne books continue to evoke great nostalgia from many adults to whom much vastly superior modern Canadian writing is unknown.

The most telling criticism of this type of Canadian writer comes from E.K. Brown. In speaking of Ralph Connor, L.M. Montgomery, and Robert Service (for whom we could substitute here Marshall Saunders), he points out that 'they were all more or less agressively unliterary; and their only significance . . . is the proof they offered that for the author who was satisfied to truckle to mediocre taste, living in Canada and writing about Canadian subjects was perfectly compatible with making an abundant living by one's pen.' ('The Problems of Canadian Literature', *Masks of Fiction*, A.J.M. Smith ed.)

Their books had idealized characters and sentiments, and their workaday writing style was characterized by a superior moral tone and some archness. However, at least these writers had *some* style. (It is rather sad to be confronted by characterless ten-word sentences and two-sentence paragraphs in so much modern writing for children, no matter how laudable the intention to make reading easy.) At least their morality was an integral part of the story; it was often less hard to take than today's more artificial and disguised didacticism. In this light *Canadian Crusoes* is a far better book than, say, Lyn Cook's *Bells on Finland Street* or *Little Magic Fiddler*. Traill's religious beliefs cannot be separated from her story, whereas Cook, in trying deliberately to press for a Canadian mosaic, loses her story as she preaches. The writers of the nineteenth century also had a flowing story line—a kind of narrative propulsion that might be envied by writers today. Many modern Canadian children's books have what Claude Bissell, in referring to adult books that succeeded the nineteenth-century output, has described as 'a conscientious flatness and humdrum realism' (Introduction to *Masks of Fiction*).

The older books were also remarkably free from the antiseptic quality that is prevalent in most modern Canadian books for children. Perhaps because the stories were so highly moral in tone, adults were often shown with human weaknesses, even with cruelty in their nature. In Egerton Ryerson Young's *Duck Lake*, for example, a father is shown in the act of giving his small son a beating. All turns out well, of course, but the reader is not spared the horror of the moment. Harsh reality is not lacking in the writing of Haig-Brown, Mowat, and Walker, but it is hard to find elsewhere.

There is also much to be said for the picture of the Indians that is given in these older books. While most of the modern writers on this theme look back at the Indians through history, many writers of the nineteenth century could write about them from first-hand knowledge—and with genuine respect. Thus their Indian characters are not just primitive warriors; they are often shown in their natural contemporary role as masters of woodcraft and as guides for white men in the forest. In Egerton Young's *Three Boys in the Wild North Land*, the Indians, while kind to the three boys in their charge, mock at their ineptitude, and in his *Duck Lake*, one Indian is shown to be far more sensitive and generous and good than most of the adult white characters.

Certainly the writers of the nineteenth century need yield to none in the authenticity of their Canadian background. In such books as De Mille's B.O.W.C. stories, the boys were much more natural participants in their environment than the children presented in the 'Secret Circle' series, the 'Canadian Career' series, or in such individual works as Louise Riley's *The Mystery Horse*.

The themes of many of these early books—exploration, fur-trading, fighting the wilderness, fighting the Eskimo, endurance, survival—are much the same as those of present-day books. The treatment, however, is significantly different. The nineteenth-century writers did not seek to escape the strong emotions and cruel realities that can be found in ordinary life. The children's world of the nineteenth century was not a world apart. Those who write for children today might find much to learn from these books of the past.

Books published from the 1920s to the 1940s warrant only a brief review. The most striking fact about this period is that new Canadian children's books were still scarce. For 1921-2 *The Canadian Catalogue* lists only five novels, five in 1923, and none at all in 1935. The other significant factor about this period is the preponderance of historical fiction and of books on the North and the West.

A few books had some lasting popularity and acclaim. *Kak, the Copper Eskimo*, by Vilhjalmur Stefansson and Violet Irwin (1924), is a convincing portrayal of an Eskimo boy, and Charles Clay's *Fur-Trade Apprentice* (1940) combines the exciting aspects of an old theme with a lively, modern style. Muriel Denison's *Susannah, a Little Girl with the Mounties* (1936), with its pert little girl who wins her red coat by helping to bring in a 'wanted' man, needed nothing but its plot to make it popular. It had little to offer in other ways, for it is just a junior edition of *Rose-Marie*.

The 1940s brought a fine group of books on Canadian themes by American authors, proving that nationality gave Canadian writers no particular advantage in writing about Canada. Holling Clancy Holling's *Paddle-to-the-Sea* (1941) is still read in Canada. Although strictly speaking a book of information, it is conceived with such imagination and is so splendidly illustrated that it deserves a place with our best books for children. An Indian boy sets adrift a toy canoe at the head of the Great Lakes and the book describes its journey through the lakes and down the St Lawrence River to the Atlantic Ocean; there are maps and illustrations portraying the country through which it passes. Virginia Watson's *Flags Over Quebec: A Story of the Conquest of Canada* (1941) is excellent historical fiction on a subject avoided by Canadian writers, and Robert Davis in *Hudson Bay Express* (1942) wrote with authenticity and feeling a story of a white boy and an Indian boy who own and train the first dog team to carry passengers and freight through the Hudson Bay country. But nothing at the level of these books came from Canadian writers.

American writers also wrote the best non-fiction relating to Canada. Genevieve Fox's *Sir Wilfred Grenfell* (1943) is a warm and convincing account of Grenfell's childhood, his work in the London slums, and his great achievements in Labrador, described in a way that brings out the character of the man as well as the adventurous nature of his life. Louise Hall Tharp, in *Champlain, Northwest Voyager* (1944) and *Company of Adventurers: The Story of the Hudson's Bay Company* (1946), wrote Canadian history for children as it should be written, turning historical source material into thrilling stories of courage without suspect fictionalization.

Our own Roderick Haig-Brown distinguished himself in the forties. With his books the modern period begins.

BALLANTYNE, R.M. *The Red Man's Revenge: A Tale of the Red River Flood.* London, J. Nisbet & Co., 1880. 264 pp.

BALLANTYNE, R.M. *Snowflakes and Sunbeams; or, The Young Fur Traders. A Tale of the Far North.* London, T. Nelson and Sons, 1856. 429 pp. (Cover-title: *The Young Fur Traders: A Tale of the Far North.* The first part of the title was dropped in subsequent editions.)

BALLANTYNE, R.M. *Ungava: A Tale of Esquimaux-Land.* London, T. Nelson & Sons, 1858. 509 pp.

BALLANTYNE, R.M. *The Wild Man of the West: A Tale of the Rocky Mountains.* London, Routledge & Co., 1863. 408 pp.

BURNHAM, JOHN HAMPDEN. *Jack Ralston; or, The Outbreak of the Nauscopees: A Tale of Life in the Far North-East of Canada.* London, T. Nelson & Sons, 1901. 448 pp.

CLARKE, GEORGE FREDERICK. *Chris in Canada.* London, Blackie & Son [1925]. 224 pp.

CONNOR, RALPH (pseud.). See GORDON, CHARLES W.

DE MILLE, JAMES. *Among the Brigands.* Boston, Lee and Shepard, 1899. 328 pp. ('The Young Dodge Club'.) First published in 1871.

DE MILLE, JAMES. *'B.O.W.C.', The* [Brethren of the White Cross]: *A Book for Boys.* Boston, Lee & Shepard, 1869. 322 pp.

DE MILLE, JAMES. *The Boys of Grand Pré School.* Boston, Lee and Shepard, 1871. 348 pp. ('B.O.W.C. Series'.) First published in 1870.

DE MILLE, JAMES. *Lost in the Fog.* Boston, Lee and Shepard, 1871. 316 pp. ('B.O.W.C. Series'.) First published in 1870.

DE MILLE, JAMES. *Picked Up Adrift.* Boston, Lee and Shepard, 1872. 335 pp. ('B.O.W.C. Series'.)

DE MILLE, JAMES. *The Winged Lion; or, Stories of Venice.* Boston, Lee and Shepard, 1899. 323 pp. ('The Young Dodge Club'.) First published in 1876.

GORDON, CHARLES W. *Glengarry School Days: A Story of Early Days in Glengarry* by Ralph Connor (pseud.). Chicago, Fleming H. Revell Co., 1902. 340 pp.

GORDON, CHARLES W. *The Man from Glengarry: A Tale of the Ottawa* by Ralph Connor (pseud.). Toronto, Westminster Co. Ltd, 1901. 473 pp.

HENTY, GEORGE A. *With Wolfe in Canada; or, The Winning of a Continent.* London, Blackie & Son, 1887. 384 pp.

MCCLUNG, NELLIE L. *Sowing Seeds in Danny.* New York, Doubleday, Page & Company, 1908. 313 pp.

MARRYAT, FREDERICK. *The Settlers in Canada. Written For Young People.* London, Longman, Brown, Green & Longmans, 1844. 2 vols.

MONTGOMERY, LUCY MAUDE. *Anne of Green Gables.* Boston, L.C. Page & Company, 1908. 396 pp.

OXLEY, J. MACDONALD. *Fife and Drum at Louisbourg.* Boston, Little, Brown, 1900. 307 pp.

OXLEY, J. MACDONALD. *L'Hasa at Last.* London, Ward, Lock & Co., 1902. 301 pp. First published in 1900.

PHILLIPPS-WOLLEY, CLIVE OLDNALL. *Gold, Gold, in Cariboo; A Story of Adventure in British Columbia.* London, Blackie & Son [1894]. 288 pp.

SANFORD, M. BOURCHIER. *The Trail of the Iroquois: A Pioneer Romance of Canada.* Toronto, Longmans, Green, 1925. 256 pp.

SAUNDERS, MARGARET MARSHALL. *Beautiful Joe: An Autobiography.* Philadelphia, American Baptist Pub. Soc., 1894. 304 pp.

Snow Drop, The; or, Juvenile Magazine. Montreal, Lovell and Gibson, vols 1-5, 1847-53 [?].

TRAILL, CATHARINE PARR (STRICKLAND). *The Backwoods of Canada.* Toronto, McClelland and Stewart, 1966. ('New Canadian Library'.) First published in 1836.

TRAILL, CATHARINE PARR (STRICKLAND). *Canadian Crusoes: A Tale of the Rice Lake Plains.* Toronto, McClelland and Stewart, 1923. 322 pp. First published in 1852.

TRAILL, CATHARINE PARR (STRICKLAND). *Cot and Cradle Stories.* Edited by Mary Agnes FitzGibbon. Toronto, William Briggs, 1895. 239 pp.

TRAILL, CATHARINE PARR (STRICKLAND). *Lady Mary and Her Nurse; or, A Peep Into Canadian Forests.* London, 1856. (Later published as *Afar in the Forest; or, Pictures of Life and Scenery in the Wilds of Canada.* London, T. Nelson and Sons, 1869. 207 pp.)

TRAILL, CATHARINE PARR (STRICKLAND). *The Young Emigrants; or, Pictures of Canada. Calculated To Amuse and Instruct the Minds of Youth.* London, Harvey and Darton, 1826. 168 pp.

YOUNG, EGERTON RYERSON. *Children of the Forest: A Story of Indian Love.* New York, Fleming H. Revell, 1904. 282 pp.

YOUNG, EGERTON RYERSON. *Duck Lake: Stories of the Canadian Backwoods.* London, The Religious Tract Society [1905]. 227 pp.

YOUNG, EGERTON RYERSON. *Thee Boys in the Wild North Land.* Toronto, William Briggs, 1897. 311 pp.

book-of-the-year awards

This award, in the form of a bronze medal, is presented by the Canadian Association of Children's Librarians for the best children's book by a Canadian author. Only awards for English-language books are listed here. (For several years the award was given two years after the date of publication.)

1947 *Starbuck Valley Winter* by Roderick L. Haig-Brown. New York, Morrow, 1943.

1948 *Kristli's Trees* by Mabel Dunham. Toronto, McClelland and Stewart, 1948.

1949 No award.

1950 *Franklin of the Arctic* by Richard S. Lambert. Toronto, McClelland and Stewart, 1949.

1951 No award.

1952 *The Sun Horse* by Catherine Anthony Clark. Toronto, Macmillan, 1951.

1953 No award.

1954 No award.

1955 No award.

1956 *Train for Tiger Lily* by Louise Riley. Toronto, Macmillan, 1954.

1957 *Glooskap's Country and Other Indian Tales* by Cyrus Macmillan. Toronto, Oxford, 1955.

1958 *Lost in the Barrens* by Farley Mowat. Toronto, Little, Brown, 1956.

1959 *The Dangerous Cove* by John F. Hayes. Toronto, Copp Clark, 1957.

1960 *The Golden Phoenix and Other French-Canadian Fairy Tales* by Marius Barbeau. Retold by Michael Hornyansky. Toronto, Oxford, 1958.

1961 *The St Lawrence* by William Toye. Toronto, Oxford, 1959.

1962 No award.

1963 *The Incredible Journey: A Tale of Three Animals* by Sheila Burnford. Toronto, Little, Brown, 1961.

1964 *The Whale People* by Roderick L. Haig-Brown. London, Collins, 1962.

1965 *Tales of Nanabozho* by Dorothy

M. Reid. Toronto, Oxford, 1963.

1966 *The Double Knights: More Tales From Round the World* by James McNeill. Toronto, Oxford, 1964.

1966 *Tikta'liktak: An Eskimo Legend* by James Houston. Toronto, Longman, 1965.

1967 *Raven's Cry* by Christie Harris. Toronto, McClelland and Stewart, 1966.

1968 *The White Archer: An Eskimo Legend* by James Houston. Toronto, Longman, 1967.

1969 *And To-morrow the Stars: The Story of John Cabot* by Kay Hill. New York, Dodd, Mead, 1968.

1970 *Sally Go Round the Sun: 300 Songs, Rhymes and Games of Canadian Children* by Edith Fowke. Toronto, McClelland and Stewart, 1969.

1971 *Cartier Discovers the St Lawrence* by William Toye. Toronto, Oxford, 1970.

1972 *Mary of Mile 18* by Ann Blades. Montreal, Tundra, 1971.

1973 *The Marrow of the World* by Ruth Nichols. Toronto, Macmillan, 1972.

1974 *The Miraculous Hind* by Elizabeth Cleaver. Toronto, Holt Rinehart and Winston, 1973.

AMELIA HOWARD-GIBBON AWARD (FOR ILLUSTRATION)

1971 *The Wind Has Wings: Poems from Canada* compiled by Mary Alice Downie and Barbara Robertson. Illustrated by Elizabeth Cleaver. Toronto, Oxford, 1968.

1972 *A Child in Prison Camp* by Shizuye Takashima. Montreal, Tundra, 1971.

1973 *Au-delà du soleil* by Jacques de Roussan. Montreal, Tundra, 1972.

1974 *A Prairie Boy's Winter* by William Kurelek. Montreal, Tundra, 1973.

---

*Two awards in the same year because of a change of policy in award procedure.

index OF AUTHORS, TITLES, AND ILLUSTRATORS